Heroes of the Indian Wars

Heroes of the Indian Wars
Congressional Medal of Honour Winners During the Indian Wars

compiled by
Walter F. Beyer &
Oscar F. Keydel

Heroes of the Indian Wars: Congressional Medal of Honour Winners During the Indian Wars
compiled by Walter F. Beyer & Oscar F. Keydel

Leonaur is an imprint of Oakpast Ltd

Material original to this edition and presentation of the text in this form copyright © 2011 Oakpast Ltd

ISBN: 978-0-85706-761-6 (hardcover)
ISBN: 978-0-85706-762-3 (softcover)

http://www.leonaur.com

Publisher's Notes

The views expressed in this book are not necessarily those of the publisher.

Contents

Extract From Regulations Relative to the Medal of Honour 7
The Indian 9
Thrilling Incidents From Arizona 12
The Minnesota Massacre 21
The Chivington Butchery 34
Saved From Starvation 36
The Fetterman Massacre 51
Thirty-Two Against Three Thousand 56
On the Arickaree 59
Exciting Scout For a Trail 66
Coolness Prevented a Disaster 73
Death of Chief Black Kettle 79
A Well-Planned Surprise 85
The Sixth Cavalry and the Indians 92
Six Men Against 400 Comanches 95
Daring Single-Handed Combat 102
Where the Comanches Were Put to Flight 105
The Battle in the Lava Beds 109
Rescuing the Germaine Girls 122
With General Miles Through Texas 129
Hand-to-Hand Fights With Indians 142
Snatched From a Horrible Fate 145
Chasing Indians by Railroad 148
Adventures With Indians in 1875 154
The Little Big Horn 159
Three Daring Couriers 188
Battle of Wolf Mountain and Cedar Creek 192
Capture of Lame Deer's Village 203

Campaign Against the Nez Perces	209
Battle of the Big Hole	217
Chief Joseph's Camp Surprised	222
The Battle of Milk River	229
Hunting Indians in the Snowdrifts of Montana	238
The Surrender of Rain-in-the-Face	244
Pursuit of Chief Victoria	250
Tularosa Saved by Twenty-Five Cavalrymen	254
Saved From Annihilation	260
The Treachery at Cibicu Creek	267
Treachery of the Scouts Avenged	276
Chasing Geronimo and Natchez	285
Hazardous, But Successful	292
The Indian at Last Subdued	314
The Memorable Outbreak of 1890	316
The Perils of Winter Campaigning	332
Fought Three Mexicans Single-Handed	340
The Bear Island Uprising	343
An Officer's Devotion to His Men	347

Extract From Regulations Relative to the Medal of Honour

By direction of the President, the following regulations are promulgated respecting the award of Medals of Honour:

Medals of Honour authorized by the Act of Congress approved March 8, 1863, are awarded to officers and enlisted men, in the name of the Congress, for particular deeds of most distinguished gallantry in action.

In order that the Congressional Medal of Honour may be deserved, service must have been performed in action of such a conspicuous character as to clearly distinguish the man for gallantry and intrepidity above his comrades service that involved extreme jeopardy of life or the performance of extraordinarily hazardous duty. Recommendations for the decoration will be judged by this standard of extraordinary merit, and incontestable proof of performance of the service will be exacted.

Soldiers of the Union have ever displayed bravery in battle, else victories could not have been gained; but as courage and self-sacrifice are the characteristics of every true soldier, such a badge of distinction as the Congressional Medal is not to be expected as the reward of conduct that does not clearly distinguish the soldier above other men, whose bravery and gallantry have been proved in battle.

Recommendations for medals on account of service rendered subsequent to January 1, 1890, will be made by the commanding officer at the time of the action or by an officer or soldier having personal cognizance of the act for which the badge of honour is claimed, and the recommendation will embrace a detailed recital of all the facts and circumstances. Certificates of officers or the affidavits of enlisted men who were eyewitnesses of the act will also be submitted if practicable.

In cases that may arise for service performed here after, recommendations for award of medals must be for warded within one year after the performance of the act for which the award is claimed. Commanding officers will thoroughly investigate all cases of recommendations for Congressional Medals arising in their commands, and indorse their opinion upon the papers, which will be forwarded to the Adjutant-General of the Army through regular channels.

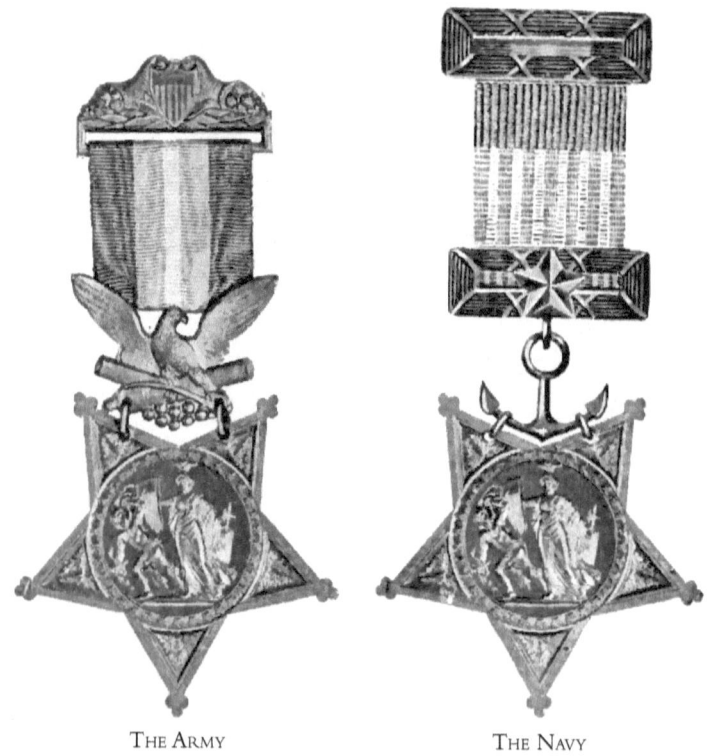

THE ARMY   THE NAVY

The Indian

The Indian, now practically civilized, has always figured prominently in our country's history. The pioneer as he gradually spread out and settled on new land, thus advancing civilization, was in continual conflict with him. The stories of many of these encounters are thrilling and fascinating, revealing deeds of self-sacrifice and fortitude which cause the blood to run warmer. Ever since the first white men settled in North America there had been a constant clash between them and the red men, until now what remains of a once numerous and hardy race is huddled together upon small reservations in various sections of the United States.

A retrospective view of the early struggles with King Philip's tribes, the Seminoles, the Black Hawks, etc., makes these events seem less bloody than they actually were; but the Indian outrages and massacres of later years, still fresh in our minds, abound with treachery and cunning and a fiendishness that in some instances is positively indescribable. It is these later wars, from 1860 down to a recent date, that bring out more prominently the true character of the wily red men, showing them to be a most picturesque, interesting and withal an intelligent race. Their character was so diverse from their white aggressors that it was difficult to understand them, and therefore they seldom got the benefit of just criticism from their foes.

So long as the red man could roam in freedom over the vast hunting grounds from the shores of the Atlantic to the shores of the Pacific, he was happy and contented; but when the exterminating process was begun he was gradually driven toward the setting sun, and as his confines were narrowed down to smaller and smaller areas he resisted the action of the white men, put on his war paint and proceeded through the settled portions killing, burning and laying waste. This pillaging, together with the fights between tribes which are hereditary mutual enemies, necessitated the continual presence of troops to quell these outbreaks.

If we judge the Indian by his morals we find that originally he stood fairly high. He is acknowledged at first to have been trustworthy and hospitable; in the prominent tribes like the Sioux the women enjoyed an excellent reputation for virtue. Their institutions were all thoroughly democratic, not only in theory but also in practice, and fitting the wants and views of a people who appreciated liberty and freedom.

The evil change in the red man's character came with the advent of the white *desperadoes* on the frontier. These white men, reckless and unconcerned, belonged with very few exceptions, to the very scum of their race, and their behaviour towards the redskins was that of brutal, inconsiderate bullies. Many wars on the frontier were brought on by the actions of these white men: and when the provoked Indians finally took the warpath, in the instincts of their savage nature, they committed unspeakable outrages, and were denounced as treacherous wild beasts who should be hunted down as such.

In later times, after the establishment of Indian reservations, it was often the dishonesty of the government agent which deprived the reservation tribes of their subsistence and caused their suffering, want and starvation. All these evils were seldom counted in favour of the Indians by the men on the frontier. The red man's best friends in these remote regions were the United States troops, the men who had to fight him hardest after he had taken the warpath.

Not often was the sensible advice heeded which went to Washington from the military commanders at the frontier posts; when the agent had stirred up the red skins and could no longer control them he would try in time to save his own hide and pack up, while the soldiers had to round up the raiding Indians in most fatiguing and relentless warfare.

The campaigns and scouts against the Indians from 1860 to 1898 in the following pages are arranged in chronological order, with particular attention given to those fights in which some of the brave regulars won the Medal of Honour.

Thrilling Incidents From Arizona

COL. BERNARD J. D. IRWIN

Arizona, the sunniest part of the Union and the home of numerous tribes of Apaches, had been "opened to civilization" up to 1861 by but few frontiersmen. The desperate resistance of the Indians had allowed these daring settlers to gain but little foothold, and even the almost continuous warfare with Union troops could not intimidate the treacherous redskins, who aimed to drive the hated whites out of their domain. At that time the territory was unexplored, and, excepting the military road passing east to west, through the southern part from Fort Thorn, New Mexico, *via* Tucson to Fort Yuma, California, and a short one from Tucson to Sonora, there were no public highways. The region embraced between the Rio Grande on the east and the Colorado River on the west, and from the international line on the south to the country of the Navajoes on the north, was then but little known a veritable *terra incognita,* inhabited by

---

The Medal of Honour which was awarded to Colonel Bernard J. D. Irwin ranks in chronological order as the first one on record, he having earned it by his voluntary, hazardous trip to rescue besieged soldiers in Apache Pass. Arizona, February 13 and 14, 1861. The act of Congress creating and awarding the medal, approved March 3. 1863, included all exceptional deeds of valour performed during the years 1861 and 1862.

nomadic tribes of hostile Apaches, embraced under the various tribal designations of Mescalero, Mogollon, Cayatero, Tonto, Pinaleno, Yuma, Mojave, Hualapi and last—but the most savage of all—the Chiricahua. The Pueblo or Montezuma Indians—Pimas, Maricopas, Papagoes and Moquis—lived from time immemorial and still live in the villages or fixed habitations, and have always maintained friendly relations with their white neighbours, but were obliged to defend themselves against the constant raids of the predatory Apaches.

The usual home or rendezvous of the Chiricahuas, when not roving over the border in the Sierra Madre, Mexico, was in the mountain range situated in the southern part of Arizona and named after that tribe. This range had been their stronghold for many years and they always felt secure when, being chased by troopers, they had managed to reach it. From there they made forays in quest of plunder, or they laid in wait ready to pounce upon small parties of incautious travellers *en route* to Mexico or California. Such parties were usually ambushed, the men slaughtered, and the women and children subjected to bondage and ill-treatment much worse than the most cruel death.

The chief of the Chiricahuas at that time was Cochise, after whom one of the counties of Arizona has been named. He was then in the prime of life, tall and well-formed in face and figure, about thirty years old, and at least six feet in height. His presence was bold and warlike, presenting the attributes of a superb specimen of robust, physical manhood. Conscious of the evil reputation of his tribe, and fearing that retribution for their many wicked deeds might overtake him, he declined all overtures and offers made to induce him to visit the military posts. The highway leading to and from Apache Pass was dotted with the graves or stone *tumuli* that covered the remains of the victims of his treachery, slaughtered by his bloodthirsty followers, who were ever on the lookout from their mountain fastnesses for the approach of the careless wayfarers, constrained to enter the dreaded pass in quest of water and transit through its range of heights.

Early in 1861, while Captain Ewell was encamped at the pass, endeavouring to conciliate the Chiricahuas with presents, two young Mexican girls—part of the spoils of a recent foray over the border—were discovered in their possession, and were rescued by purchase from their cruel fate and restored to their parents. While detained there, awaiting the pleasure of the independent and haughty chief of the tribe, he was aroused one night by a courier seeking his aid to succour a party consisting of three discharged soldiers and their families who had left the post of the Seventh Infantry shortly after his departure, and desiring to get through the dreaded pass, on their way to the States, while he was encamped there, had been attacked.

Two of the men, who had served as sergeants in the army during many years, were killed while defending their wives and children. Their horses and mules had been carried off by a party of savages who had joined and camped with them during the night and partaken of breakfast, after which they withdrew to the screen afforded by a neighbouring ravine, from where they attempted the destruction of the party whose hospitality they had enjoyed only a few moments before. Such was the character of the Apache Indians of Arizona in 1861. One and all were then alike treacherous, bloodthirsty and cruel, and ever on the alert to ambush small parties or incautious travellers, without risk to themselves, the chances being always in favour of their success.

Men had been waylaid and shot down within 300 yards of the only post guard-house in the territory in 1860, and the government herds had been stampeded repeatedly by Indians who lurked in the ravines and bushes in the vicinity of the military post, watching for a favourable opportunity to make a dash upon the coveted animals. All of that, and much more of a similar character, occurred before the arrival of the Seventh Infantry in the territory. A raid upon a beef contractor's cattle, which were trailed to the mountain home of Cochise, brought the Seventh Infantry in contact with these murderous Indians, in February, 1861, and gave an excuse to punish them as they deserved.

The owner of the stock, Mr. Wadsworth, had followed the

trail of the stolen cattle until he became satisfied that they had been taken by the Chiricahuas. He came to the post and reported the robbery, and his convictions that the marauders were of that tribe. The commanding officer of the station, Colonel Pitcairn Morrison, directed Lieutenant George N. Bascom to take sixty men of that regiment and follow up the trail until the cattle were found and recovered. If the trail were found to enter the camp of Cochise, Bascom was ordered to demand the immediate restoration of the stolen property, and in the event of refusal to use the force under his command in recovering it.

Lieutenant Bascom having followed the trail of stolen cattle to the stronghold of the Chiricahuas, marched his command to the mail station situated within the pass and in the vicinity of the only water in that neighbourhood. A station employee named Wallace, who was acquainted with Cochise, volunteered to go to his village to apprise him of the nature of the duty which had caused the troops to visit that place. That having been done, the chief, accompanied by several of his people, visited Lieutenant Bascom's camp, but when demand was made upon him for the restoration of the stolen property he scoffed at the idea of force having been brought there to compel obedience on his part.

Argument having failed to produce any effect upon the disposition of the chief, Lieutenant Bascom then determined to detain him and some others of his party as hostages, until the tribe should deliver up a captive boy, carried off with the herd, and surrender the stolen animals. That determination was only reached as a *dernier* resort and after every effort at peaceful persuasion had proved futile. When Cochise was informed that he would not be allowed to depart until after the demand made by the representative of the government had been complied with, he arose from where the party was seated and, yelling to his companions to follow him, boldly dashed through the bystanders, and with some of the warriors escaped into the adjacent ravines, from where they, with others who had been waiting to learn the outcome of the visit, opened fire upon the occupants of the mail-corral.

Next day a squaw was dispatched with a message informing the chief that the hostages detained would be taken to Fort Buchanan, and confined there until the captive and the cattle were restored.

The overland mail coach from California could not be apprised of the situation by the garrison in time and on entering the pass that night was attacked by a well-prepared ambuscade, but, after a wounded horse had been cut adrift, miraculously escaped. The driver, with a shattered leg, and with one of his passengers shot through the chest, finally succeeded, with the remaining horses, in bringing the coach into the corral.

There being several wounded soldiers at the station, one of them volunteered to lead a mule over the steep and untraveled hillside and endeavour to escape during the night towards Fort Buchanan in quest of aid. The brave man having succeeded in creeping through without detection, reached the mail station at Dragoon Spring early next day, and, after receiving a remount, arrived at the post the second night of his weary and dangerous journey. On the same day, in response to the message sent him, Cochise approached the mail station with a white flag and called for a talk with the "Soldier Captain," which was accorded, Lieutenant Bascom, two soldiers, Wallace and two other mail employees meeting the chief with an equal number of his followers at a point about 150 yards from the corral.

The *parley* had hardly commenced when a sentinel posted on the roof of the station house discovered a large number of Indian warriors crouching from view in a ravine close behind Cochise. The soldier called an alarm, and had scarcely concluded his warning when a dash to surround Bascom's party and cut off his retreat was made, the warriors in the ravine opening fire on him as he fell back. He escaped without injury, although several rifle bullets passed through his clothing and one through his hat. Wallace and his companions, presuming upon their intimacy with the Indians, incautiously advanced too far and were seized and dragged into the ravine, after which they were not again seen alive.

At that critical moment the hostages attempted to escape from guard. One of them was shot and killed, and another knocked down and transfixed by the bayonet of a sentinel, the weapon passing through his abdomen without wounding the viscera, as evinced by his speedy recovery and his ability to walk with other prisoners a mile and a half to the place of execution, where he and five other warriors were hanged seven days later.

At that time there had been quite a heavy fall of snow at the pass, which was used until it became impracticable to melt a sufficient quantity of it to supply water for the men and animals at the place. It then became necessary to resort to the spring, situated about 8,000 yards from the corral.

On the third day after this outbreak part of the herd was driven from the station to the spring, but ere the mules had reached the water the Indians pounced from all directions and succeeded in stampeding the animals. During this affair several of the guard and quite a number of warriors were shot down. As the attack had been expected, half the mules were to be detained to be sent forward after those sent to be watered should have returned, but through an error all got out at once.

The daring soldier who during the darkness of the night had stealthily scaled the steep and pathless mountain side and groped his way out to the plain where his command was surrounded by several hundred blood-thirsty savages, had meanwhile reached the post and related the events which had just taken place.

There being no mounted troops at Buchanan, an order was at once sent to Fort Breckenridge to dispatch two troops of cavalry to the assistance of Bascom's force. Assistant Surgeon B. J. D. Irwin, who was to accompany them at once, volunteered to take a small but picked number of men through the Apache Pass direct to Fort Breckenridge, about 100 miles north of Buchanan. Fourteen reliable infantrymen were selected for the hazardous service. James Graydon, a discharged soldier. who was ever ready for an adventure, joined the party, which, mounted on mules, set out in the face of a heavy snow-storm on February 13.

As 100 miles had to be traversed to reach the pass, two days

They were tied to the wheels and burned to death

were required to accomplish the weary and fatiguing journey, sixty-five miles of which—to Dragoon Spring—were made during the first day's march. On the Second day, February 14, while crossing the plain west of the Chiricahua range, a party of Indians, evidently returning from a raid, were discovered driving a herd of cattle and horses. They were pursued, and after a long and exciting chase, including a running fight of several miles, abandoned the stock, consisting of some thirty ponies and forty cattle, all of which, with three Indian warriors, were captured.

Knowing that Bascom's party was short of provisions, it was determined to drive the animals along, as well as for the further reason that, in the event of being attacked within the pass, escape would be facilitated through the desire of the enemy to stampede and recapture the large drove. The prisoners were secured and every precaution taken for defence while passing through the long and tortuous canyon leading to where Bascom's party was beleaguered.

On arriving at the entrance of the canyon a train of five wagons was found plundered and burned in the road. To the partially consumed wagon wheels the naked remains of eight human bodies were lashed the unfortunate and unsuspecting victims having been captured, stripped, tied to the vehicles and then slowly tortured to death by the burning of the outfit.

By a fortunate incident the little party under Irwin escaped destruction, which would have been inevitable had the Indians guarded the western entrance to the pass. After the success the Indians had in driving off the stock from the spring they drove the animals out on the west side of the mountain range, and, while running them to the northwest they discovered a company of infantry on the march changing station from Fort Breckenridge to Fort Bliss, on the Rio Grande. Suspecting that that force was marching to the east side of the pass for the purpose of attacking them in the rear, they followed that command and thereby left the western entrance unguarded.

The arrival of the relief party at the mail station was hailed with shouts of joy, as it was feared that they had been intercepted and wiped out. The wounded were attended, and two days later, on the arrival of two troops of cavalry, a scout through the southern part of the mountain range was made, but on seeing the concentration of troops for their punishment the Indians had vanished in various directions. Two more days were spent in seeking the camp or village of Cochise, which was found and destroyed.

While on the march in quest of his home a flock of buzzards was observed some distance to the right of the trail leading to the chief's favourite camping ground, and on riding over to the place from where the birds had flown the ghastly remains of six human bodies, upon which the vultures had been banqueting, were discovered. The evidence was indubitable that the skeletons were those of the unfortunate Wallace and his companions and three other prisoners who had fallen into the power of the savages.

It was then and there determined to execute an equal number of Indian warriors confined at the mail station in retaliation.

The punishment was an extreme mode of reprisal, but was demanded and justified by the persistent acts of treachery and the atrocious cruelties perpetrated by the most treacherous and intractable tribe of savages infesting the territory.

When some six months after the events related the same troops again traversed the pass the bodies of the Indians executed still dangled in the oaks over the graves of the murdered men, and the debris of the train burned at the entrance to the can yon gave sad evidence of the devilish work perpetrated at that point before the execution of the Indian warriors.

By the untiring energy and perseverance of such officers as Generals Crook, Crawford, Lawton, Gatewood, David, Maus, Wood and others, the Chiricahuas were finally brought to bay, and through the efforts of General Miles were transported from the scenes made memorable by the perpetration of their diabolical cruelties.

The Minnesota Massacre

The Minnesota Massacre, perpetrated by Winnebago and Blackfeet Sioux in August, 1862, on the Upper Minnesota, ranks among the darkest and bloodiest episodes in the life-destroying struggle between Indian and white man on the North-western frontier. The saddest feature of it was that this wholesale butchering of some 700 whites of all ages and sexes was undoubtedly the result of the shameful unscrupulousness and dishonesty of some of the representatives of our government in the latter's immediate dealings with the savages of those regions.

The treaty which existed between the Indians and the United States as to lands abandoned by the former in Minnesota, stipulated that the sum granted by our Government was to be paid annually in gold, per head of their members, to the tribes concerned. Those Indians, like most of the red men of those days, knew the value of money, and, furthermore, being superstitious, would not touch or accept paper money. In accordance with their wishes, it was promised that they should receive their annuities in gold.

When pay-day arrived, in 1862, the Indians were assembled in the two agencies, the Upper and Lower Agency of the Upper Minnesota Valley. The paymaster was present and began with the paying of that part of the annuity that consisted of *"naturalia"* and *"materialia,"* ammunition, blankets, and so forth. When this was finished, the official produced paper money to settle the cash account. The Indians promptly refused to accept it. In vain were they told that the paper had the same practical value as gold. They were not to be convinced. Finally they were quieted with the promise that the paymaster would go back to fetch gold and would return in a short time.

Weeks passed and no paymaster returned. The Indians grew restless. Not only their belief in having been cheated, but their actual want, rendered them unusually excited. Add to this that the traders in the agencies denied them credit, that the buffalo was not to be found in that region at this time of the year, and the need in the villages of the Indians grew daily, until finally the bucks had to go begging at the settlements. The farmers, mostly Germans, gave them willingly what they had to spare, hoping thus to keep on good terms with the starving and despairing red men.

Soon after there came warnings that serious trouble was to be expected from the Indians. A fair-minded Indian by the name of Other Day brought word to some settlements that his kinsmen were holding secret gatherings in which the protests against the faithlessness of the white men grew louder and more menacing every day, and that an outbreak was immediately pending. Other Day ran the risk of being declared a traitor to his kin; from the last and decisive meeting of his red brethren he had to flee, leaving his hat and coat behind. He arrived at the Upper Agency, which was farthest away from the nearest point of possible refuge, and saved sixty white people, men, women and children, by leading them over out-of-the-way tracks to a point of safety.

The Civil War, which was then raging in its most fearful intensity, had necessarily deprived this North-western country of almost all military protection. The whole effective force of the defence on the entire frontier from Pembina to the Iowa line did not exceed 200 men, and most of them militia.

There were thirty soldiers at Fort Ridgley, thirty at Fort Ripley, and a company of some fifty men at Fort Abercrombie, the rest scattered in similarly small details along the line.

On August 17, 1862, the Chiefs Little Crow, Little Priest and the ill-reputed Inkpaduta, a Winnebago marauder, met in council and decided to cut loose.

Now it was learned that an uprising had taken place at the agency, and most all whites there killed and their properties destroyed. The savages had immediately branched out and were on their way to capture and destroy New Ulm. They were coming in large bands on all roads and murdered and pillaged whatever came into their way.

The little town of New Ulm, founded by Germans, was the main settlement, and distant about eighteen miles from Fort Ridgley. The inhabitants of this place and the surrounding settlers, mostly Germans and Scandinavians, had not the slightest fear of an outbreak, as they had all aided the distressed and starving Reds to their best ability and felt sure of their friendship.

On the 17th of August the citizens of this peaceful town were startled by the appearance of a company of volunteers, mostly half-breed Indians, which had been mustered in by Uncle Sam's officials for the protection of the agencies. This troop was escorting one of the foremost government officials, who declared that urgent business called him to Fort Snelling, 100 miles away. It was hardly credible that this man was not informed of the coming storm; anyway he took the greater part of the protecting force, which was insignificant enough as a whole, away with him.

On the 18th of August a fleeing white man aroused the people of New Ulm, with the terrifying cry that the Indians were on the warpath and were coming. At his heels came fugitives, men, women, children, pouring into the little town, helpless, half dead from fright and exhaustion.

On the forenoon of this day a recruiting party for the United States Army had left New Ulm in wagons, with a band, to go to Milford, a small town some eight miles away. This party was just crossing a bridge over a gully near Milford, when a volley was fired into them from the surrounding bushes, and three of the people in the first wagon fell dead to the ground; they were the first victims of the Indians from New Ulm. Several others were wounded; the remnant of the party, taking their wounded with them, fled back to the town, where one of the neighbouring

New Ulmer citizens behind barricades

settlers, who had watched the dastardly murder from a distance, had preceded them with the alarming news.

The New Ulmers now felt that time was precious and hurried to the utmost in establishing a defence. The sheriff appointed a courageous citizen, Jacob Nix, as commandant of the town, and all the available men were organized. They formed three companies, one of rifles, under Louis Theobold, another one of men with double-barrelled shot guns, under E. F. Brunk, and a third one, under J. Chaikowitz, armed with all sorts of guns, mostly old-fashioned. Besides there were some twenty men with guns, who wished to act independently. As a reserve they had a number of men with hay-forks and similar weapons.

Barricades were erected in haste at the extremities of the main streets. New Ulm, with its 1,000 inhabitants, was not to be easily defended, the 200 houses being rather widely scattered. Within a day some 600 women and children had arrived as fugitives.

On the afternoon of the 19th the alarming news was spread that a party of farmers from near Cottonwood had been cut off on their way to New Ulm and was now being surrounded by the Indians about a mile from the town. Theobold's sharpshooters were despatched to the scene, and later on Brunk's company too, to bring the endangered party in.

This news of the Cottonwooders, however, had been a "canard," which came near settling the fate of the New Ulmers. The dispatched men had hardly been away half an hour, when the Indians were sighted by Engineer Brockmann, stationed with a telescope on top of a brick building. The savages, with infernal yells, immediately rushed upon the town. They made for one of the barricades behind which the greater part of the tiny force of defenders was lying. The ensuing fusillade proved serious enough; the citizens lost two dead and several wounded.

The situation became most desperate. The few men already contemplated plans to kill their women and children and themselves before allowing the red devils to take them prisoners, when a dispatched detail, on its return, brought help, just in the nick of time. Deployed as skirmishers, the undaunted men, mostly former citizens from Cincinnati and experience 1 sharpshooters, attacked the savages from the rear and scattered them, for the time being, in all directions. Soon the detached men united with those within the town, and fresh hope was instilled in the brave little band.

The renewed attacks of the Indians grew more reckless and daring, and the ammunition of the citizens began to run short. The women gathered casks of shot from the different stores and melted the lead into lumps from which they casted bullets for the rifles. The loss of the whites had now reached a serious proportion, and it took all the courage and steadfastness of the leaders to keep up the spirits of their men.

It was at 4: 30 in the afternoon, when an unforeseen ally in the shape of a thunderstorm broke loose with all the force peculiar to the electric storms of this region. It grew dark, and the superstitious Indians, taking this explosion of the forces of nature as a bad omen, lost heart and withdrew. At 5 o'clock the firing had ceased. During the fight the Indians had managed to set fire to six houses.

The citizens, and especially their leaders, Roos and Nix, who had served against Indians as leaders of militia companies before, knew that the red men would leave them alone during the night, so these hours were devoted to the wounded and the women and children, who during the day had been gathered and taken care of by Dr. C. Weschke. The defences were also strengthened.

It was estimated that over 900 Indians had been in the attack of the 19th. It proved afterwards that their repulse by the brave little band of settlers decided the fate of the Upper Minnesota Valley. Had New Ulm fallen, the next important town. Mankato, twenty-eight miles below New Ulm, and situated in grounds entirely unfavourable for any defence, would have undoubtedly shared the same fate; the red men would have been masters of the valley.

In the morning it was found that the Indians had left and

were on their way to capture Fort Ridgley. The joy of the inhabitants may better be imagined than described. A feeling of safety came over the harassed population, strengthened through the arrival of twenty-five mounted citizens from St. Peter and the neighboring country, under Captain Bordman. This detail came in on the evening of the 19th, just after the firing had ceased and was enthusiastically received.

But the country surrounding New Ulm did not escape as luckily as the little town. All the farms and settlements were heaps of ruins, the inhabitants were massacred, the women having suffered outrages too horrible to describe.

Fort Ridgley, garrisoned by Captain Marsh and one company of the Fifth Minnesota Volunteers, received the first news of the Indians being on the warpath, from the Upper Agency, some forty miles above the fort, which asked for help. Brave Captain Marsh took fifty men and started forthwith, Before the command reached the Lower Agency, which was situated about twelve miles above the fort, they had gathered in a great number of fugitives, mostly women and children, who had taken temporary refuge in the cornfields. At the ferry, running between the two banks of the Minnesota, the little band of soldiers ran into an ambush; thirty-seven men, among them Captain Marsh, were killed; the remaining thirteen men reached the fort. The command here then fell to a sergeant of the regular army, by the name of Jones. He had about twenty men left, including the survivors from Captain Marsh's detachment.

But re-enforcements arrived; armed farmers, some of them ex-soldiers, flocked into the fort for protection, and a company, under Lieutenant Sheenah, ordered back from Fort Ripley, reached Ridgley at about the same time. Besides there were some fieldpieces left by the former garrison, which formed the most important part of the defence.

On the 20th the redskins were discovered in front of the fort and proceeded to the attack. They had no chance of success here. Although the garrison suffered a loss of several killed and many wounded, the sound of the cannon soon took all the

The siege of New Ulm, Minn.

heart out of the Indians. They retreated in the afternoon, taking, according to their fashion, their dead and wounded with them. Their loss could, therefore, not be ascertained, but was estimated at from fifty to seventy.

Meanwhile the menaced New Ulm had received more re-enforcements; armed detachments from St. Peter and Mankato arrived at midnight of the 19th, under the command of the worthy Judge Flandreau, who was one of the most esteemed settlers in the district. The command of New Ulm was transferred to him. During the night and the following day more aid arrived.

The Indians, however, did not appear again until the 23rd of August, when, undaunted by their second repulse before Ridgley, they renewed the attack upon New Ulm. At 10 o'clock in the forenoon they began to advance under cover of the smoke of fired fields and outlying buildings. In their first effort they succeeded in taking possession of the Turner Hall, a building on a rise of ground overlooking the town. It was a commanding position. Not far from this building and on the same elevation was a large windmill, occupied by the commands from Mankato and Le Sueur. These held the enemy in check and were supported by citizens holding the post-office, a brick structure, which afforded good covering against the deadly fire of the savages, who were splendidly armed and seemed to be amply supplied with ammunition.

The south and southeast sides of the town were the weakest points in the defence. and cunning Little Crow, the chief who directed the hostiles again on this occasion. was not slow in noticing it, The southeast side was formed by the German Park, a piece of ground then covered with high grass, just the place where the red men could display the cleverest side of their warfare. They were soon thick in this park and managed to push forward towards Minnesota Street until they reached abandoned houses in the latter street, from which they opened a deadly fire into the centre of the town.

Towards noon two men, Captain Dodd from St. Peter and a former German soldier by the name of Krieger, of Milford, attempted a daring reconnoissance in that direction. They had hardly galloped 200 yards before they were both shot. Krieger managed to ride back to town, but Dodd had to be rescued by a party of daring citizens, of whom one paid with his life for his devotion. Dodd died after a few hours, Krieger succumbed to his wounds after several months of suffering.

The Indians were gaining ground step by step. Towards 4 o'clock they occupied a large blockhouse at the southwest corner of Minnesota and Centre Streets. This was the strongest position in that part of the town. The conviction forced itself upon the defenders that they must drive the enemy from it or perish. Judge Flandreau and Captain Nix gathered some seventy men and made a most desperate attack on the redskins, some 200, who were in this blockhouse. The savages were driven out, but the attackers lost five killed and eighteen wounded.

It was now necessary to sacrifice all the outlying buildings by firing them, in order to deprive the enemy of the chance of again gaining strong positions. The great glow of the burning town was a magnificent sight that night.

Later on in the morning the Indians in the Turner Hall, anticipating correctly a determined attack by the settlers, fired the building and fled.

Then firing on their side ceased entirely, and the besieged commenced to fight the flames. The greater part of the town was in ruins. Only the centre, where the women, children and wounded were sheltered, remained—not more than thirty houses.

On the 24th of August the Indians were held at bay and withdrew. But the besieged found their stay in the ruined city unsafe, and, although some of them bravely objected, an organized exodus of the whole population took place on the 26th of August. The column reached Mankato the next morning, without further hardship. The Indians, after being twice repulsed, did not show up again before New Him, which was reached and occupied by Captain Dean and a company of United States volunteers on the 27th.

On the 29th of August the inhabitants began to return; the first ones finding troops and not Indians in possession of the destroyed town.

Details of affairs at Fort Ridgley were then learned, which disclosed the fact that the Indians had again retreated to that place and had made a most determined assault, which had forced the besieged garrison to seek shelter within the buildings and every spot where concealment against the shower of bullets was possible.

Probably five hundred Indians were engaged in the assault, There had been no time to construct any defensive works, or to remove or destroy the wooden structures or haystacks behind which the enemy could take position and shelter. And to render the situation of the beleaguered garrison still more critical, the magazine was situated some twenty rods outside the main works on the open prairie. Men were at once detailed to take the ammunition into the fort. This perilous duty was performed while Indian bullets rained across the open space over which they had to pass, until the last ounce was safely within the barracks.

Many deeds of bravery were exhibited during this fight and the men, although wounded, would not leave their places even when ordered to do so by their commander.

The fight continued until dark, the artillery all the while shelling the ravine at close range, and the rifles and muskets of the men dropping the yelling demons like autumn leaves. Meantime the Indians had gotten into some of the old outbuildings and had crawled up behind the haystacks, from which they poured heavy volleys into the fort. A few well-directed shells from the howitzers set fire to their places of shelter, and when night closed over the scene the bright light of the burning buildings shot up with a fitful glare, revealing to the watchful eye of the sentinel the head of each one of the foe as soon as it appeared. The Indians retired with the closing day, and were seen in large numbers on their ponies, making toward the agency.

All the vast region over which the savage up to this time had carried desolation and death was abandoned by the inhabitants

ALTHOUGH WOUNDED, THE MEN WOULD NOT LEAVE THEIR PLACES

who survived. During that entire week, over all that wide region, the midnight sky was red with the flames of burning buildings and stacks. In two days a population of 30,000, scattered over some eighteen counties on the western border of the state, on foot and horseback, with teams of oxen and horses, under the momentum of panic, had fled to places of safety.

After the described attacks the red devils retreated towards the northwest, their path being marked by death and destruction. Several small villages were burned to the ground, sharing the fate of New Ulm.

United States troops were now on their way to put an end to such atrocities. Fourteen hundred soldiers, under command of Colonel H. H. Sibley, were hurried from Fort Snelling in pursuit of Little Crow and his followers. A succession of desperate fights on both sides followed, which always ended in favour of the troops. Such defeats as were inflicted upon the Indians at the battle of Birch Coolie, which was the most bloody of any in which the forces were engaged, and also that at Wood Lake, where 300 Indians were terribly cut up by the troops, put an end to all hopes which Little Crow had entertained.

A large number of his warriors, and especially those of the Wapeton tribe, surrendered, but the notorious chief and his outlaws managed to escape and continued the war until the following year. Deprived of all comfort and deserted by his followers, he roamed through the woods and prairies, accompanied only by his son, until fate brought him before the gun of a white hunter, whose bullet finished his bloody career.

Had Little Crow been caught alive, his fate would have been the same as that of the ringleaders of the outbreak, thirty-eight of whom, after having received a regular trial, were hanged on one gallows. The hanging of these thirty-eight murderers at the same time was most gruesome, yet picturesque, and the punishment administered to the tribes thereby bore the best of results, as it taught them that every crime would be punished as it deserved.

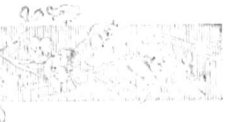

The Chivington Butchery

The Minnesota massacre had matured an intense feeling for revenge in the white man against the Indian. The question as to where was the real right or wrong found seldom a place for consideration in these strifes; it was simply a matter of to be or not to be between the frontier settlers and the red man beyond.

Consequently a force set out into the Platte country as soon as the slackened strain of the ebbing of civil war granted a chance.

This force, amounting to 750 cavalry and artillery, started one night late in November, 1864, from Bison Basin towards the northwest. The weather was so bitterly cold that old trapper Jim Beckwith, the guide, gave out and a half-breed had to take his place.

After a march of some 200 miles the head of the column came upon the village of 120 Cheyennes and eight Arapahoe lodges, stretching along the bank of a little river, the Sand Creek. The command bore down upon this hapless camp just before sunrise; only a few of the redskins had risen from their night's rest when the clattering of the cavalry became noticeable in the distance.

The camp was practically surprised, and the enraged soldiery proceeded to one of the most merciless butcheries ever committed by white men in recent times. Not only were the women and children ruthlessly destroyed, but, if reports of eye witnesses may be trusted, there were numerous cases of scalping of murdered women and even children, and many of those who tried to surrender were shot down like animals and mutilated in a manner rivalling the brutality of the red man himself.

Two squaws and five children were the only prisoners taken. About 300 Indians were slaughtered, half of whom were women and children.

The loss of the whites was seven killed and forty-seven wounded, seven of the latter mortally.

The ferocious acts on the part of the white soldiery at this bloody affair had naturally much to do with the subsequent relentless fierceness which the red tribes of the Northwest showed during the intense struggle lasting all through the latter sixties, the seventies and eighties, and ending with the battle at the Wounded Knee in 1891.

The man who planned and superintended this ill-renowned and atrocious deed on the Sand River was Colonel I. M. Chivington of the First Colorado Cavalry, under whose name it is generally known.

Saved From Starvation

CHARLES L. THOMAS

The Powder River expedition, lasting from June 20 to October 7, 1865, was planned to punish the various Indian tribes, notably the Sioux, Comanches. South and North Cheyennes, the Arapahoes, Kiowas and Apaches, who were continually harassing and obstructing the newly opened Platte and Arkansas overland routes. Only a month before the expedition started the Indians had at tacked a train on the Arkansas River, killed five men and robbed and destroyed the train. A station on the Smoky Hill route was attacked, stages were burned and cattle and stock carried off. Every day brought news of some act of hostility and treachery on the part of the Indians, and summary action became imperative.

The situation in reference to Indian matters about this time was a peculiar one. The Indians complained of great wrongs inflicted upon them by their agents. Some of the tribes claimed that they had received the government annuity but once within the past ten years, and they knew that it had been sent them regularly.

Other tribes asserted, with much apparent truthfulness, that they had received only a moiety of what was intended for them.

It was, as General G. M. Dodge expressed it, dishonestly frittered and speculated away by agents. This, of course, bred hatred and incited the Indians to many of their outrages.

Previously treaties were made which neither party would carry out, and were therefore easily broken. A spirit of independence and rebellion had grown up among the tribes, which manifested itself in ever-increasing atrocities. Life and property of the white man were nowhere safe in sections where any of the above-mentioned tribes were located.

Such was the situation at the time of the Powder River expedition, which was conducted by Major-General Dodge. The plan of the expedition was this:

General P. E. Connor was to move against the northern Indians in three columns; General J. B. Sanborn in three columns against the southern Indians, and two separate columns were to move to the country between the Platte and Arkansas Rivers to protect the great overland routes.

One of General Connor's three columns, under Colonel Nelson Cole, consisted of eight companies of the Second Missouri Light Artillery, equipped as cavalry, eight companies of the Twelfth Missouri Cavalry and a train of 140 six-mule wagons. The total number of men was about 1,400. The artillery comprised one section of three-inch rifled guns, manned by men of the Second Missouri Light Artillery.

On July 1 this command took up the line of march towards Columbus, on the Loup Fork of the Platte, following the line of the Pacific telegraph. From Columbus the route left the Platte and followed up the north bank of the Loup, leaving the last vestige of civilization at the Pawnee Mission, 110 miles from Omaha.

After passing the Mission a lieutenant's escort brought dispatches from General Connor containing full instructions as to the destination and route of the columns, which up to then were not known.

It was unquestionably an act of prudence on the part of either General Dodge or General Connor to have kept the leader and men in ignorance as to the nature of the expedition. For, had they known in advance through what desolate country they were to march, what obstacles they were to overcome, what deprivations they were to suffer, many of them who now started on the march with cheerful heart and expectant mood might have hesitated to participate in the hardships, and Colonel Cole's difficulty would have been increased a hundred-fold.

After much hardship they reached the Loup River, where wood, water and grass were found in plenty, and with few exceptions scarcely any serious obstacles to the march were encountered. Anticipating the frequent use of tools in the construction of bridges and cutting of embankments, a company of the Second Missouri Light Artillery was organized as a pioneer company. By keeping this company some distance in advance with the guides the road was prepared with sufficient dispatch to occasion but little delay in the movement of the column. After the first 150 miles had been traversed few creeks or rivulets emptied into the river. Near the head of the Loup the wood gave out entirely and the command was forced to resort to buffalo chips, of which a very limited quantity could be found.

Serious misgivings as to the practicability of moving the command across the country, which according to the best information obtainable was a barren, sandy desert, without fresh water, wood or grass, were harboured by the commander, and two parties were sent out, one on Lieutenant Warren's trail and another to the north or most direct line to the Niobrara River, to reconnoitre. The former reported an impassable route, the latter a practicable one with grass and water in abundance.

The latter course was adopted. This part of the country consisted of ridges from 200 to 500 feet in height, of deep, loose sand, which made the draught heavy on the mules, necessitating the frequent dismounting of the men, and the pulling of the guns and the army wagons with drag ropes. Continuous marches brought the command to the head of Antelope Creek, and thence it proceeded to the White Earth River; from there through Les Mauvais Terres to the South Fork of the Cheyenne

River. Recent rains rendered the crossing of this stream very difficult. The banks were submerged and made almost impassably miry, compelling the construction of corduroy roads before the trains could be gotten over.

Here, not far from camp, was discovered the first trail of a small party of Indians, indicating the recent passage of some roving band. On the march through the Bad Lands they had found no water fit for use until reaching the South Fork of the Cheyenne, but here again there was a scarcity of grass.

Many trails, evidently five or six days old, of parties of from five to fifteen Indians were seen; older and heavier trails, tending down the valley, were observed, denoting it to be one of their highways.

Scurvy had now become prevalent in the command, and the absence of the usual scorbutic remedies resulted in many fatal cases.

From here to the westward the troops moved over a gently undulating country, without water, save that in a couple of holes, which, with its brackish taste and thick consistency, was almost unfit for use. It was nearly night when the head of the column arrived at the edge of a cliff in sight of the Powder River. This cliff was hundreds of feet in height and no place of descent could be found. It seemed utterly impossible to traverse the rough and broken country, and it was decided to move into the valley of O Fallon's Creek, where, happily, a small pool containing possibly half a dozen barrels of brackish water, which the buffalo had been within a short time wallowing in, was discovered. The intense heat of the day, along with the dust-laden air, had created too strong a thirst among the men to cause them to hesitate at drinking the water discovered, although it was impregnated with the excrement of these animals. Of forage there was none to be had, and the stock had to be tied up the entire night without water or grass.

At 3 o'clock the next morning they moved to the edge of the cliffs again, where the guides discovered an Indian trail leading down to the lower plain. By cutting along this path, across divides and through canyons the trains were advanced about three miles that day. It was necessary, however, to station men on the sides of the hills with ropes to steady the wagons, which were frequently on the point of upsetting upon the mules or sliding sideways down the numerous precipices along the brinks of which they were compelled to pass.

The following day was intensely hot, and the great labour of working through canyons and over masses of rock, ofttimes necessitating the men to dismount and pull the fieldpieces and wagon by drag-ropes, together with the excessive dust, intensified the weariness and exhaustion of the entire command. The valley was reached at a point about fifty miles from the Yellowstone River.

The instructions given by General Connor were to proceed to Panther Mountains, at the base of which, on the Tongue River, there was to be found a depot of sup plies. Rations by this time were nearly exhausted, and it was necessary to communicate with the general as soon as possible to procure a fresh supply. To expedite this Lieutenant Hoagland, Second Missouri Light Artillery, with Raymond, a most reliable guide, and a detachment of twenty men, was sent to scout across the Tongue River, to ascertain the best route by which to move the column; also, if possible, at what point General Connor was lying with his command.

The scouting party returned September 1st. They had travelled fifty miles and reported no depot of supplies in sight, nor any indication of any having been around there at any time before. Panther Mountains were simple masses of red volcanic rock without the slightest sign of vegetation.

Upon the receipt of this report the rations were ordered to less than one-half. No Indians, nor any traces of any, had lately been seen.

Presently a report was brought that the Indians had attacked the men herding stock a mile distant from the camp and had driven off some of the animals. Immediately the entire command was ordered out, save sufficient to guard the camp. The advance engaged the Indians and succeeded in recovering most of the captured stock. Captain Rowland, Second Missouri Light Artillery, with a party of seven men, reached the ground first and pressed the Indians closely, killing a number of them. He was pursuing one of the small detached bands when another party of about forty-five suddenly dashed upon him and his men from a ravine to their right and killed or mortally wounded all of the small detachment, with the exception of Captain Rowland himself.

When the main body of the command reached the scene of action, the Indians fell back out of sight rapidly, and the troopers, with their broken down horses, could not pursue. The result was a loss of four men killed and two mortally wounded.

The greatest bodies of Indians were seen in the direction of the Little Missouri River and the most of them retreated along the trail through the " Bad Lands." During the afternoon a column of smoke was seen distinctly rising toward the mouth of the Powder River. Knowing that there were hostile Indians in the neighbourhood, the commander felt satisfied that there was a large body of warriors or a village on the Yellowstone River.

It was concluded that the smoke was evidently a signal made by the Indians, or else General Connor, unable to get down the Tongue River Valley on account of its barrenness, had availed himself of the fertile valley of the Big Horn to reach the Yellowstone and was endeavouring to attract attention by signal fires. Either case being true, it was the proper course to pursue to move in that direction, especially since it was expected to find there game in plenty and with sufficient buffalo to feed the command.

On the morning of September 2nd they crossed to the west bank of the river and followed the trail of Colonel Walker, Sixteenth Kansas, who marched about three miles ahead of the main force, through a country that offered nothing but cottonwood bark for forage.

After marching for about twenty-five miles, scouts were sent out to examine the territory. The waters of the stream sank into the sand about eight miles away and the bed was comparatively dry. The Indian trails scattered and were lost in the quicksands of the river, where the horses could not for an instant control themselves. During the night a terrible storm set in, a kind of storm that is liable to sweep over this country in any season and during which the temperature of the atmosphere suddenly changes from intense heat to extreme cold.

The want of nourishing forage, the exhaustion from the intense heat of the day's march, together with the effects of the storm, proved fatal to a large number of horses. Very reluctantly the command turned back on the next morning, September 3rd, to the point where they started and where they could at least find some grass for the dying stock. During this march down the river and back to grass 225 horses and mules died, and in consequence a number of wagons had to be destroyed, as also a considerable amount of now superfluous quartermaster's stores.

On the following morning Indians were discovered in large numbers in the hills to the west.

Larger detached parties showed themselves on the adjacent hills and many hundreds were discovered in the ravines be-

HAULING THE FIELD PIECES BY DRAG ROPES

yond, who thus far had not shown themselves. Large bodies also moved up the valley toward the south and a considerable force manoeuvred on the east bank of the river.

The Indians made efforts to attract small parties of men from camp and frequent attempts to get at the horses of the men who were on foot on the skirmish line, but the gallantry of the men and the excellence of the Spencer arm invariably frustrated these designs.

On one hill a large number of them had collected; a red flag and the constant use of their signal glass a piece of looking glass flashed in the sun—denoted it to be their headquarters. Guns were trained on that particular spot, which drove the Indians out of sight. Continuing up the river on September 8th, Colonel Walker, who was still three miles in advance of the main body, sent information that he was being attacked by between 3,000 and 4,000 Indians, who were driving him back. The command was rapidly pushed forward, and by quick action drove the Indians in all directions, then the river was crossed and a camp was formed of both commands.

After getting into camp a storm blew up, which grew worse as night came on and finally became terrific in its fury. From rain it turned to hail, then in succession it snowed and sleeted, yet freezing all night long. Picket officers were forced to march their men in circles at the reserve posts to prevent them from being frozen to death, as fires were not admissible. Nothing could be done to protect the stock from the peltings of this terrible storm, and whole numbers of them died during the night.

When daylight dawned it had not abated in the least, and owing to the unsheltered position of the camp was especially severe on the men as well as the stock, so much so that it was determined to move to some point within a few miles where shelter could be secured in heavy timber to save the remnant of the rapidly failing animals. Two miles and a half of march route were marked with dead and dying horses and mules. During the thirty-six hours of the storm 414 animals perished at the picket ropes or along the roads between the camps.

On September 10th the command was compelled to cross the river under cover of artillery fire, for the Indians had, vulture-like, hovered around the exhausted and starving command and made a detour around to a position on the bluff in the rear, prepared to dash down and finish up. However, a generous amount of shells thrown among them kept them at a respectful distance.

Fatigue and starvation had now done their work on both men and stock so that they were unfit to pursue the savage foe that circled around their starving way through this desert. The rations by this time had been reduced to less than quarter rations, and the horse and mule flesh was used to sustain life.

At this critical juncture there appeared like a messenger from heaven a stranger—a mere youth—in Colonel Cole's camp, and by his timely arrival and valuable information, of which he was the bearer, an entire command was saved from an almost inevitable fate of death and destruction.

This man was Sergeant Charles L. Thomas of Company E, Eleventh Ohio Cavalry. He came, a courier from General Connor, to apprise Colonel Cole of the proximity of the general's camp and point out a way of safety amidst the dangers that beset the colonel and his helpless troops and lead him along an avenue of escape.

How the wonderful feat of the brave soldier, whose presence seemed like a miracle to the downcast command, was accomplished, and for which a Medal of Honour was awarded him, is told in the hero's own narrative, as follows:

"We had marched 400 miles northeast to the Powder River, established a stockade fort called Fort Connor, at a base of supplies, proceeded in the same direction to Clear Creek, where another fort—Fort Carney—was constructed, and marched to the junction of the Tongue with the Yellowstone River, where on August 22nd our scouts reported the location of a large Indian village. A detachment was sent after daybreak to attack the habitation, which was pillaged, burned and destroyed, many Indians being killed and about 700 horses and mules captured.

"Our chief guide was a Major Bridge, and a better guide or better posted pilot through this territory could not have been found, for he had spent forty-two years of his life in this section and among the Indians. In fact, he had a wife in every tribe and children galore.

"On September 7th we reached the Yellowstone River, where we were to meet Colonel Cole's command.

"Not finding the division at this place, General Connor was greatly concerned and worried as to its whereabouts, because he knew that by this time Colonel Cole would have exhausted his rations and feared that he was in a serious plight. Scouting parties were at once sent out, but they all returned and reported the surrounding country full of swarming Indians, to such an extent, even, that it was impossible for a small command to get to the Powder River. Reports also came in to the effect that artillery firing, the roar of cannons, could be heard distinctly somewhere along the river. All agreed that no human help could reach Colonel Cole, as he was surrounded and completely hemmed in by thousands of Indians.

"General Connor knew that Colonel Cole must be apprised of the location of his own camp and base of supplies or perish with his entire force, even should he escape the clutches of the 6,000 or 7,000 Indians.

"He asked for volunteers to go to the colonel's relief.

"On the morning of September 12th I went to the general and offered my services. General Connor was pleased.

"'Go get your breakfast, fill your canteen with coffee, take some buffalo-jerk and all the ammunition you can carry, and prepare yourself for your journey. I expect there will be others to join you,' he said.

"I did as he bade me and waited, but not another man came forward to undertake the mission.

"General Connor ordered me to appear before him, and, emphasizing the dangers of the task I had volunteered to accomplish, asked me if I still was willing to carry out an undertaking so hazardous, yet, if successful, so eminently important.

"I said I was. And why shouldn't I? I was young—22 years old—vigorous, considered a good horseman, and admittedly the best shot in the regiment. I was recklessly fearless and could stand almost any amount of hardship. I rather liked an errand like that.

"My captain gave me two of his most reliable Pawnee Indians to take along, as he did not want to see me go alone to my almost certain death.

"We rode out of camp on September 12th, at 8 o'clock in the morning, and for an hour and a half saw no Indians, and then observed only a few who were too far away to shoot at. We rode as fast as the condition of our horses would permit.

"By 3 o'clock we had reached the top of the divide between the rivers and met two Indians with a *travis*, upon which they carried a wounded warrior. We made them drop their comrade, and one of my Pawnees jumped from his pony, gave his tribe's war-whoop, struck the helpless Indian in the face with the handle of his whip, placed his foot on the brave's neck and in an instant was holding his scalp high in the air. A shot through the head put the finishing touch on the mutilated foe. My proud Pawnee companion then remounted and we rode on, exchanging frequent shots with numerous Indians whom we met on our dashing ride.

"When darkness fell we could observe the small Indian camp-fires and had no trouble in avoiding them. Yet, I dreaded to encounter a party of these Indians in the dark, and therefore entered the first draw I found leading into the river. How I missed the elbow touch of a white comrade that night. Here I was almost deserted in a wild, unknown country, surrounded by hordes of bloodthirsty Indians riding on madly through the dark, pursued by the hideous howls of the hungry wolf and hostile Indians.

"I reached Powder River just at daybreak. At the mouth of the canyon, along which I and the Pawnees were riding, a horse appeared and immediately afterward an Indian came out from under the shelving rocks where he had been sleep-

WHAT IN GOD'S NAME ARE YOU DOING HERE?

ing. He was less than ten feet from me as he raised up, threw his blanket off his shoulder and held his rifle in his left hand. I shot him dead. The incident was sudden and made me and my Pawnees somewhat excited. It was too bad, for had I kept my head a second Indian, who likewise appeared from behind the rocks, would have shared his fate. But this Indian got away by jumping over the embankment, a distance of fifteen feet, and escaping into the dense bushes.

"We rode for about six miles along the banks of the Powder River. Then in a comparatively cool spot we let our horses drink and rest up a little. Now we could hear distinctly the signal calls of the Indians from six or seven different directions. It was apparent that our presence was known to the Indians, so I decided to push on as fast as I possibly could, realizing that lingering would mean almost certain death with no show for a defence. So riding out into the valley we discovered Colonel Cole's trail leading in a southerly direction, or up the river, and followed this trail, hurrying on our horses to the greatest possible speed.

"We pushed on unmolested by Indians until about 9 o'clock, when we struck a small stream. The valley below was strewn with carcasses of horses and mules. The sight brought the cold sweat to my brows. I thought Colonel Cole's entire command had been massacred down there, but soon reassured myself when I rode down into the valley and found that there was not a single human corpse among these bodies, and also discovered that the animals had all been shot in the head. Shortly after leaving this ghastly valley I noticed an Indian riding into a chaparral alongside of the trail. There was no way of avoiding an encounter.

"Neither could we tell whether that Indian was alone. We drew revolvers and charged right past the chaparral. We were immediately followed and fired on by seventeen Indians. Answer was given with shots from our rifles, which killed one Indian on a horse and drove the others across the river. As we continued on our course, these Indians recrossed and followed in our rear, increasing in number as we proceeded until there were too many of these red skins on our heels to count. For mile after mile, hour after hour, a hot chase and running fight was kept up. The longer this chase continued the more excited it grew. At every crook and turn in the trail I expected to find Colonel Cole.

"This fighting, running, shooting, chasing at break-neck speed lasted from 10 o'clock in the morning until 3 o'clock in the afternoon. Then, away in the distance where the valley was narrow, I saw a body of men drawn across the trail. I was sure they were men of Colonel Cole's command, and my heart beat faster as I urged my horse on to still greater speed. But what a disappointment when, on coming closer. we found them to be Indians—a large body of Sioux!—and no alternative but to break through that file or fall in the attempt. I realized that some scalping would be done, and rather anticipated that my own head would have to furnish such a trophy.

"Nevertheless I was determined to sell my life as dearly as possible, and, instructing my faithful Pawnees, rode up to within fifty yards of this line of Indians. Then we fired our rifles at them. One Indian dropped to the ground dead; the others ran hither and thither, opening the way for us to make a swift dash. We dismounted two more warriors, when the rest fled as if Satan himself were on their heels. Still another Indian was struck by our bullets, and he fell off his horse in the trail. He was tied to his pony by a hair lariat and was dragged along for some distance. I separated him from his horse and took the animal to have a remount should my own horse give out or get shot, which I expected every moment.

"I discovered that the Indian's horse I had taken belonged to a member of the Sixth Missouri Cavalry. I still found his letters and pictures in the saddle-pockets. There was also in one of the pockets a tintype picture of the Indian himself and $95 in United States notes. How I longed to scalp this fellow! But my time was too precious to indulge in acts of vengeance. After riding for a short distance I saw a white man lying behind a stone and small sage-bush. I rode up to him.

"'What in God's name are you doing here?' I asked him.

"He stammered, hardly audibly, that he was one of Colonel Cole's command. 'I'm played out. My feet are full of thorns and thistles. Would that the Indians only come and end my misery!'

"I got him on my reserve horse and carried him along. We still had a distance of four miles to cover until we reached camp, and had to fight every inch of our way. It was sundown when we finally arrived at the picket-line. I at once reported to Colonel Cole and was able to direct him to Fort Connor, about 150 miles distant.

"I found the men of the command in a most deplorable condition—they were a starved, discontented body of men.

"I left Camp Connor with over 350 rounds of ammunition and had 17 shots left when I arrived at Colonel Cole's camp. My horse, which had carried me throughout the expedition, came down with lockjaw the next day, and I was compelled to shoot the faithful animal."

The Fetterman Massacre

The rush of settlers to the Northwest, following the disbandment of the large armies of the civil war, made it necessary to build roads in that remote region, the undisputed home of the most warlike tribes of American Indians. To protect these roads forts had to be constructed.

Fort Phil Kearney, built by General Carrington in the year 1866, was one of the line of forts intended to protect the Montana Road from the attacks of the Dakotas, or Sioux. At that time the most dreaded savage in the Powder River region was Red Cloud, the leader of the Ogalallas.

Fort Kearney was one of the largest posts ever erected in the wilderness, and was surrounded by an extensive stockade. While the building was in progress the soldiers at work were continually harassed by the roaming savages. The commander of the troops in the fort, which consisted of two small detachments of cavalry and infantry, was Colonel Fetterman.

An important part of the military life around the new post was the cutting of the timber for the new buildings and palisades, and the soldiers had to do this work, so that the protection of these wood-cutting details from the surprises of the hostiles became one of the trying tasks of the garrison.

On December 6, 1866, the wood-cutters were attacked in the timber, two miles from the fort. Colonel Fetterman, who hastened to their aid with a detail of cavalry, was lured into an ambush and escaped from disaster only through the timely arrival of support under General Carrington himself.

Lieutenant Bingham and several soldiers were on this occasion killed by the Indians.

On December 21st it became necessary to obtain a large quantity of timber, and a force of some ninety men was detailed to cut it. Colonel Fetterman secured the assent from the general to look after their protection.

The wood cutters had hardly left the stockade when Indians were appearing in the surrounding woods, first in clusters of three and four, but soon in considerable numbers. Only a short time after the wood-cutters had left the lookouts from the signal station reported that the detail was surrounded by savages and had gone into corral to defend itself. Colonel Fetterman started immediately for the relief with a combined force of cavalry and infantry, counting, including himself, three officers and eighty-two soldiers.

The command soon disappeared in the woods and its effect upon the Indians was apparent, when the lookouts from the signal bluff reported that the wood-cutting detail had broken corral and was on its way back.

Nothing was observed of Fetterman's command until, towards noon, heavy firing was heard in the distance. As it kept increasing in intensity, General Carrington sent all the rest of the garrison available towards the sound of the firing. This party reached a ridge from behind which the firing seemed to come. But when the troops were crossing it the firing had ceased.

From the crest of the ridge the soldiers could see dense swarms of Indians in the woods in front, the redskins challenging the troops with provoking boldness to come down and fight. From Fetterman's party nothing could be detected.

The officer in command of the supporting troops went determinedly down and attacked the savages, who retreated after a short and not very vigorous resistance.

After a short advance the soldiers came to a large boulder, and on the ground around this boulder, within a space of perhaps fifty feet square, they found the butchered remains of forty-eight of Fetterman's detachment and the body of the of-

The massacre of Colonel Fetterman's command

ficer himself. Nearly overcome by the ghastly sight, the relief party had had hardly time to count the dead when the Indians came on again in a furious attack. Their numerical superiority was such that the little force was compelled to withdraw back to the fort, which was reached at nightfall.

After this longest of winter nights had passed in depressing dreariness and sorrow for the people in the fort General Carrington went out, as soon as the sun came up, with a detachment of eighty men, determined, if possible, to obtain the full de tails of the tragedy. This time the Indians were not inclined to resist. The troops reached the fatal spot unmolested. In vain did they send out searching parties for possible survivors; all the searchers found were the bodies of Lieutenant Grummond, two civilian volunteers and thirty-two soldiers lying towards the further end of the divide.

Lieutenant Grummond had been in command of the cavalry detachment, the civilians had volunteered in their eagerness to test a couple of Henry rifles, which were at that time a much admired novelty in the Northwest.

Colonel Fetterman and the third officer, Lieutenant Brown, lay close together at the foot of the boulder, each one with a shot through the left temple. This led to the conjecture that in the last moment both took each other's life in order to escape capture and torture. But one cannot help thinking it strange that in the midst of bloody slaughter the swarm of undisciplined savages should have spared the two officers to the last just to give them a chance to escape being taken by blowing each other's brains out.

The bodies were horribly mutilated; such butchery had never been known before, on even Indian murder-fields. The rocks around the fatal spot were strewn with torn-out eyes, knocked-out teeth, hacked-off heads, limbs, ears, noses; the life less trunks were filled with arrows; in one of the bodies were counted no less than thirty-seven. This was the devilish work of the Indian boys after their elders had done the killing.

The eighty-five bodies, or rather what remained of them, were buried around the spot where the men had fallen.

Shocking as this horrible massacre was, the climax of the evil-doings of its perpetrators was yet to come. Red Cloud, who instigated this murder and led his bands into committing it, found his own deviltry outstripped by his tribesman, Sitting Bull, when the latter, nearly ten years later, slaughtered brave Custer and his men at Little Big Horn.

Thirty-Two Against Three Thousand

When the government in 1866 decided upon the necessity of constructing a road through some of the Indian reservations in Dakota to Montana, consent was obtained from the Sioux, through whose territory the proposed highway was to run. The concession was granted and a treaty signed by all the Sioux chiefs, except one—Red Cloud. He regarded the demand of the "Great Father in Washington" as an invasion and succeeded in gathering about himself a formidable force of Sioux and Cheyennes, upon whom his fierce eloquence, firm attitude and warlike spirit had made a great impression, and who like Red Cloud himself were determined to resist the proposed "invasion" to the bitter end.

In the meantime the government had built in July, 1866, a fort right in the heart of the Sioux domain and called it Fort Phil Kearney. Red Cloud and his hordes placed every obstacle possible in the way of the construction of the fort, attacking small detachments sent out to cut wood, lying in ambush for small details and ready at all times for a coup to annihilate an inferior force. The Fetterman massacre was the sad result of this treacherous conduct.

In February, 1867, Sergeant George Grant, of Company E, Eighteenth United States Infantry, came near falling into the hands of these savages and losing his life, when he voluntarily undertook to deliver a dispatch from the newly constructed fort to Fort C. F. Smith in Dakota. His sufferings from the hardships of very severe weather, lack of food and the dangers of an invisible, yet powerful, merciless enemy made his trip one of the most heroic and the success of his mission a grand achievement.

About the latter part of July of the same year Captain James Powell, of the Twenty-seventh United States Infantry, left the fort with fifty-one men and one officer, Lieutenant J. Jenness, to protect a "wood party," which, under the eye of a contractor, was cutting fuel for the garrison.

The contractor had two encampments of lumbermen, one in the centre of a small plain well situated for effective defence, another on the other side of Little Piney Creek, near the foot of the mountains. Both encampments were about a mile apart. The captain detailed part of his soldiers to protect the working parties and to escort the wood trains on their trips to and from the fort.

With wise precaution Captain Powell, who had a force of one lieutenant, twenty-six men and four civilians left at his disposal, made his position on the plain as strong a defence as he could.

He had fourteen empty wagon-beds, top parts of large wagons, the running gears of which were being used to haul wood, which he placed on the ground in such a manner as to form an oval-shaped fort. At the point on each side a wagon on wheels established the connection between the beds. Those wagons contained the necessary supplies for the troops.

Red Cloud's warriors were swerving ominously about the vicinity of the corral, but for three days everything was quiet. Then came the clash the final and last clash, which forever crushed the Indian chief's ambitious hopes.

On August 2, 1867, 200 Indians attacked and drove off the men in charge of the herd attached to the camp; 500 attacked the train on the foot of the mountain, compelling the men to flee, and burning the wagons. A number of soldiers were killed and wounded, few arriving at the fort.

Then followed a concerted attack on Captain Powell's corral. The Indians, numbering some 3,000, were certain of their prey. Indeed, they had brought their squaws along to assist in the torturing of their victims and add zest to their enterprise. As they lined up, garbed in their war costumes of many colours, parading hither and thither, they were a picturesque and repulsive set.

Now the attack began. Captain Powell was fully prepared—each man had his instructions, each his designated post. "Fight for your lives now," was the commander's last admonition before the charge.

Eight hundred Indian horsemen came dashing on with the force of a whirlwind. When they were within 100 yards of the corral, Powell commanded "Fire!" and a sheet of flame from behind the wagon-beds was the answer. Another volley and still another, and of the charging savages nothing could be seen but a mass of dead bodies, and a number of wounded on the ground and a few fleeing in confusion toward the hills. That was the end of the first charge. Red Cloud was watching awe-stricken the destruction wrought to his braves from a mysterious arm so cleverly handled by the soldiers. It was his first acquaintance with the breech loading gun, which had just been introduced in the army.

He now began to encircle the corral, sending out first his sharpshooters, who, creeping forward, dodging behind stump and boulder, hiding in the hollows, slowly came nearer and nearer to the wagon-beds, and by constant firing occupied the attention of the few defenders. Charge after charge was made, five times in succession, every time with the same result—death and defeat before the murderous gun of the accurately firing soldier.

For three long hours did Red Cloud lead his horde of followers before the fatal muzzles of the mysterious gun, but when hundreds of his braves had been slain on the field, hundreds wounded and he had lost nearly half his force either by death or wounds, he desisted from further attack and gave up the hopeless task. He retired to the hills, just as re-enforcements arrived for Captain Powell and his band of heroes, who had lost one officer—Lieutenant Jenness—and five men killed and two wounded.

On the Arickaree

When after the War of the Rebellion disbanded soldiers and others flocked in great numbers into the northwest and the railroads began to build their lines, the warlike Indian tribes who considered that vast region their own and indisputable territory became greatly aroused. From mere excitement and turbulence to actual aggressiveness it was only a small step with these fierce aborigines. Towards the end of 1866 the situation on the border was ripe for the crisis, and from many signs and sources the military garrisons took their warning and prepared the best they could for the gathering outbreak. The storm centre was felt developing within the haughty and powerful Sioux nation, and particularly among the Cheyennes.

At Fort Ellsworth, in Kansas, the commander of the post, General Palmer, had an important conference, a "big talk," with the Cheyenne chieftains, Black Kettle, the superb Roman Nose and some others. The demeanour of the Indians was defiant in the extreme; they declared unanimously that if the building of the railway through their country was not stopped immediately and for good it would be war. "This is the first time," said the towering giant, Roman Nose, "that I shook the white man's hand in friendship; if the railway is continued I shall again be his enemy for evermore." General Palmer was unable to promise anything, but assured the indignant warriors that he would faithfully submit their complaint to the Great White Father in Washington.

The next move on the part of the government was to send

General Hancock with a mixed force of some 1,500 troops into the endangered region, with strict orders to avoid bloodshed if possible, but to announce to the Indians in unmistakable terms that they must henceforward refrain from any acts of molestation or depredation, and keep away from the lines of travel.

The Indians answer was a number of raids and murders committed among the white frontier settlers. All the Cheyennes and Sioux between the Arkansas and Platte went upon the warpath.

In the summer of 1867 General Hancock was relieved by General Phil Sheridan; the latter had on his staff Brevet-Colonel George A. Forsyth, a trusted aide during the civil war, a man of iron will, iron constitution and absolute fearlessness. The emergency required quick action, and General Sheridan directed Forsyth to hire fifty civilians, if possible expert frontiersmen, at the rate of thirty-five dollars per month, each to bring his own horse and equipment, receiving forty-five cents per day for its use, but to be supplied with arms, ammunition and rations by the government, Forsyth did not lose any time and soon had his force in readiness. It was sent out at once to the aid of white settlers between Harbinger Lake and Bison Basin, who were in immediate danger from large Indian war parties.

On the march the command, or rather posse, discovered traces of criminal acts of some of these Indians near the head waters of Beaver Creek. Forsyth took up the pursuit of this band, and on the 14th of September his men struck a fresh trail of a large force of hostiles. From all signs their proximity was evident, and the command inarched with all necessary precaution. On the afternoon of the 16th the whites had no more provisions left except biscuit for one day, and their leader was extremely anxious to close in with the enemy.

Forsyth's good judgement led him into camp on this day at about 5 o'clock, instead of marching on till nightfall. He wanted to give the horses rest and good fodder so that they should be fresh the next day on which he hoped to catch up with the hostiles. It was afterwards found out that only three miles from where he halted the Indians were lying in ambush for him in such a position that had Forsyth run into it his force would undoubtedly have been annihilated.

Forsyth's camp was close to the bank of the Arickaree, a tributary of the Republican. In the middle of the stream, which had a depth of only a few inches, was a sandy island fringed with willows and with a few stunted trees distributed over its surface. The surrounding country was an undulating plain, with the nearest divides about one mile away. The place offered good grazing, and the horses, carefully picketed and under guard, were soon enjoying it. When night came the men lay down near their horses, with arms in hand.

The commander was up and reconnoitring long before daylight. While peering through the gloom of early morning twilight he saw some indistinct figures stealthily creeping over the plain towards his camp. His men were quietly notified that the enemy were coming; everybody secured his horse and prepared for the attack.

Presently the Indians rushed in, howling and shaking blankets and buffalo robes with the intention of stampeding the horses, their usual introductory act at battle. They were not successful; a few well-aimed volleys drove them off. When day broke it was at once seen that the enemy were overwhelmingly superior in numbers, and Colonel Forsyth began forthwith to transfer his camp to the sand island. This was about 200 by 40 feet in extension. The horses were tied to the scanty shrubbery, the men distributed in a circle, and set at once to the digging of rifle pits, which was soon accomplished in the sandy ground. In the meantime a few good marksmen on the main bank of the river kept advancing crowds of hostiles at bay.

Forsyth stood unprotected among his men, and only after several Indian bullets had barely missed him he consented to protect himself in a pit which one of his men had dug.

Shortly after 9 o'clock the Indians proceeded to the first great assault. In the distance the men on the island could distinguish the magnificent Roman Nose by the crimson sash which

General Palmer had presented to him on the occasion of his visit at Fort Ellsworth. Roman Nose organized his mounted braves, who were to deal the decisive blow in the attack. Swarms of dismounted Indians, with breech-loading guns of latest pattern, and even boys armed with bows and arrows, preceded the onrush of the mounted force, covering the island with a perfect fusillade of missiles. The men on the island were directed by their leader not to answer this galling fire, and they obeyed to the letter.

Presently the Indian women and children who as spectators fringed the slopes of the flanking elevation, started a terrific, ear-tearing yelling and whooping, and the mass of mounted warriors, with Roman Nose far in the van, came thundering on in all their savage splendour. At about 200 yards from the river they all let loose their unearthly war-whoops and urged their ponies to the utmost speed. Forsyth had warned his men earnestly to wait with their fire until they should hear his command.

When the roaring wave of redskins was not farther away than fifty yards the colonel's command rang out: "Now!" The sharpshooters bullets crashed into the dense column of horses and men with unerring directness; volley after volley swept with lightning-like rapidity into the fast-moving ranks. The horses went down in rows and the riders fell in heaps. Some bodies of men and horses lay right in the stream, only a few yards from the rifle pits. But the great mass, wavering a moment, split in two under the fearfully telling fire, and, describing wide, flanking curves to the right and left, swept back into safety.

Right in front of the rifle pits, the shallow waters of the Arickaree rippling about the lifeless bodies of rider and horse, lay Roman Nose, the wicked and merciless hater of the pale-face, superb and defiant even in death.

The Indians, discouraged though they were by the collapse of their daring attack, resorted to their boldest tricks to recover the body of this renowned warrior, but the guns on the island held them in check.

Roman Nose's death meant a fatal blow for the hostiles. Twice in the course of the day they repeated the attack, but

The Indians proceeded to the first great assault

their energy did not nearly come up to their first effort; both attempts were easily frustrated by the steady hands and the cool heads behind the guns in the sand island's rifle pits.

The brave white men had suffered severely. Lieutenant Beecher, of the Third U. S. Infantry, second in command, having been shot through the abdomen, died in great agony; the doctor of the outfit was killed early in the day; Colonel Forsyth was dangerously wounded in three places. Before 10 o'clock a bullet pierced his right thigh; later another shattered his left leg at the knee, and in the afternoon a third one grazed his skull, scooping the bone. Two other men were dead, two mortally and sixteen more or less severely wounded. Every horse and mule had been killed.

Towards evening a drizzling rain began to fall, adding to the discomfort, dreariness and hopelessness of the situation. Fort Wallace, the nearest place from which help might be obtained, was almost 100 miles away.

But the little band, encouraged by the marvellous example of their leader, did not despair, They dug a well through the sand, stripped meat off the dead horses and mules and strengthened their line of defence with saddles and the bodies of the dead animals. Towards midnight two men, Pierre Trudeau and John Stilwell, left the camp to reach Fort Wallace, if possible, and summon relief. By unusual care, combined with good luck, they accomplished their task. Wearing *moccasins* they had made from boot-tops and with blankets wrapped around them Indian fashion, they managed to crawl through the lines of the hostiles in the first night, making three miles.

The next day they spent lying hidden in a washout between the Arickaree and the South Republican. During the second night they continued their dangerous trip, meeting and avoiding several parties of Indians, and towards daybreak they reached the South Republican. The next day they spent like the first, lying concealed under the river bank; the Indians swarmed all around them, and it was a wonder to themselves that the wily savages failed to discover them. During the third day they were lying in a bison swallow when some scouting Indians came within thirty yards of their cover and Stillwell had to quiet an alarming rattle snake by spitting tobacco juice on its head. The following night Trudeau, who was an elderly man, came near breaking down. But they kept on, and on the fourth day, towards noon, they met two mounted couriers going to Colonel Carpenter at Lake Station, which was about sixty miles from Forsyth's camp. Colonel Carpenter, as soon as these two men informed him, started with his whole command and relieved Forsyth on the ninth day.

The Indians had given up the siege on the fifth day, but Forsyth's command was by that time in such a state of exhaustion that nobody could move. The relief party found the men helpless and near death, lying among the dead animals in an atmosphere rendered pestilent from the decaying bodies.

The day after Carpenter reached this veritable island of desolation a second relief force arrived from Fort Wallace. The sufferers were transported to the latter place, but some of them never recovered. Scout Trudeau died in the following spring; Forsyth had to have his shattered leg amputated and was put on the retired list.

The Indians said afterwards that their whole force against the fifty men had amounted to 900 warriors, of whom 75 were killed.

Exciting Scout For a Trail

Edgar L. Aston & William G. Cubberly

A pretty little Indian story tells of the dangers which beset the explorer who in days not far remote dared to follow an Indian trail.

The scene of action was in picturesque Arizona. The time was in the early spring of 1868 a few months before the great Indian uprising.

The Apaches had become unruly. They harassed and annoyed the settlers and stole and plundered. An expedition was expected to restore peace and safety and punish the offending savages.

Two cavalry troops, B and L, of the Eighth United States Cavalry, and two companies of the Fourteenth United States Infantry, left Camp Verde, Arizona, sometime during the latter part of May, 1868, on their mission. A large pack train, conveying a sufficient supply of rations, ammunition and other accessories to an expedition, greatly impeded the progress of the command, especially since the route itself offered an abundance of obstacles. The destination was the Tonto Basin, where the rebellious Indians were supposed to be in hiding. The march to the edge of the Basin consumed five days. The first stop was made at San Carlos River not far distant from the edge of the basin; just near enough to remind the troops that they were almost within sight of their field of operations, and to make some of the soldiers, who knew the Indians only by reputation, tremble with fear. Seven men of Troop B stole away from camp and deserted.

Trouble began at the edge of the basin, which was a mass of gigantic walls of solid rock, with no path or passageway leading to the bottom. Yet the descent had to be made, though it would take nearly all day, and was the occasion of many a thrilling escape from death. The descent began early in the morning; in the evening camp was pitched 4,000 feet down the valley near a running stream. The presence of the Apaches was soon made known to the troopers, for they announced themselves early in the evening by shooting innumerable arrows into the camp, but without inflicting any damage except to kill a horse. A detachment of forty cavalrymen was sent after them, but the wily Indians got away and kept out of sight.

On May 27th Troops B and L left the camp at San Carlos River and started on a two days scouting tour, leaving the infantry and the pack train behind them in camp.

Four cavalrymen were ordered to remain with the pack train: Sergeant Richard Fisher, Corporal William Thomas and Privates Edgar L. Aston and William G. Cubberly.

There was also attached to the train an old trooper, a most original and quaint character called "Cap" Shere, who acted as a guide. He, Aston and Cubberly started out to find a passable trail.

"On the morning of May 28th," says Private Aston, "'Cap' Shere saddled up his mule. Without saying a word the old fellow got ready to leave camp.

"'Say, Cap, what are you going to do?' I asked him.

"'Hmm,' he replied, without looking up. 'Going to hunt up a trail. There must be some way to git out o' this here valley, I reckon.'

"The idea struck me as an excellent one, but neither I nor my friend Cubberly wanted to see the old man go alone, so we obtained permission to go along with him.

"We had left the camp and journeyed about a mile, when at the foot of the hills we struck Indian signs, and, of course, continued on the trail a mile or two farther, till we could see that there was quite a large party of redskins at least nineteen ahead of us.

"We followed the trail down a very steep decline in a canyon and then turned abruptly to the left. The tracks of the Indians were now fresh and plain.

"Every moment I expected a big Indian to jump out and swing his tomahawk. I needn't say that I did not feel quite comfortable.

"Cap Shere halted. 'Look here, you fellows,' he said to us; 'do yer want to go on or do yer want to go back?'

"'You're running this trip. Whatever you say goes,' I replied, and Cubberly nodded assentingly.

"'Well, then,' Cap remarked, 'I ain't satisfied yet about this here trail. What I want to find out is, what becomes of the trail at the top of the hill.' That settled it. We continued our lead, Cap going at the head, Cubberly and I bringing up the rear.

"Before we reached the top of the hill the old man discovered that the Indians had left the trail, and once more he halted to ask us whether we still wished to go ahead. Our reply was the same as before. Then Cap declared himself:

"'Now,' said he, 'it's just about like this: if we turn back the Indians'll surely think we're afraid, and jump on us, and if we go ahead, they'll git ready and lay fer us. You kin bet your lives they'll try to git us, if they kin. If you fellers are a mind to stick by me, we kin give 'em all the fight they want. I'm fer goin ahead.'

"Having delivered himself of this speech, he faced about and on we went for another six miles till the top of the hill was gained and the best kind of trail leading out of the valley found. We now concluded to retrace our steps.

We made our Spencer carbines talk

"We fully knew, of course, that our troubles would now commence and we prepared to find the Indians lying in wait for us.

"But we had to go back no matter how great the danger.

"The thought that our discovery of a passable trail was of great importance inspired us with courage and hastened our return.

"The six miles back from the top of the hill was about the most uncomfortable six miles I ever made in my life, and when we arrived within about a hundred yards of the place where we first stopped old Cap halted and gave us the following orders:

"He was to take the lead and Cubberly and I were to follow. But we were first to turn our animals loose and drive them down to him, so that he could lead them off as they reached the bottom of the hill.

"Cap started, but the Indians did not molest him.

"Cubberly and I, however, had not proceeded more than 150 yards, when the redskins suddenly appeared and with a whoop and yell opened up on us. We continued on our retreat, but also made our Spencer carbines talk.

"How we did fire! The Apaches, too, were furious and sent arrows and bullets after us, till we were in a shower of missiles.

"We managed to reach the bottom of the hill without injury, and after crossing the canyon to the other side knew that we were safe from further attacks. We halted to make an inventory. Cubberly's mule was shot through the nostrils, my horse was wounded along the tail, the bullet passing clean through the intestines. Cap had a lock of hair cut off his forehead as nicely as though it had been done with a pair of scissors. His forearm was also slightly injured.

"There is no doubt but what we would have been killed had we taken to our heels and simply ran, and that only by keeping up a hot fire we held the Indians at bay."

Privates Aston and Cubberly were both rewarded with the Medal of Honour for the valuable information which enabled the troops to follow the Indians with their wagon train after the encounter.

From this time on to the end of October troops B and L

were constantly engaged in encounters with the Indians, but the principal work was done and the greatest hardships endured during the months of August, September and October.

The Apaches kept all Arizona in a state of terror by their depredations, and it was only by the most persistent hammering that the troops, particularly B and L, kept the territory open to the settlers. During these three months the Indians were murdering men, women and children mercilessly and stealing live stock and other property, and all real progress in the territory was prevented. The Apaches did not give battle to the troops except when cornered by them; their idea being primarily to steal, and then to kill without being killed. Many times were these two troops, amounting to not more than fifty or sixty men, attacked from ambush, and before the startled troopers could respond the redskins fled to their mountain strongholds, where if by chance they succeeded in carrying a prisoner they would inhumanly torture him.

But this method of warfare did not deter the troopers, who, although they spent the greater portion of every twenty-four hours in the saddle, and were exposed to the treacherous fire of the Indians, nevertheless persistently kept at them until they finally drove them into subjugation.

For their gallantry in these actions against the Apaches and their successful efforts in keeping the territory open to the settlers the following men of the Eight U. S. Cavalry were awarded the Medal of Honour:

    Thomas Carroll, Private. Company L.

George Carter, Private, Company B.

Charles Crundle, Private. Company B.

Charles Daily, Private, Company B.

William Dougherty, Blacksmith, Company B.

James Dowling, Corporal, Company B.

Henry Falcott, Sergeant, Company L.

Thomas P. Higgins, Private, Company D.

John Keenan, Private, Company B.

Albert Knaak, Private, Company B.
James Lawrence, Private, Company B.
Thomas Little, Bugler, Company B.
Bernard McBride, Private, Company B.
James McDonald, Corporal, Company B.
William Shaffer, Private, Company B.
Andrew J. Weaher, Private, Company B.
George G. Wortman, Sergeant, Company B.
Daniel Farren, Private, Company B.
William H. Folly, Private, Company B.
Nicholas Foran, Private, Company L.
Charles Gardner, Private, Company B.
Thomas H. Gay, Private, Company B.
Patrick Golden, Sergeant, Company B.
John Hall, Private, Company B.
Clamor Heise, Private, Company B.
Daniel McKinley, Private, Company B.
Charles H. McVeagh, Private, Company B.
George W. Miller, Private, Company B.
John O'Callaghan, Sergeant, Company B.
Michael O'Regan, Private, Company B.
Lewis Phife. Sergeant, Company B.
John A. Sutherland, Corporal, Company L.
Benoni Strivson, Private, Company B.
John Kay, Private, Company L.

Coolness Prevented a Disaster

John B. Babcock

The patience of the government with the Indians had reached its limit; forbearance with them had ceased to be a virtue. The boldness and audacity of some of the largest tribes had reached a point that demanded prompt and immediate attention; they had committed atrocities and acts of barbarism which aroused public indignation throughout the country, and from all quarters came the cry for retaliation. Within a few years no less than 800 white men had been butchered by these savages, scores of women had fallen into their hands to be mutilated, outraged or dragged into captivity, where their sufferings were too horrible and revolting to relate. The Indians had torn away the infants from their mothers and tortured them before their parents eyes; older children they simply carried along and brought them up amidst the dismal surroundings of their miserable villages.

They devastated farms, pillaged small, unprotected settlements and looted and destroyed many thousands of dollars worth of white men's property. These deeds were always perpetrated during the summer. In the winter these marauding bands retired to the snow-covered deserts and prairies, where they felt fairly safe from attack and prosecution, as military operations in the severe climate of these regions were deemed impracticable. Here they would pass the winter months in celebrating and glorifying their robberies and butcheries and in practicing and inventing new cruelties to torment the captive white women. Winter over, they would again start out and renew their deviltries. This had been going on for years, the Indians growing bolder, more daring, more audacious, more bloodthirsty with every succeeding year.

Finally, in 1868, the government called a halt to further depredations, slaughter of human life and outrages of women. It was decided to punish the Indians, and punish them hard. They were to be taught a lesson which they would not soon forget, At that time Lieutenant-General Phil H. Sheridan was commander of the military division of the Missouri, and as such had charge of all military operations within this large district, which, at the time, included all the territory extending from the British boundary on the north to the Mexican frontier of the Rio Grande on the south, and from Chicago on the east to the western boundary of New Mexico, Utah and Montana on the west.

In this territory there were living some ninety odd Indian tribes, the principal ones being the Sioux, Northern and Southern Cheyennes, Crows, Chippewas, Poncas, Assinaboines, Flatheads, Piegans, Gros Ventres, Bannocks, Shoshones, Utes, Arapahoes, Pawnees, Winnebagoes, Pattawatomies, Omahas, Kickapoos, Miamis, Otoes, Kiowas, Comanches, Apaches, Navajoes, Pueblos and others. Of these the Sioux, Cheyennes (both tribes), Kiowas, Comanches, Arapahoes, Utes and Apaches had shown themselves most hostile toward the whites; others had only occasionally transgressed into the white man's domain, while still other tribes remained peaceful and lived up to the treaties.

General Sheridan was entrusted with the execution of the government's resolution to punish the offending tribes, and formulated a plan which was calculated to make order of lasting effect. He organized a campaign for the winter of 1868, fitting out three expeditions which, starting out in November, trailed and met the Indian at his own home village at a time when he least expected an attack and was least prepared for one.

This campaign was highly successful; about 12,000 Indians were surrendered at the various military posts, while over 300 of them were killed, 89 wounded and 53 captured.

The next year, 1869, the campaign was continued with equal vigour and lasted all summer and the following winter. It was during this campaign that an occurrence took place which forms the subject of the following narrative:

One of the expeditions organized by General Sheridan was commanded by General E. A. Carr. In the spring of 1869 General Carr was directed to proceed with a column of seven troops of the Fifth United States Cavalry across the country from the Arkansas to the Platte and carefully patrol the valleys of the intermediate streams and round up all the roving bands of Indians he found lurking there.

The expedition started on its long march from Fort Wallace, Kansas, May 10th, and three days later struck the first Indian trails at Beaver Creek.

The advance guard under Lieutenant Ward made a reconnoissance and observed a large Indian village some eight miles from Elephant Rock. Their presence, however, was discovered by a party of Indians who had been hunting, and within an incredibly short time they found themselves surrounded by an overwhelming force of warriors. The detachment had to charge through the ranks of Indians to avoid capture, which every soldier knew would mean torture, scalping, death.

Another incident, still more thrilling, occurred three days later, on May 16th. The command, learning of Lieutenant Ward's experience, proceeded to attack the Indians, and found them massed to cover the retreat of their families. A charge was ordered and the redskins were completely routed. Their camp was destroyed, twenty-five Indians being killed and fifty wounded. The loss to the command was three soldiers killed and four wounded. General Carr followed up his brilliant victory with energy, following the trail of the fleeing Indians, until he arrived at Spring Creek, Nebraska. Here the command was rested to water the animals and forage.

Before breaking up General Carr decided to feel his way cautiously and carefully, and ordered Lieutenant J. B. Babcock to scout the country with his troop "M."

Realizing that the expedition was over a country comparatively unknown and full of hostile bands of Indians, he detailed that expert of all scouts, William F. Cody, to accompany the lieutenant. Babcock pushed on about two miles, when he detailed Lieutenant Volkmar with four men to go in advance a short distance to survey the topography of that section of the country. The latter was carrying out his order when suddenly and without the slightest warning he found himself confronted with a large force of Indians. From all directions they came; they seemed to be literally growing on the ground.

Volkmar and his companions lost no time in rejoining Lieutenant Babcock's detachment. The Indians followed in still increasing numbers and were preparing for an onslaught on the whole command. The sudden appearance of so many yelling and howling Indians created no little consternation among the few men of Babcock's command. Some of the soldiers were badly rattled and began to retreat, others were frightened, and but a few kept their nerve in the face of the wild-eyed, yelling, devilish looking foe. Lieutenant Babcock realized that his command could be saved only by the most determined and prompt action. To retreat would lead to a rout and bring disaster. The only salvation was to meet the attack and face the Indians, even though they outnumbered his men about one to ten. His command: "Forward!" brought the wavering men to their senses. "Trot!" he commanded next—and all further confusion within the ranks ceased.

He led his troop to the top of the slope, thus selecting the most favourable ground to repulse an attack. Here he quickly ordered the men to dismount, form into a circle and shield themselves behind the prostrate bodies of their horses, which served them for breastworks, each man holding the bridle-rein over his right arm. "Now let the red devils come!" Lieutenant Babcock exclaimed. "In the position you are now, boys, you can whip any number of Indians."

THE INDIANS COMMENCED CIRCLING

This talk, together with the coolness displayed by the lieutenant, who alone remained in the saddle, occupying the most conspicuous position in the middle of the circle and directing the fire of the men, had a most reassuring and encouraging effect upon the latter.

Then the Indians came. First singly, then in groups they swarmed around the human circle. A well-directed fire kept them at a respectful distance. Every man was aiming as accurately as he could; every shot told in the ranks of the savages.

Scout Cody, known as a crack shot, coolly picked off the Indians one by one as they came within the range of his rifle. Some of the braves, more daring than the others, threw themselves over the necks of their horses, thus shielding themselves behind the bodies of the animals, and ventured closer to the circle. A well-directed bullet paid them for their daring. This manner of fighting was continued for some time, the Indians being held at bay in spite of their superiority of numbers.

Lieutenant Babcock remained steadfastly on horseback in his dangerously conspicuous position and refused to yield to the urgent pleas of his men not to expose himself in such manner. Calmly he directed the fire of his men, now cautioning this one of the approach of the Indian, now commanding that one to fire into a group of advancing warriors. It was almost miraculous that he himself escaped the deadly missiles of the foe, whose easy target he seemed to be. His horse was shot and fell just as a large body of cavalrymen sent in all haste by General Carr, who had heard the firing, came to his rescue.

Upon arrival of the re-enforcements the Indians desisted from their attack and reluctantly left the small detachment, the members of which they had counted on as their prey. They retired before the new arrivals and disappeared behind the many small hills of the prairie.

Lieutenant Babcock's coolness and presence of mind had saved the day and averted what would unquestionably have turned out to be a disaster. A Medal of Honour was the reward for his conduct on this occasion.

Death of Chief Black Kettle

A tremendous punishment administered to the hostiles in the memorable winter campaign of 1868-9 was carried out by General George W. Custer against the notorious Chief Black Kettle and his numerous followers while they were encamped for the winter. The hostilities carried on by the Indians, described in the foregoing story, had reached their climax, and these atrocities they expected to continue until the approach of winter, when the inclemency of the weather would give them ample security, and they could live on their plunder, glory in the scalps taken and the debasement of the poor unfortunate women whom they held as prisoners.

Depredations of this character for many years, with comparative security to themselves, had made the Indians very confident and bold. To disabuse their minds of their fancied safety, and to strike them at a period when they were helpless, became a necessity, and a winter campaign was authorized, which was commenced October 9, 1868.

At this time the operations of the Indians had been mostly transferred to the line of the Arkansas River and Santa Fé Road, owing to the presence of troops under Colonel Forsyth, General Bradley and General Carr, north of the Smoky Hill River and on the Republican, as well as to the near approach of winter, which caused them to work in the direction of their families, then supposed to be on the headwaters of the Red River.

To make this campaign General Getty was directed to quickly organize a small column at Fort Bascom, New Mexico, General

Eugene Carr to organize a column on the Arkansas River, while a third column composed of eleven companies of the Seventh Cavalry, twelve companies Nineteenth Kansas Cavalry, and three companies of the Third and one company of the Thirty-eighth Infantry, were directed to concentrate at the junction of Beaver Creek with the North Canadian, 112 miles south of Fort Dodge.

On November 5th the Nineteenth Kansas was in readiness and moved from Topeka *via* the mouth of the Little Arkansas to Camp Supply the point before alluded to at the junction of the North Canadian and Beaver Creek; and on the 11th of November the Seventh Cavalry and Third Infantry moved from Dodge to the same destination. The column from Bascom had already moved, and Carr's column from Lyon was ordered to move on November 12th. The main column from Camp Supply—was expected to strike the Indians either on the headwaters of the Washita, or still further south, on the Sweetwater and other branches of the Red River. A furious snowstorm commenced on the evening of November 21st, which continued during the night and next day, making the situation very gloomy, especially on account of the non-arrival of the Nineteenth Kansas, expected to reach Camp Supply about this time.

Indians were seen by General Sheridan, who was then on his way to Camp Supply, and two days after he arrived he directed General Custer to move his regiment, storm or no storm, on the morning of November 23rd. This order was responded to with alacrity by the officers and men of the Seventh Cavalry, and on the morning of the 23rd the regiment moved at daylight, although the snow continued to fall with unabated fury.

General Custer, on the evening of the 26th, struck the trail of the war-party, which had passed north. This party was composed, as was afterwards learned, of Black Kettle's band of Cheyennes and some Arapahoes. They had been north, killed the mail carriers between Dodge and Larned, an old hunter and two express men. As soon as Custer struck the trail he corralled his wagons, left a small escort with them and followed the Indian trail, which was very fresh and well marked in the deep snow, until it led into Black Kettle's village. The next morning, before daylight, the Osage Indian trailers discovered the village and stock of the Indians and notified Custer, who at once made a most admirable disposition of his command for the attack and capture of the village. At dawn the attack was made, the village captured and burned, 103 warriors killed and 53 women and children captured, the horses and ponies being killed in accordance with orders.

While this work was going on, all the Indians for a distance of fifteen miles down the Washita—Cheyennes, Comanches, Kiowas and Apaches—collected and attacked Custer, but were driven down the stream for a distance of four or five miles, when, as night was approaching, Custer withdrew. The loss at the attack on the village was Captain Louis M. Hamilton and three men killed, and three officers and eleven men wounded. Unfortunately, Major Elliott, of the regiment, seeing some of the young bucks escape, followed with the sergeant-major and fifteen men, to capture and bring them in; after capturing them, and while on their way back to the regiment they were surrounded and killed.

No one, so far as could be learned, of those with the regiment knew of their having followed the Indian bucks; no one heard the report of their guns, and no one knew of their exact fate until they were discovered, some two weeks afterward.

The first news of the whereabouts of the Nineteenth Kansas was brought to Camp Supply on November 25th by Captain Pliley and about thirty men. The regiment had lost its way, and becoming tangled up in the deep snow of the canyons of the Cimarron, and running out of provisions, could not make its way out, and was in a bad fix. Provisions were immediately sent, along with guides, to bring it in. It had been subsisting on buffalo meat for eight or nine days, and as buffalo were plenty no great suffering was occasioned for want of food. November 30th, Colonel Crawford, commanding the regiment, came into Camp Supply with four companies, and a few days after the remainder of the regiment arrived in a crippled condition.

Although Custer had struck a hard blow and had wiped out Black Kettle and his murderous band, the work was not yet finished. The Indians were to see fully how helpless they were, even at this season, when the government was in earnest. So on the 7th of December, after getting the Kansas regiment as well up as possible, a movement towards the head waters of the Washita was commenced.

Snow was on the ground and the weather very cold, but the officers and men were cheerful, notwithstanding the men were supplied with shelter tents only. They moved south until they struck the Washita, near Custer's fight of November 27th, the thermometer registering about eighteen degrees below zero.

The next day the troops started down the Washita, following the trail of the Indians, and crossed numerous ravines by digging and bridging with pioneer parties. This was continued until the evening of the 16th, when they came to the vicinity of the redskins—principally Kiowas. They did not dream that soldiers could operate in such cold and inclement weather, and the troops marched down on them before they knew of their presence in the country. After night they saw their fires, and by means of relays communicated with General Hazen, and obtained a letter from him saying that the Kiowas were friendly. This was a pretty good joke, as Sheridan's troops had just followed their trail from Custer's battlefield, and a section of this band had just come from Texas, where they had murdered and plundered in the most barbarous manner.

Sheridan did not strike these Indians on account of General Hazen's letter, and because he did not at the time know the extent of their guilt. As soon as they found he was not going to attack them, the old system of lying and deception was revived, by their proposing that all the warriors should join his column and march with it to Fort Cobb, while their villages moved to the same point on the opposite bank of the Washita. But this was a decoy, as toward night all the warriors slipped off, as they said, to help the women along with the villages, leaving only about twenty chiefs and principal men, and early the next morning these escaped, except Santanta and Lone Wolf, the head chiefs, whom Sheridan ordered Custer to arrest.

On reaching Fort Cobb that evening, he found that the villagers, instead of moving to Fort Cobb, as they proposed, were going down toward the main Red River, west of the Wichita Mountains, in an opposite direction, as fast as possible, and that some of them were nearly 100 miles distant; and that the proposition of Lone Wolf and Santanta was a decoy to get their villages out of the way. Sheridan immediately issued orders for the execution of Lone Wolf and Santanta, unless the villages came back in two days and delivered themselves up at Fort Cobb. They all came back eventually under this pressure, and at a gait as fast as that of their flight, and Santanta and Lone Wolf were saved.

At Fort Cobb Sheridan found most of the Comanches and Apaches; they had hastened into the reservation after the fight with General Custer. While these operations were going on, Lieutenant-Colonel A. W. Evans moved, as heretofore mentioned, from Bascom up the main Canadian to Monument Creek, there established his depot, and with the most commendable energy struck off to the south, on the headwaters of the Red River, where he discovered a trail of hostile Comanches, who had refused to come in, following it up with perseverance. On the 25th of December he attacked the party, killed, as near as could be ascertained, twenty-five, wounded a large number, captured and burnt their village, destroyed a large amount of property, and then moved in to a point about twelve miles west of Fort Cobb, where Sheridan communicated with him.

Meanwhile, General Carr was scouting along the main Canadian, west of the Antelope Hills, and the country was becoming so unhealthy for Indians that the Arapahoes and the remainder of the Cheyennes concluded to surrender and go to the reservation designated for them. The operations of the troops had forced these bands over into the eastern edge of the Staked Plains, where they surrendered and agreed to deliver their people at Fort Cobb as speedily as possible.

The Arapahoes were faithful to their promise, and delivered themselves up under their head chief, Little Raven. The Cheyennes broke their promise and did not come in, so Sheridan ordered Custer to move against them. He found them in a very forlorn condition, and could have destroyed most of the tribe, certainly their villages, but contented himself with taking their renewed promise to come into Camp Supply, and obtained from them two white women whom they held as captives. The most of the tribe fulfilled this latter promise as to coming into the vicinity of Camp Supply, and communicating with the commanding officer; but Tall Bull's band again violated the promise made, and went north to the Republican, where he joined a party of Sioux, who, on the 13th of May, 1869, were attacked and defeated with heavy loss, whereupon the remainder of the tribe moved into Camp Supply.

Meantime, while the Arapahoes and Cheyennes were negotiating with Sheridan to surrender, the Oua-ha-da, or Staked Plains Comanches, sent a delegation over to Bascom. General Getty arrested the delegation, who were ordered to Fort Leavenworth, and finally returned to their people on condition that they would deliver themselves up on the reservation at Medicine Bluff or Fort Sill. This was complied with, thus ending a successful campaign.

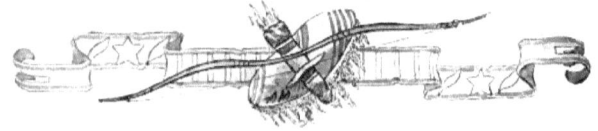

A Well-Planned Surprise

WILLIAM F. CODY

A quiet June evening in 1870 found the troops stationed at Fort McPherson, Neb., enjoying a well-earned rest after many a hard chase and expedition. Of the stirring incidents that brought their brief recreation to a sudden termination, Colonel William F. Cody has this to say:

"I was chief of scouts under General Phil H. Sheridan, and knowing the boys well, having led them on many a dangerous journey, joined them to enjoy the refreshing breezes of the evening. A detail had left the fort to water the government herd of horses and mules in the nearby Platte River, when presently shots were heard. Everybody was on his feet the next moment and we learned that a war-party of Sioux Indians had dashed from among the cottonwood trees on the little islands in the river, shooting, shouting and waving blankets, which stampeded the herd of about 400 animals. The Indians also killed two of the herders and wounded another.

"Some of the herd ran for the corral, where they were accustomed to going for the night, but the Indians got away with about 200 and started for the bluffs south of the fort. In less time than it takes to tell it, all was excitement at the fort. All knew it was an Indian attack. As was my custom, I had my war horse, old 'Buckskin Joe,' near at hand and was mounted in time to note the ravine or canyon in which the Indians disappeared with the government stock. General William H. Emory, who was in command, immediately ordered his bugler to sound boots and saddles, and by the time I returned for instructions, five troops of cavalry were busy saddling up, getting their arms, ammunition belts, etc. Company I, Fifth United States Cavalry, was the first troop saddled and ready for the chase.

"Their officer, a young lieutenant by the name of Earl D. Thomas, just from West Point, was delighted when he received the order from General Emory to take his troop and follow me. The general stated that he would be supported by the other troops as soon as they were ready, but ordered him to follow the Indians and recapture the animals. By this time the Indians with such of the herd as did not get away from them were at least five miles away in the hills. Thomas at once counted fours, 'fours right, trot, gallop, march!' and we were off. Striking the trail, it was followed in a gallop till dark, but it did not bring us in sight of the Indians, and the tracks of their horses showed that they were still on the run.

"The lieutenant called a halt to rest the puffing horses and to consult me as to what he should do. His orders were to follow the Indians and recapture the animals, but his men had had no supper and had neither rations nor water and the way the Indians were headed it was still thirty miles to water. I told Thomas that it was possible to follow the trail all night and awaited his answer. He said he was told to follow me, and where I went he proposed to go.

"'Mount and forward!' was at once the order, and the chase was continued. During the night the Indians repeatedly doubled on their trail, with all the horses. They would drive them in a circle, and use every means known to a crafty Indian to throw anyone who might be following off the trail, and several times during the night it took some time to get the trail straightened out. While this was being accomplished, the troops would get

BOTH INDIANS FELL TO THE GROUND DEAD

some sleep. Such delays, however, increased the distance between us and the Indians, and we did not reach the head of Medicine Creek, where we got water for men and horses, until 11 o'clock next day. Here we consulted again while the horses were drinking and nibbling a few mouthfuls of grass, and some of the men, with empty stomachs, caught a few minutes sleep. The trail of the Indians showed that they were several hours ahead of us and headed southwest in the direction of Red Willow Springs, about thirty miles distant.

"There is no water between Medicine Creek and Red Willow Springs, and this made me feel sure that the Indians would make a stop at the latter place, for it was many miles from there to the next water. This was well considered by the lieutenant as we talked over the situation. No one in the little party had had anything to eat since dinner the day before, and there was no possible way of getting any before the next morning, and then only by overtaking the Indians, surprising them, whipping them and capturing what dried meat they had. These were long chances, but we decided to take them.

"Again the order: 'Bridle up, mount, forward!' was given. Nearly all the Fifth Cavalry soldiers knew the country, as they had followed me through those dry, hot sand hills on many a scout. Thirty miles to water and no canteen in which to carry any, nor anything to eat in twenty-three hours, and nothing in sight, was a hard proposition for our little troop, yet no one demurred at the thought that every mile took us farther into those hot sand hills. Most of the men were in their shirt sleeves and had not even a blouse to protect them from the night air. When we left the green grass that bordered the creek and entered the dry sand hills I listened to hear if there should be any complaints.

"Not a word. Grim, silent, like sleuthhounds they came. They were on a hot trail for Indians. Indians who had killed their friends. They were ready to starve, to thirst, if only the prospects of a tight were good. They were American soldiers of the Indian-fighter type, Sheridan's cavalrymen. Soon after leaving the creek the Indians began their old tricks of trying to hide the trail, but no attention was paid to this, for we now knew the next stopping place and were as familiar with that part of the country as they were. We kept straight on for the springs, with the exception that occasionally we went out of the direct line to keep in low places between the sand hills, so as not to be seen.

At 9 o'clock that night we halted about four miles from the springs. I advised Thomas to allow the men to unsaddle and unbridle, letting each second man hold two horses by their halters and so let them feed on grass. By changing the men every two hours they could get some sleep. Meanwhile I was to disguise myself as an Indian, locate the hostiles and be back in time so that we could attack them at daylight. No fires were to be lighted. All must be silent until my return.

"Tired men go to sleep quickly, and before I left half of my little band were slumbering. I took the saddle and bridle off from old Joe and left him to graze, knowing he would not leave. One hour later I found the Indians just where they were expected to be. The tired horses, some grazing, some sleeping, were corralled. Four Indians were guarding them and one sentinel or scout was lying down on a little sand hill back from camp on the trail peering into the night to signal our coming. I knew every inch of ground around the spring, and knew where to bring the troop for an attack. Going back I found the boys as I had left them. Quietly they were called to saddle up, and told what they were to do, those who were to capture the herd and the ones who were to attack the camp being instructed in their duties.

"I had estimated the Indians to number thirty, and there were forty-two of us. Ten of these were to creep up to the sleeping Indians on foot, while twenty, besides the lieutenant and myself, were to charge on horseback, and the other ten were to bring up the remaining horses, take care of the mounted Indian herders, and round up the animals. We were to attack them just at the break of day, which we did, and a more surprised lot of Indians never awoke to face the woes of this world. The very next moment nine of them went to sleep again forever. Indians on the warpath always keep their war horses near them and some of these redskins got to their horses and thus escaped. I saw two Indians mount one horse, and they were on none other than my favourite war horse, 'Powder Face,' which was with the government herd when captured by the Indians.

"I gave chase as soon as I saw that we had won the fight, which took less time than it takes to tell it, but by this time the two Indians on 'Powder Face' were half a mile away heading for the hills. I knew my old friend to be nearly as swift a horse as 'Buckskin Joe,' but he had double weight to carry and Joe soon began to gain, so that within a few minutes I was getting near enough for a shot.

"The Indian who was riding behind kept shooting back with a revolver, but I feared to chance too long a shot for fear of killing or wounding 'Powder Face.' By this time we were in the rough sand hills, and as they were about to go out of sight over a mound I fired, with the result that both Indians fell to the ground, the bullet having passed through both of them. I soon caught 'Powder Face' and returned to our little battlefield, where the boys were then in high glee. They had found a lot of dried buffalo and deer meat, which they ate hungrily, between copious draughts of spring water. A detail was sent to bury the dead Indians and gather up all the stock.

"Certainly the results of our chase raised the spirits of our brave troopers to a point of enthusiasm hardly to be described. I felt great sympathy with these courageous fellows, and knew that on our trail would soon be following the support that General Emory said would be sent, presumably in command of at least a major. If this supporting command reached us, Lieutenant Thomas and his brave boys would have to share their glory with others. It was my intention to prevent this by getting away as soon as possible, and by not taking our trail back to the fort.

"We kept a few miles away from our former route so that the supporting troops could not see us, and thereby succeeded in avoiding a meeting. The supporting troops had the unenvied pleasures of following our entire trail, on the second half of which they certainly noticed the scheme. When our boys 'tumbled' to what was being done they gave me a hearty cheer. We reached the fort the next evening much fatigued but joyful.

"The lieutenant and his men were complimented by special order, and shortly afterwards I had the distinction of receiving a Medal of Honour."

The Sixth Cavalry and the Indians

With the coming of spring in 1870 the Indians in Northwestern Texas became extremely dangerous and daring. White outlaws in great numbers kept the small detachments of troops then stationed in the vast region amply occupied, and the Indians saw the time was opportune for an assault upon the mail stage.

Their attack upon the stage began in early July, and the troops were sent from all sides to chastise the bold marauders.

Captain C. B. McLellan, of Troop L, Sixth United States Cavalry, commanding a mixed detachment of three officers and fifty-three men of Troops A, C, D, H, K and L of said regiment, was the first to come across the Indians and force them to fight.

He left Fort Richardson, Tex., on the 6th of July in pursuit of a party of Indians who had captured the mail at Rock Station, sixteen miles west from the post. Marching generally in a north-westerly direction, passing Rock Station and picking up information and evidence of the doings of the marauders while he went along, McLellan reached the Middle Fork of the Little Wichita on the 9th of July.

The weather was bad; heavy rain-storms visited the detachment several times. A severe one kept the command in camp at the last-named place until the 12th of July, when camp was broken. The troops moved in a westerly direction, with the heavy rain pouring down, and came upon the Indians towards noon. The latter were recognized as superior in numbers, but the captain deployed into line and intended to charge them, when hostiles were discovered on both flanks threatening the pack-train left in the rear. The troops halted, dismounted and opened fire, which was promptly answered by the enemy. Within half an hour the Indians nearly surrounded the detachment, and the necessity of retreating to some stronger point of defence caused McLellan to move his force slowly back to some crests where he thought he could meet the redskins on equal terms.

This retreat was far more difficult than was anticipated.

The country was a rolling prairie interspersed by marshy places which threatened to cut off outlying details of the command. For four hours and a half the small hand of soldiers moved slowly back from one crest to the next under a heavy fire, without finding a spot where they might hope to cope successfully with the ever-increasing swarms of Indians.

According to Captain McLellan's opinion there were some 250 of them against his fifty odd soldiers.

The retreat, always under a hot fire and over unknown ground, was stopped between 3 and four o'clock in the afternoon, when the Indians gave up hope and withdrew. Two American soldiers were killed, the surgeon and ten other men wounded. All the wounded were saved, but the killed fell into the savage enemy's hands. The Indians lost fifteen killed; the number of their wounded could not be ascertained.

The order, discipline and devotion shown throughout this remarkable action are indicated by the fact that the swift and clever Indians were unable to get hold of any of the property of the command except some baggage belonging to the officers, which they themselves decided to abandon to avoid unnecessary exposure of their men. Twelve non-commissioned officers and soldiers earned the Medal of Honour for exceptional gallantry. They were recommended by Captain McLellan in his official report as having "made themselves conspicuous in acts of bravery in the engagement." They were:

First Sergeant A. Stokes, Sergeant Thomas Kerrigan, Corporal John Connor, Corporal Charles Smith, all of Company H; Farrier Samuel Porter, Bugler Clarion Windus, Corporal James Watson, Private Solon Neal, Sergeant John May, of Company

L; Sergeant William Winterbottom, of Company A; Sergeant Geo. Eldridge, of Company C, and Corporal John Given, of Company IV, Sixth Cavalry.

At noon of July 14th the detachment reached Fort Richardson, after having marched 200 miles.

The department commander complimented this expedition in a general order, concluding with the words that "this engagement doubtless saved the frontier counties in North-western Texas from a most destructive raid from a band of 250 Indians."

But the Indians, in ignorance of the fact that more troops were to be encountered, pushed their boldness further. They were all from the Fort Sill Reservation and infested the entire north-western part of Texas, where outrages increased in number and atrocity.

Another expedition against the red fiends started from Fort Richardson on September 26th under Captain Rafferty and twenty-two men. They were all of Company M, Sixth Cavalry. They marched towards the headwaters of the Trinity River, passing over part of the ground of Captain McLellan's exploit. A few Indians were seen and pursued, but they escaped into the trackless fastnesses of the rocky desert. On October 4th a new trail, discovered by Scout Dozier, was followed, and on the 5th of October the command came up with the Indians near the Little Wichita, early in the morning.

The soldiers attacked without delay and surprised the red skins. It was a war-party of about fifteen. Two were killed and one wounded, but the latter crawled in the underbrush and made his escape with the rest of the band. Eighteen horses were captured by the detachment, together with a considerable quantity of clothing and property belonging to white settlers, showing that the red devils were just returning from a raid.

For this exploit, the success of which was due in great measure to the efficiency of Scout Dozier, the latter received the Medal of Honour, together with five enlisted men: Sergeant Michael Welch, Corporals Samuel Bowden and Daniel Keating, and Privates James Anderson and Benjamin Wilson.

Six Men Against 400 Comanches

R. G. Carter

For ten years or more immediately following the close of the War of the Rebellion the entire borders of Texas, Kansas, Montana, Nebraska, Wyoming, Arizona, Utah and neighbouring territories were ablaze with Indian wars. One raid followed another, and many depredations and massacres were committed by the Sioux, Cheyennes, Arapahoes and other affiliated bands of Kiowas and Comanches, followed by fire, rapine, pillage and plunder.

In September, 1871, the Fourth U. S. Cavalry had returned from a long and arduous expedition against Kicking Bird's and Lone Wolf's bands of hostile Kiowas, when Colonel Ronald S. Mackenzie, commanding the regiment, learned that a band of hostile Oua-ha-da Comanche Indians, under Mow-wi, the "Hard-Shaker," and Para-o-coom, the "He Bear," were in the Pan Handle of Texas, outside the reservation.

It was said that they held several white captives, among them two boys and one little girl, stolen some time before near San Antonio, Texas, besides many horses and herds of cattle driven off during the almost constant raids. Colonel Mackenzie reorganized the command at Old Camp Cooper, the former reservation of the Comanches, on Tecumseh Creek, near Fort Griffin, Texas, and on the morning of October 3rd the column moved out with wagon and pack trains for the purpose of beating up this nest of freebooters, recovering the captive children, and either destroying the village with its accumulated plunder or driving the Indians back into the reservation, from which they had been absent for years in utter defiance of the government.

Lieutenant Henry W. Lawton, regimental quartermaster of the Fourth Cavalry, was in charge of the wagon train. On October 7 Duck Creek was reached, where a permanent supply camp was established. It was determined to surprise the village by moving at night and attacking at daybreak. About 7 o'clock on the morning of the 8th Troops A, B, F, G, H, I, K and L left the supply camp with a pack train of about eighty mules for this purpose. The village was supposed to be somewhere on the Freshwater Fork of the Brazos River, or up on the numerous canyons of the Staked Plains. The Ton-Ka-Way scouts had been sent out on the night of the 7th for the purpose of locating it.

About midnight, after a hard march over a very rough country, further progress of the command was blocked by a precipitous bluff, which in the impenetrable darkness it was found impossible to scale, and the command bivouacked on the trail. At daybreak the march was resumed by passing around the obstacle. The Freshwater Fork was reached about 9:30 a.m. of the 9th, too late for any decisive action. The locality was recognized as being near the spot where Lieutenant P. M. Boehm of the Fourth Cavalry had a skirmish with this same band two years before. The command unsaddled and got breakfast.

In the afternoon Captain E. M. Heyl, with a squadron, was sent out on a reconnoissance. The Ton-Ka-Way scouts sent out from Duck Creek came in, but while hastening along some ravines on high ground unexpectedly ran upon a group of Comanches busily intent upon watching the reconnoitring column. The scouts reported the village to be up Cattish or Canyon Blanco

(White Canyon), nearby. At 3 p. m. the command saddled up, moved across and clown the Freshwater Fork, Captain Clarence Manck with one squadron being left behind on guard with instructions to join the advance later. After proceeding two miles or more a shot was heard.

Colonel Mackenzie immediately rode to the rear, sending word to Captain Wirt Davis to counter-march the column, but after proceeding some distance, on discovering that it was an accidental shot by a careless soldier, the march was resumed. Much valuable time had been lost. The country was rough with foothills and small ravines or *arroyos*, making frequent halts necessary, so that it was nearly dark before the command was fairly straightened out and ready to go into bivouac.

The absent squadron was sent for, and under the shadow of a line of abrupt hills, scarcely 100 yards from the stream, the command camped. The horses were staked out and the men were allowed to make small fires. The missing squadron came in after dark, and, not finding much room, crowded up pretty close to the rear company, the horses being huddled upon their grazing ground. It was a long picket, with the line of small bluffs or hills close to camp on one side and the treacherous quicksand stream on the other; an excellent camp provided there were no Indians about.

Shortly after midnight the camp was attacked by a large body of Indians who rode along the line of hills referred to, and by tiring, yelling, shaking dried buffalo robes and ringing bells, succeeded in stampeding the horses. As the fire was immediately returned the flashes of carbines and pistols showed, at intervals, that the ridge which skirted the entire camp was alive with Indians, riding and yelling like so many demons. The cry rang out above the tumult: "Every man to his lariat! Stand by your horses!" Pandemonium reigned for a few moments.

At every flash the horses and mules, about 600 in number, could be seen rearing, jumping, snorting and running, with a strength that terror and brute frenzy alone could inspire, while ropes could be heard snap like the cracking reports of pistols.

Iron picket pins were whistling through the air, more dangerous than bullets; men, crouching as they ran, vainly endeavoured to seize the pins as they whirled and swished, only to be dragged and thrown among the heels of the animals, with hands lacerated and burnt by the ropes running so rapidly through their fingers. The herd thundered off in the distance; the yells of the retreating Indians came back on the midnight air with a peculiarly taunting ring, telling all too plainly that the Oua-ha-das, Mow-wi's wild band, had been found at last.

As soon as the confusion had somewhat subsided, orders were given for a portion of the command to saddle up, and Captain Heyl and Lieutenant W. C. Hemphill were ordered with detachments from their respective troops, K and G, to scout about the camp for the trail of the stampeded horses, of which some sixty-five or seventy had been driven or "circled out" by the Indians. At daybreak Lieutenant R. G. Carter, then second lieutenant, Fourth Cavalry, while engaged, by order of Colonel Mackenzie in inspecting the picket posts, and endeavouring to find the trail of the outgoing horses, heard a shot, then a loud shout.

Riding in that direction, he met Captain Heyl and Lieutenant Hemphill galloping from different directions, both riding towards the sound of the shot. Upon looking down a long and narrow valley from the ridge they were on, a small party of Indians was seen running off some eight or ten horses. All gave chase. About two miles from camp the detachments came to a break or abrupt shelf in the prairie. Here the Indians suddenly released the captured horses, being then under pistol fire from their pursuers, and turned toward quite a prominent bluff or butte. Lieutenant Hemphill, with most of the men of both detachments, stopped here, as it was a difficult place to cross. Captain Heyl, however, with some six or seven men of his own troop, jumped, and scrambled through this abrupt break, closely followed by Lieutenant Carter and Sergeants Jenkins and Foley and Privates Gregg, Downey and Melville of Troop G.

It was not yet light enough to see far, and the ground for 300 yards or so gradually ascended. As the pursuers passed over

THE INDIANS IMMEDIATELY CLOSED IN UPON THE DETACHMENT

this slight rise, terminating in an open, smooth prairie ridge or knoll, they suddenly came upon the main body of Indians, variously estimated at from 400 to 600, and but five to six hundred yards distant. The Indians gave one shrill yell of intense satisfaction and moved out rapidly to cut off the retreat of the detachment, All drew rein on the ridge as one man, and without a word each looked at the other, and then raised a simultaneous shout of surprise.

It was like an electric shock. For a moment the blood fairly congealed and the heart of every man in that little party stood still. All realized what the ruse of the Oua-Ha-Has had meant, knew that they had been drawn into an ambuscade, and the almost hopelessness of their situation. Capt. Heyl, who was riding near Lieutenant Carter, exclaimed: "Heavens, look at the Indians, we are in a bad nest!" Lieutenant Carter, while fully realizing the danger of all, quickly suggested that the men dismount immediately and open fire, to gain time until Colonel Mackenzie could hear the firing and come to their relief. Captain Heyl gave orders to this effect. There was no shelter whatever, it was nearly three miles from camp, and the horses were almost exhausted from the long run over rough ground.

It was certain death to one and all should they turn and seek shelter in the ravine they had just left, now some 500 or 600 yards to the rear, for the Indians had already commenced circling and were endeavouring to get around the flanks of the little party. Captain Heyl, who was more than 100 yards to Lieutenant Carter's right, with his men in line, dismounted, deployed and firing, upon observing this movement of the Indians, without giving Lieutenant Carter any other instructions, or without notifying him of his intentions, suddenly mounted, and with his men started on a run for the ravine. The Indians, seeing this, charged down upon Lieutenant Carter, who, seeing that it would be certain death to all should he join the retreating party, mounted his five men, gave them instructions to keep well deployed, maintain a rapid fire and to commence falling back, but on no account to turn and run.

The leading Indians, led by Para-o-coom himself, in black war paint—stripped to his breech-clout—wearing a full war bonnet of feathers reaching to his horse's tail, and mounted on a coal black pony, immediately closed in upon the detachment. Private Gregg of Troop G was killed by the chief, and Private Downey of the same troop was slightly wounded. All would undoubtedly have been killed in a few moments, although all were determined to sell their lives dearly, had not Lieutenant P. M. Boehm, with the Ton-Ka-Way Indians, of whom he had charge, gallantly come to their rescue. He had met Captain Heyl at the ravine, and with the men who had halted there when the pursuit first commenced together with two citizens, Messrs. Stockton and James, who had accompanied the expedition to identify their stock if found in all about twenty-five or thirty, he had reached the scene of action at just the right moment.

The dust of the column could now be seen coming out of an adjacent valley, and the Indians, fearing they might be attacked from the rear in open ground, and by a superior force in front, commenced falling back into the hills. A running skirmish was kept up for nearly half an hour until the arrival of Colonel Mackenzie with the column. It is believed that this decisive action of Lieutenant Carter, in temporarily checking the pursuit by the Indians of Captain Heyl and his fleeing men until Lieutenant Boehm's arrival, saved the lives of the entire party, excepting the unfortunate man who was killed, and it was because of such prompt, brave action, that Second Lieutenant R. G. Carter was brevetted first lieutenant, who was also, for "most distinguished gallantry in this action," granted the Medal of Honour.

Daring Single-Handed Combat

JOHN NIHILL

It was nothing new when, on the morning of July 13, 1872, a Mexican ranchman rode into the military post at Camp Crittenden, in the extreme southern part of Arizona, and reported that a band of Apaches with large herds of stolen cattle had passed his ranch, for all summer the Indians had been committing all kinds of depredations and terrorizing the inhabitants. The military protection was somewhat inadequate, only a small force—one company, Troop F, Fifth U. S. Cavalry—being stationed at the post, and three-fourths of these few men were usually disabled and laid up by fever, chills and other physical ailments due to the climate. Thus the military post exerted little deterring influence and furnished slight protection.

However, when this Mexican came in with his complaint, Lieutenant W. 13. Hall immediately started in pursuit of the thieving Apaches. His detail consisted of First Sergeant Henry Newman and seven privates. The chase is described by Private John Nihill, who was one of the participants.

"The trail," he says, "was found within 600 yards from the

post, and, as it had been raining the day before, the ground was soft, so that there was little difficulty in following it while in the open country.

"It headed towards the Whetstone Mountains, which were distant about fifteen miles, southeast of the post. We travelled as rapidly as the nature of the ground would permit, hoping to overhaul them before they reached the mountains. As we approached the mountains our progress was necessarily slow. The Indians had in several places split up their band, so as to throw us off the trail, which invariably came together again at some given point.

"Late in the afternoon we passed some cattle that the Indians abandoned in a deep ravine, as they were thoroughly exhausted and unable to travel any farther. This caused us to make as much haste as possible, for we knew that they would strike into some of the deep canyons in the mountains, where it would be almost impossible to follow them.

"About two miles from where we passed the cattle the trail led into a deep can yon, where Ave had the greatest difficulty in following it, and then could only do so by dismounting and leading our horses.

"We had advanced in this manner about a mile when we were suddenly attacked by some forty Indians, who were concealed behind rocks 800 feet above us. The side of the ravine where the Indians had taken up their position was nearly vertical, so that it was almost impossible to get a shot at them. At the time the Indians made the attack I was following the trail of some who had gone up the opposite side of the canyon, and had taken a position behind a small tree, which had a fork about five feet from the ground; in this fork I rested my carbine to steady it. I watched for every opportunity to fire at an Indian, but they were so well concealed behind rocks that it was almost impossible to catch more than a fleeting glance of them. During this time some of our party were wounded, and to make matters worse the Indians commenced to roll rocks down from the top of the cliffs with such force and noise that the horses became unmanageable.

"It was then that Lieutenant Hall made up his mind to retreat and gave the men orders to do so, he and First Sergeant Newman taking the post of danger, in the rear, assisted by Private Michael Glynn, who displayed great courage and bravery throughout the fight, thus giving the wounded men a chance to get out first. Glynn alone drove off eight of the hostiles, killing and wounding five. I was watching a chance to get a shot at an Indian who was dodging behind the rocks on the opposite side of the canyon, and did not notice that I was being left behind until our detail had got a considerable distance ahead of me. However, I started to catch up. I was dismounted, with the bridle-rein over my arm, and my carbine in readiness for whatever might turn up.

"After I had gone about 300 yards I was fired at by an Indian, but the gun missed fire, and before he could make a second attempt I fired and dropped him. In the meantime, three others rushed down the side of the canyon, with the intention of cutting me off from the remainder of the detail. One of them stopped long enough to shoot at me, but missed. I returned his fire, and was fortunate enough to bring him down also. The other two concealed themselves behind rocks, directly in front of me. I turned my horse loose and drove it ahead to draw the fire of the Indians.

"Then I moved about thirty or forty yards to the right of my horse, making as little noise as possible. When within about thirty yards of the redskins they came crawling around the rocks to the side where they were ex posed to me, and just as soon as they discovered me I fired, killing one; the other jumped into a ravine and I saw him no more. I kept on and rejoined the detail, which was waiting at the mouth of the canyon."

Sergeant Newman and Privates Nihill and Glynn were awarded the Medal of Honour for the active part they took in this action.

Where the Comanches Were Put to Flight

DAVID LARKIN

Although no general Indian war took place in 1872, there were several expeditions and crusades against bands of savages. The number of murders, outrages and depredations by small parties of redskins was greater than the preceding year, especially in Kansas, Nebraska, Minnesota and Dakota, and those states where the building of railroads marked the advent of a new era of civilization. About this time the Northern Pacific Railroad had reached the Missouri River, and the surveyors were at work as far west as the Powder River, 200 miles beyond the Missouri. The Santa Fé and the Southern Pacific Railroads were both in course of construction, and small groups of surveyors, engineers, contractors, etc., were scattered all over this large territory, challenging the attention of certain tribes of Indians who were always on the lookout for plunder and murder, and ready to go on the warpath at the slightest provocation. The dawn of a new civilization, which the building of these roads signified, furnished a sufficient pretext for many a chief to gather his braves and look for trouble.

An expedition commanded by Colonel Mackenzie was consequently ordered to scout over the Staked Plains of Texas to locate some of the turbulent hostiles camps, and started out, marching as far as Fort Bascom, N. M., without detecting the presence of Indians in any considerable number. Owing to the exhausted condition of the horses and the prevalence of disease among the men, the command returned to the supply camp, arriving there September 27, 1872.

The day following Colonel Mackenzie left his camp again, having provided himself with new operating material in men and horses, taking with him Companies A, D, F, I and L of the Fourth United States Cavalry.

After riding one day at a good steady gallop, the command reached the North Fork of the Red River, where a camp of Comanches of considerable size was sighted. A charge was ordered and the command swooped down upon the lodges, numbering 250, with vigour and dash. The Indian pony herd stampeded and made a mad rush for the village, giving the first alarm of the approach of the troopers to the unsuspecting redskins, who at once prepared to resist the sudden attack.

Lieutenant Hudson with Troop I led the advance, and in jumping from the bank to the bed of the river the lieutenant's horse and the horses of some of the men got stuck in the quicksands and could neither advance nor retreat. Colonel Mackenzie ordered Sergeant William Wilson of Troop I to take command of the troop, continue the charge and hold the right of the village.

This order Wilson executed with skill and bravery and complete success, holding his position until recalled at sunset. In the meantime the remainder of the command attacked the left of the village, and after a fierce and bloody fight of three hours defeated and routed the Comanches, who had to flee to avoid annihilation. The entire camp outfit, 300 squaws and over 3,000 ponies, fell into the hands of the troopers, whose loss consisted of one man killed, three wounded and a number of horses shot. The bodies of twenty-three Indians were gathered up and buried.

This stinging defeat so discouraged the Mow-wi tribe of Comanches that they subsequently gladly surrendered at Fort Sill, after having been on the warpath for seventeen years.

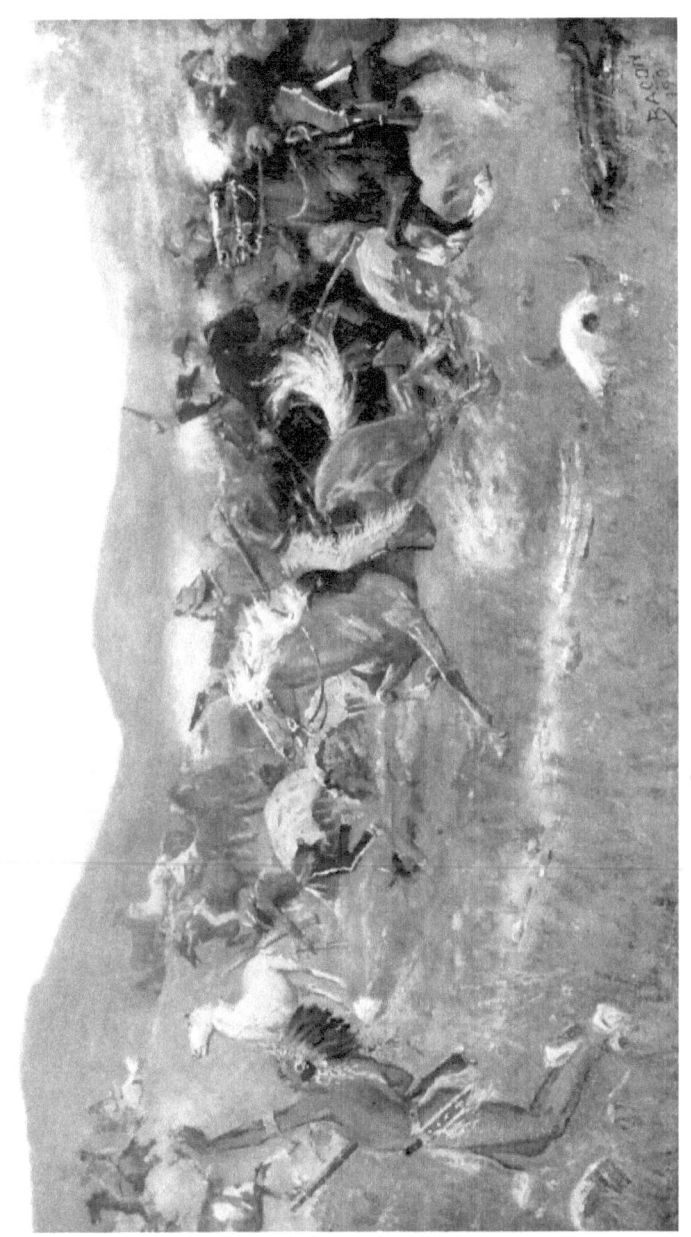

SURPRISED — AN ATTACK AT DAWN

Besides Sergeant Wilson the following men distinguished themselves in this encounter: First Sergeant William McNamara, Sergeant William Foster, Privates Edward Branagan and William Rankin, Farrier David Larkin, of Troop F; Corporal Harry A. McMaster, of Troop A; Corporal William O'Neill and Blacksmith James Pratt, of Troop I.

Sergeant Wilson, a few months previous, on March 28, 1872, had a fight with Indians which furnished him an opportunity to distinguish himself, and for which he likewise received a Medal of Honour.

This fight occurred on the Colorado River near Fort Concho, Texas, when he and twenty privates of Troop I attacked a band of Indians and Mexican cattle thieves. After a short engagement the hostiles were driven off with a loss of four killed, several wounded and one prisoner in the hands of the sergeant himself. In addition, the marauders lost their entire camp equipage. Sergeant Wilson's capture proved to be important, as much valuable information in reference to the location of hostile camps was obtained from his prisoner.

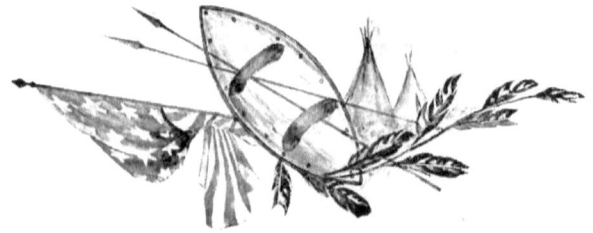

The Battle in the Lava Beds

JOHN GREEN

The south-western part of Oregon was formerly the home of the powerful Indian nation of the Klamath. A large, narrow stretch of lakes, the Upper and Lower Klamath, run nearly parallel to the mountains which reach ever the frontier down to California. East of the lower Klamath, divided by the frontier, lies a third lake, the Tule, into which the Lost River empties its waters.

In 1873 the Upper Klamath touched towards the north east, the southwest corner of the Indian Reservation of the Klamaths, who counted among one of their offshoots the warlike tribe of the Modocs. The Modocs, then under the leadership of Captain Jack, did not live on the reservation, but occupied a stretch of land about the Lost River.

This region was the original home of the Modocs. But after the government road had been laid through the heart of their country and the immigrants began to come, trouble naturally arose. There was a massacre of seventy-five whites in 1852, and a treacherous murdering of forty-one Modocs, who had been invited to a peace council, as retaliation for the former act.

In 1864 the Klamaths, Modocs, Yakooskins and Snakes gave up their territory, as agreed to in a treaty, for the exchange of the above named reservation farther north. The Modocs, it seems, were the ones who meant to keep most strictly and faithfully to their agreement; they began to cultivate the land assigned them with skill and diligence. But the Klamaths, now their immediate neighbours, annoyed them so that they simply left, after only a few months stay, and returned to their old home.

In 1869, after having been given all sorts of promises and assurances of protection against the Klamaths, they let themselves be coaxed into coming back to the reservation and started anew, with earnest effort, to create for themselves new homes. But the promises of the government's representatives proved to have been wind, and the provocations and annoyances by the Klamaths grew more unbearable than ever, they going so far as to claim tribute for fish, grass, timber and water. The Modocs were helpless themselves, as the Klamaths far outnumbered them. So they appealed to the White Father, through his Indian Agent. This man, instead of following the appeal with protection and help, simply removed the guiltless Modocs again to another place; they went there, insulted and taunted by their overbearing enemies, and losing all the work and time spent upon their former grounds.

The Klamaths did not leave them alone in their new country, and again the Modocs appealed to the government agent. The latter, instead of checking their aggressors, tried to move the Modocs again, to still another place. But their patience was exhausted, especially as the new region appeared to them altogether unsuitable. They left the reservation for their old hunting grounds. Here in the meantime the whites had settled more or less thickly, and there was no longer room for the homeless red man. Soon difficulties arose, and complaints against the Indians were frequent. Then—this was in 1871—the Superintendent of Indian Affairs tried, by sending a special commission, to induce them to return to the reservation. They refused and declared their wish, to settle with the superintendent in person and permanently. They wanted to be separated from the Klamaths and claimed a small reservation on Lost River for their home.

MAJOR JOHN GREEN RESCUED THE WOUNDED

Demonstrations against them were of no avail; the white settlers grew more and more urgent in their demands to have the Indians removed, as they, Indian fashion, could not resist from committing all sorts of minor offenses and misdemeanours, which rendered them dangerous and highly undesirable neighbours.

It happened that the command of the Department of the Columbia was then in the hands of Brigadier-General E. R. S. Canby, a soldier of great professional experience, natural tact and thorough comprehension of the situation, and consequently eminently qualified to deal with it.

When a joint petition of the white settlers of the Lost River district and the Indian Agent asking for the removal of the Indians reached the superintendent he took the side of the settlers and communicated to General Canby the desirability of removing the Modocs by force.

General Canby investigated. In a short letter, which proved afterwards his remarkably good judgement and true conception of the state of affairs, he recommended moderation. He was not heeded. In the fall of 1872 the agent demanded directly and peremptorily from the Modocs that they should comply with his wishes and return forthwith to the part of the reservation assigned to them. They defied him. The next step was an appeal by the agent, in the name of the Central Office in Washington, to the commanding officer at Fort Klamath to furnish a force sufficient to compel the Modocs to return to Camp Yainak. The commanding officer, Major John Green of the First U. S. Cavalry, had to comply, and detailed Captain Jackson with about thirty men for the purpose Jackson left Fort Klamath on November 28, 1872, and thus started the Modoc War.

On the 29th the troop reached Captain Jack's camp before daylight; the Indians were still asleep. The clattering of the hoofs of the United States cavalry horses among their tents brought them quickly to their feet.

A short "talk" ensued, during which Captain Jackson endeavoured to point out to Captain Jack the imprudence of resisting the United States Government, and urged him to accept the request of the Indian Agent and to return to the Klamath Reservation. The officer promised that the Modocs would this time be protected against any transgressions whatever from the Klamaths. But Captain Jack, having apparently become too distrusting by preceding events, would not listen. Jackson finally ordered the Indians present to lay down their arms. Some of them complied, but a warrior by the name of Scar Faced Charlie refused to obey, and when an officer approached him with a cocked pistol in hand two shots were fired; the Indians claimed the officer had fired first, and the military claimed that the Indians had been the aggressors. A fight was the result, in which a party of citizens joined as opponents of the red men. Nine warriors lost their lives, the rest were driven into the hills; one soldier was killed and seven wounded.

The Indiana selected as their stronghold a stretch of country known as the Lava Beds, south of Tule Lake, a most inaccessible region. The Lava Beds comprise an intricate net of gorges, crests and crevices, amply supplied with water from Tule Lake, and covering a surface of four by seven miles.

The next expedition was started against the hostiles towards the middle of January. It numbered some 400 men, officers included; 225 were regulars, the rest volunteers. After the commanding officer had obtained a true insight of the almost absolute inaccessibility of the country and the character of his foe, things which he could not have known beforehand, he reported that 1,000 men might have been equal to the task.

During the whole fight hardly half a dozen Indians were seen by the soldiers, although the attacking force lost between forty and fifty killed and wounded.

While on this occasion many deeds of valour on the part of the troops came to light, the most conspicuous personage during the whole fight was Major John Green, the commander at Fort Klamath, whose conduct won the admiration of all who observed him.

Major Green commanded a line of skirmishers. As the battle ground was of such peculiar formation that an unbroken line of skirmishers would a few minutes later find itself split up in small detachments cut off from one another by impassable crevices and exposed to sudden flanking fire from an unseen enemy, extreme precaution was required to avoid disaster. The rank and file, who felt their prey continuously slipping away from them, between their fingers, so to speak, while the hostile shots told only the more severely, were likely to lose heart and confidence in themselves.

So it happened that, when the command came to advance, the men in some part of Major Green's line appeared none too eager to execute the orders; they had sustained severe losses without any visible counter effect upon the Indians, and the position then held was a sheltered one. Major Green, seeing this, at once stepped forward and commenced walking coolly up and down, fully exposed to the enemy's fire, showing his men by his own example that the hostile bullets were not worthy of notice. During the whole engagement he exposed himself with a recklessness that could not fail to impress his men. Under fire it is the example of the superior which inspires the soldier to disdain death and danger and to devote his whole energy to the fulfilment of duty.

As the United States forces were not at all adequate to cope with the foe under the heavy odds against them they were finally "withdrawn to their camps."

This second effort to force the Modocs back to the Klamath Reservation had thus failed.

Re-enforcements were asked for. At this stage the Central Office in Washington considered it wise to resort again to a peace commission. Then it was deemed timely to take General Canby into the confidence of the Indian Affairs Department. Can by advised that now, after the first clash had taken place, there was only one way to assure success, and that was to crush the Indians by a superior force, bring them to terms, and then, after their forced surrender, treat them fairly.

But in spite of his proposition the peace commission, consisting of Mr. A. B. Meacham, Rev. Dr. Thomas and the Indian

Agent, L. S. Dyar, arrived and conferred with the general. The latter, from his experience, foresaw the futility of an attempt to pacify the fully aroused savages now by any other means but force. On the 5th of March a telegram arrived from the Secretary of the Interior to the commission, saying: "I do not believe that the Modocs mean treachery. Continue negotiations." A subsequent meeting with the representative Indians on April 2nd showed their suspicion, fully awakened now to a degree far beyond the possible influence of "negotiation." Besides, there were the warnings of an experienced scout and interpreter by the name of Frank Riddle, and his wife, a full-blood Modoc woman, who had always been loyal to her husband and his friends, and proved to be so to the last.

But all these signs and warnings availed not with the majority of the commissioners.

General Canby had by this time assembled all his troops, surrounding the enemy's fastnesses.

After several fruitless meetings the Indians sent several of their tribe and the two famous warriors, Bogus Charley and Boston Charley, to propose a meeting the next day at a certain place, both negotiating parties to be unarmed.

They were so urgent and apparently so sincere that even the sharp Canby was deceived. It was agreed to meet on the next day; Meacham, Dyar, Dr. Thomas and General Canby were to go as the representatives of the White Father. The two Indian rogues, Bogus Charley and Boston Charley, were kept in camp over night and treated with friendly consideration and kindness. Commissioners Meacham and Dyar had their suspicions, but were overruled. Tobe, the wife of Scout Riddle, implored the commissioners not to go, as her tribesmen planned treachery and murder; but her entreaties were in vain.

Next morning the party started for the council-tent. They were General Canby, Dr. Thomas, Meacham, Dyar, Riddle and his Modoc wife, and the two warriors, Bogus Charley and Boston Charley; they carried no arms whatever; General Canby took a box of cigars with him.

At the council-tent they met six chieftains, armed; Captain Jack, Schonchin, Shacknasty Jim, Ellen's Man, Hooker Jim and Black Jim. Their pistols could be seen sticking out of their blankets. The two Charleys, who had been treated so friendly in the white camp, forthwith joined their comrades, disappeared for a while and came back armed. Canby and his companions now saw plainly that they had been entrapped. But Canby stepped forward coolly and invited everyone to sit down for the meeting. The whites sat on one side of a small sage-brush fire, the redskins on the other; Riddle and Tobe were near General Canby. The latter handed around his box of cigars, and the council farce began.

Suddenly Hooker Jim arose and, taking an overcoat from Dyar's horse, said sneeringly while putting it on, "Here is Mr. Meacharn." The commissioners thought to ignore the incident, although it was of bad enough significance; only Meacham said: "Well, take my hat, if you want to," to which the savage replied in his own language, "Just wait a bit and I will, too." The crisis was in sight.

General Canby, in a dignified little speech, explained to the Indians, through Riddle, that wherever he had dealings with them he had always looked out fairly for their interests, so that Indians of several tribes with whom he had negotiated had acknowledged to him their gratitude in various ways. He expressed the hope that some time he would also be successful in winning the friendship of the Modocs.

The chieftains received this speech with impudent sneers and contemptuous laughter.

Schonchin arose and began a harangue which was characteristic of his fierce and murderous inclinations. With loud shouts he insisted that all the soldiers should be sent home immediately and the Hot Creek region given to the Modocs as their reservation.

While he was talking, evidently only to kill time, two Modoc warriors came in, each one carrying three rifles.

Dr. Thomas, kneeling down, said: "I believe the Great Spirit

THEY TURNED AND OPENED THE ATTACK THEMSELVES

sent us here to make peace. I know my heart and those of my friends, and I know they are good; we want no more war. The Great Spirit made all men, the red man and the white man. We are all brothers and will live in peace together."

Captain Jack had quickly gotten up and, springing behind Dyar's horse, cocked his pistol. Two more armed Indians rushed upon the scene. General Canby rose and demanded sternly: "Captain Jack, what does this mean?" The answer was a shot from Jack's pistol, the bullet striking the general in the face, right under his left eye. He jumped forward, but Ellen's Man shot him through the head from behind, and Canby fell dead.

Boston Charley then sent a bullet through the lungs of poor Dr. Thomas, whose guest he had been during the preceding night. Dr. Thomas fell, raised himself again on his arm and said to the treacherous savage: "Boston, stop shooting; I am dying now."

The Indian sneered: "Damn ye! Maybe you will believe next time what squaw (Riddle's wife) tell ye," and he shattered the doctor's brain with a second bullet.

Dyar, when the shooting began, succeeded in running away, out of harm's reach. Meacham was attacked by the bloodthirsty Schonchin, who sent several bullets into him. Meacham fell and would have been scalped had not brave Tobe, Riddle's wife, suddenly raised the cry: "The soldiers are coming!" It was a ruse, but a clever one and saved Meacham's life.

The Indians fled into the lava beds. When the soldiers finally did come they were all gone.

Now, that the long-foreseen outrage had been committed and two precious lives sacrificed for nothing, the eyes of the central authorities opened sufficiently to size up the gravity of the situation, and prompt action was taken at last to make an end of the dangers and atrocities in this region forever. The Modocs must be exterminated.

The wily and desperate redskins, who must have been aware of what was awaiting them, kept still, hidden in their lava crevices.

Colonel Gillem of the First United States Cavalry, who only escaped the chance of sharing Canby's and Thomas's fate by being too ill to accompany the hapless peace-party, was ordered to attack without delay with all his available forces.

The troops, flanking the lava beds, joined at the lake front and cut off the water supply of the Indians. The latter had to come out, and desperate fighting followed, lasting three days. The troops proved too weak to prevent their foe from finding another strong position, where they again defiantly awaited further developments.

A reconnoissance was ordered, and Captain Thomas of the Fourth United States Artillery went forward, his command consisting of five officers, a surgeon, sixty-five enlisted men and fourteen friendly Warm Spring Indians. The detachment left early in the morning. The objective point was reached at noon, and as no hostile Indians had been observed, the command halted for a rest. Unfortunate men! Before they had finished an impromptu meal a volley came suddenly pouring in, well aimed, and instantly creating a panic. The men ran to escape the bullets; the officers and non-commissioned officers, with a few fearless men of the rank-and-file, rallied, made a gallant stand, and after a desperate and heroic struggle met their fate.

Some Warm Spring Indian scouts who attempted to bring succour to the ambushed party, but were by mistake fired at by the whites, rushed back to camp and reported the latter's desperate plight. Major Green, ever ready, gathered in the utmost hurry all the available forces and hastened to the spot. But of the five line officers four were found killed, Captain Thomas and Lieutenants Cranston, Wright and Howe, and Lieutenant Harris mortally wounded. Besides there were eighteen men killed and seventeen wounded of this gallant band, which when it assembled for the last stand had hardly numbered fifty men.

Major Green rescued the wounded, among whom was also the surgeon of the party, Dr. Semig, who escaped death in a miraculous way. He had been twice severely wounded and lay helpless between the rocks, hearing, while still conscious, how the hostiles endeavoured to reach him and lift his scalp. Finally consciousness fled, and when he came to he was in the hands of friends, he having lain there fully twenty hours. Major Green had come in time. The rapidly advancing soldiers kept the savages from crawling towards their intended victim, as they would have been compelled to expose themselves had they done so.

This new disaster increased the energy of the military, and on the 2nd of May General Davis reached the scene with a goodly force of fresh troops.

Two friendly Modoc squaws were sent into the lava beds as spies; after some days absence they returned with the information that the enemy had gone.

Instantly a vigorous pursuit was ordered.

The exhausted savages had not been able to make much headway in their flight, and when they became aware that the soldiers were after them they turned and opened the attack themselves. This time they were badly beaten and scattered, and Finally fell back again to the lava beds, defending every inch of the ground against the vigorously pushing troops. The latter took the enemy between two lines, and the situation of the sandwiched redskins became hopeless. They began to quarrel among themselves and split soon into two parties, both of which succeeded in sneaking out of the lava beds unseen. But soon the troops were after them.

On the 22nd of May one band surrendered, and almost immediately after this a Modoc captive, who had enjoyed Captain Jack's full confidence, betrayed the whereabouts of the latter. On the 1st of June the famous chief and his band were surprised and scatered; many of them were killed, some captured, but Jack escaped. On the 3rd of June he and three loyal followers were surrounded and gave themselves up. Jack explained stoically that he would not have been caught had not fatigue overcome him.

During these last days of desperate fighting and pursuing it was again Major John Green who, in courage, zeal, instruction and intelligence, proved a model soldier, and impressed his men more than any other officer with the idea of absolute fearlessness. Self-protection and shelter were ever secondary in his mind to the accomplishment of what he had in view, and he richly deserved his Medal of Honour.

The subdued Modocs were all brought to the Tule Lake, which place they reached on the 5th of June. Captain Jack, Schonchin, Black Jim, Boston Charley, Barncho and Sloluck, the six leaders, were afterwards tried by a military commission at Fort Klamath on the 1st of July, found guilty and sentenced to death. The sentences of Barncho and Sloluck were commuted to imprisonment for life, while the other four were hanged at Fort Klamath on October 3, 1873.

This was practically the end of the Modocs; the remnants of the band were conveyed to a small stretch of land near Baxter Springs, Kansas, where they now offer an illustration of the slowly-dying-out process, and Barncho and Sloluck withered away to their graves in the prison at Alcatraz.

Rescuing the Germaine Girls

FRANK D. BALDWIN

Many of the Indian uprisings were like the convulsive struggles of a dying race, the last efforts of a people doomed to final extinction against the irresistible and relentless march and progress of civilization. The white man's civilization was as ruthless in the removal of all obstacles and the extermination of every race or nation that proved a hindrance as the cruelty and barbarism of the savage himself, differing only in the methods. The Indian exerted his brute force, the white man his intellectual superiority; the result could be but fatal to the former.

A characteristic uprising of this kind was planned and inaugurated by the Southern Cheyennes, Kiowas, Arapahoes and other bands in the Indian Territory in 1874, and the first serious occurrences took place in June of that year, with Texas as the main scene of action. The events which led up to and culminated in the outbreak were accumulative rather than of one single and definite character.

Civilization was making rapid progress; the white man was penetrating the forests, colonizing at streams and waters and covering the plains and prairies. The establishment of military posts, trading stations and settlements, the building of railroads, gradually changed the character of whole sections of the country. Nor was this accomplished with consideration or regard for the Indian's feeling of piety and respect. Places of ancient worship were demolished, to be replaced, perhaps, by a prosaic railway station; old burying grounds, regarded by the Indian with justifiable veneration, were made to disappear by the hand of the white man, who claimed ownership of the sacred spot. The Indian's anger grew as he observed these changes in conditions, which in his eyes were but evidences of rude vandalism.

Again, the white man was depleting the Indian's hunting ground by his wholesale slaughter of buffalo. From this animal the savage derived his clothing, food and shelter; yet the white man killed them by thousands. The greed of the frontiersman, who found in the skin of the buffalo a ready article of trade, knew no bounds. Statistics show that within a few years over 4,000,000 buffaloes were killed by white hunters.

Sometime early in June the aforementioned Indian tribes met at Medicine Lodge, Indian Territory, and at a general council aired their various grievances. The chiefs were bitter in their denunciation of the invaders vandalism and reckless brutality, and war was decided upon to stop further acts of this kind. Subsequently bands of these tribes began to leave their reservations, cross the boundary lines and harass and disturb the settlers along the Texas frontier. War opened in earnest when a body of several hundred Indians advanced to attack some buffalo hunters. Fortunately for the latter, the attack was planned on a Sunday, when the hunters were assembled together for mutual rest and recreation, and thus were able to present a united front to the attacking warriors. They were crack riflemen, too, these hunters, and easily repulsed the savage foe, killing nearly one-fourth of the entire Indian force.

This sudden attack, however, induced the government to order an expedition against the rebellious tribes, and thus the Indian War of 1874 followed, during which one of the most pathetic incidents of any of the Indian wars occurred.

The Cheyennes had crossed from their reservation to the territory of Western Kansas. Their path was marked by plunder and devastation. Among the first victims were the members of a family by the name of Germaine, consisting of man and wife, a grown-up son and daughter and four smaller children, girls, aged fifteen, thirteen, nine and seven years respectively.

The Germaines originally lived in Georgia, but had later moved to Western Missouri, and now were on their way to Colorado. Although their journey was slow, they were well provided with food, carried along a fairly large stock, including several horses and an outfit of several wagons. Thus far their travels had been uneventful and free from adventure, and they were already congratulating themselves on having been spared the many dangers which in those days usually lurked in the path of the pioneer. But their joy was premature, and disaster struck them when they least expected it. A cruel fate came between them and their hopes and ended the journey of the little family.

The Cheyennes surprised them, killed Germaine and his wife, also the son, and carried off the four girls as captives, together with all their property.

For some reason or other they did not want to keep the oldest of the Germaine girls, but killed her in the presence of her trembling little sisters. These they dragged along with them on the retreat to their camp, and later kept them prisoners in their village. It is almost impossible to describe the fate to which these children were doomed among the uncouth savages. The life they had to endure, the tortures to which they were subjected, are too revolting to recite. Their innocence and tender age offered no protection from the outrages of their captors; their prayers and tears failed to move the hearts of their fiendish tormentors. They were looked upon by the males as common property and by the squaws as objects of pleasure and pastime for their consorts.

The expedition organized by the government and directed in these sections by General Nelson A. Miles began operations in June and continued all through the summer and autumn, the Indians being driven back into their reservations, wherever they showed themselves. Hostilities did not cease when winter came, but the pursuit was vigorously kept up during the cold season, and over territory where the Indians had heretofore felt themselves free and undisturbed. Wherever their trail was discovered, it was followed as long as it could be traced.

During one of these winter expeditions the command of First Lieutenant Frank D. Baldwin, Fifth United States Infantry, consisting of a force of friendly Delaware Indians, twenty-five frontiersmen, expert riflemen, scouts and men accustomed to the Indian's way of fighting, Troop D, of the Sixth United States Cavalry, commanded by Lieutenant Overton, and Company D, Fifth United States Infantry, Lieutenant Bailey commanding, at daylight, November 8, 1874, was moving through a rough country, bordering the east of the Staked Plains of the Pan Handle of Texas, when scouts, coming back suddenly at breakneck speed, reported the presence of a large Indian camp only a short distance in front in the breaks. Lieutenant Baldwin, without waiting for re-enforcements, at once closed up his command, preparatory to an attack, and sent Scout Schmalsle to General Miles to notify him that an Indian camp had been located and an attack would be made upon it immediately, regardless of the numerically vastly superior Indian forces.

After dispatching the scout, Baldwin ordered his command to advance as rapidly as possible, until it was within range of the camp. Then Company D fired a volley into the camp and drove the surprised and unprepared Indians to the brow of the hills overlooking the plain. Here the warriors rallied, and turning suddenly made a most desperate effort to repulse the soldiers and retake their camp and abandoned property.

Lieutenant Baldwin now brought the cavalry into action and once more forced the braves to flee, chasing them hotly for a distance of over twelve miles. The victory was complete and resulted in the capture of the entire Indian camp and the rescue of the two younger Germaine girls, Adelaide and Julia.

It was Chief Gray Beard's own camp of Cheyenne Indians, the very same savages who had perpetrated the outrage upon the wayfaring Germaine family, that had been captured by Baldwin.

The rescue of these two little girls was the reward of his quick and decisive action. For had he delayed the attack only for a short time, the Indians would undoubtedly have murdered their white captives and managed their escape.

Freed from the clutches of their tormentors the little girls were boundless in their joy. They cried and laughed, their eyes beamed with delight; they kissed and hugged their deliverers and knew not how to express their childish gratitude.

Those who were present when the children were led away from the camp where they had suffered so much will never forget the scene. Soldiers surrounded them; now one, now the other, would take one of the little ones in his arms and carry her along for a distance, and many a grim warrior cried as he heard the child tell her revolting experience. They clenched their fists and vowed vengeance upon the savages. "By all that is holy, there won't be a rest till we get the other two girls!" they exclaimed, and they kept their word. The two children were, under proper care, sent to Fort Leavenworth, Kansas, while the pursuit of the Indians was continued with unrelenting vigour. For two months this warfare was kept up, when at last the Indians began to weary of further hostilities and showed evidences of submission.

A trusted and friendly Indian was sent to the camp of the warriors with a message from General Miles demanding their surrender, and coupled with the further condition that they bring in alive the prisoners they had in their hands. The message made it plain that there would be no peace granted until these prisoners were restored. The Indian messenger had still another mission. He was told to find the Germaine girls and hand them a photograph of their sisters who had been liberated.

On the back of the photograph the general had written: "Your little sisters are well and in the hands of friends. Do not be discouraged. Every effort is being made for your welfare." This picture and message the faithful Indian slipped into the hands of the

They drove the surprised Indians to the brow of the hill

captive Germaine girls after his arrival in the hostile camp, and thus brought a ray of hope and sunshine to the two unfortunate girls. They had almost despaired of ever hearing of their sisters, and with sullen resignation prepared themselves to die among the savages, far away from their friends and white people.

The Indians were only too glad to have a chance to secure peace. In spite of snow and ice and the hardships of winter travel, they journeyed over 200 miles to their agency, where they surrendered. At the beginning of the march the chief ordered special care to be taken of the Germaine girls, who now were treated with the greatest kindness and consideration.

At the agency the Indians were lined up and the girls told to point out the perpetrators of the murder of their parents, brother and sister and their own worst tormentors. The girls passed along the line and pointed out seventy-five Indians. These were placed under guard and taken to St. Augustine, Florida.

The sisters subsequently were united at Fort Leavenworth, where they were educated, General Miles becoming their guardian. They each received $2,500 from the government.

That a sad story thus had a happy conclusion was due primarily to the brilliant and decisive victory of Lieutenant Baldwin, the hero of the Indian war of 1874, a man whom nature had designated to be a soldier, who was endowed with those qualities which alone prepare a man for a soldier's life gallantry and bravery. For this voluntary attack and its successful issue he was awarded the Medal of Honour.

His conduct during the War of the Rebellion furnishes additional proof of this and brought him suitable reward and recognition from the government. An achievement at Peach Tree Creek, Georgia, July 20, 1864, earned for him his first Medal of Honour.

He was captain of Company D, Nineteenth Michigan Infantry, at the time, and, under a galling fire, led his company against the enemy, entering the Confederate lines ahead of his own men where, single-handed, he took two commissioned officers prisoners and carried off the guidon of a Georgia regiment.

With General Miles Through Texas

The pursuit of the Indians in the uprising of 1874 carried General Miles's command to the Staked Plains of Western Texas, as has been related in the previous story. It now becomes necessary to describe his march briefly, leading up as it does to occurrences of more than passing importance and which form the subject of the present narration.

General Miles left Fort Dodge, Indian Territory, on August 14th, in a southerly direction, and for the remainder of the month covered a distance of many hundred miles through a country that had been devastated by a peculiar scourge—the plague of locusts—and, in addition, offered many other natural disadvantages. The almost unbearable heat of the hottest season of the year, when the mercury seldom, if ever, drops below 110 degrees in the shade, together with the large bands of ever-alert and hostile Indians, contributed to make this expedition one of the most memorable in the history of the Indian wars.

The beds of the many small rivers and creeks were completely dry. For days the troops marched without a drop of water. Sometimes the ground over which they had to pass was a mere desert, and this added to the misery of men and beasts. Sometimes, after many hours of weary marching, the soldiers, with rapturous delight, would hail the sight of a rivulet which promised the much-needed refreshment, only to find upon arriving at its inviting banks that the water was so impregnated with minerals as to be absolutely unfit for drinking purposes.

Hardships and disappointments all along the route put the military spirit, the endurance and tenaciousness of the command to the highest test, but the American soldier proved here, as always, that he was, under all circumstances, equal to the occasion, and General Miles bestowed the highest praise upon the excellent conduct of his men during this trying march. They not only braved the fatigues of weather and territory, but met the constant attacks and harassing manoeuvres of the hostile Indians with unabated courage, defeating and routing them wherever the savage hordes showed themselves.

In this fashion the march was continued towards the Canadian River in Texas, when, on August 27th, the main trail of the Indians was finally struck at the Sweetwater River. It was followed with eagerness and was of such character the day following as to lead the command to believe that they were in the immediate proximity of the long-looked-for main body of the enemy. This infused new life into the weary troops, who, incredible as it may seem, marched sixty-five miles during the next two days in their ardour to meet the redskins.

On the morning of August 30th, Lieutenant Frank D. Baldwin, the hero of the foregoing story, and his detachment of scouts, two miles ahead of the main column, were attacked by a large band of hostiles, who with the usual hideous ado sprang from their places of concealment lining the bluff which bordered the level plains, and with reckless daring charged right into the small detachment.

Baldwin's men at once took position, dropped to the ground and used their rifles with unerring and unfailing effect. With the detachment were a number of friendly Delawares under their aged chief, Fall Leaf. This veteran warrior summoned about him his faithful braves, and with glittering eyes and streaming gray hair he swung his rifle and dashed, the very picture of an Indian hero, at the head of his men against the hated enemy. The hostiles were held at bay till the main column arrived upon the scene of action, but they came none too soon, for the Indians, too, had received re-enforcements, and thus what was at first but a mere short and sharp fight now turned into a real battle, lasting for some hours and ending in a complete route of the Indians, who were driven across the Red River into the Staked Plains and pursued for more than twenty miles.

After the victory, the troops, now thoroughly fagged out, halted at the bed of the Red River, about half a mile wide at that point. A small, stagnant pool, saturated with gypsum and alkali, was the only water in sight, and that nobody could drink. How the men suffered! General Miles states that he saw some of them open the veins of their arms to moisten their parched lips with their own blood. The next day the command moved into the Staked Plains, and there, in a locality where water was abundant, rested to await the arrival of a new supply train from Camp Supply, Indian Territory.

The arrangement by which these supplies were to be transported was this: Captain Wyllys Lyman, Fifth United States Infantry, with his company, and Lieutenant Frank West, Sixth United States Cavalry, with twenty men, were sent to meet the supply train, which General Miles knew had left Camp Supply some days previously. The two detachments met September 7th, and the stores were transferred, a violent storm rendering the work rather difficult and of slow progress. The return march was eventful. At the outset the Indians made their presence felt in a most annoying manner. A teamster, for example, who had imprudently wandered away a short distance, fell into their hands, was scalped, killed, and his body left on the trail. The farther the train proceeded, the bolder these savages grew, increasing, too, in numbers all along the route.

On September 9th, just as the train emerged from a deep ravine, the Indians, who, it now appeared, were Kiowas and Comanches, who had left their reservations, attacked the rear of the train. They numbered fully 300, and, relying upon their strength, displayed unusual boldness and audacity. They came within 100 yards of the train, shot Lieutenant G. Lewis, Fifth United States Infantry, a sergeant and several soldiers. It was by almost superhuman efforts that the brave men composing the small detachment foiled the impetuous attack of the Indians.

The train continued to wend its way slowly and cautiously across the Washita River into Texas territory, and finally came to a halt one mile north of the river. Then all further progress ceased. The Indians had increased to such a strength that they were able to completely surround the entire detachment.

In spite of the most vigorous and gallant resistance, in which First Sergeant John Mitchell, Sergeants Fred S. Hay, William Koelpin, Corporal John James, John J. H. Kelly, John W. Knox and Private Thomas Kelly, of the Fifth United States Infantry, and Sergeants George H. Kitchen, Fred S. Neilon, Josiah Pennsyl and Corporals William W. Morris and Edward C. Sharpless, of the Sixth United States Cavalry, distinguished themselves, the savages would have succeeded but for the personal bravery of that daring young scout, Schmalsle.

On the second night, when darkness had fallen, Schmalsle mounted his horse and dashed through the lines of the warriors with such reckless speed as to completely surprise the braves. A number of them attempted to pursue the daring rider, but Schmalsle had the better mount and was the better rider, and proved too speedy for his pursuers.

He was chased into a herd of buffaloes and escaped in the tumult and under the cover of darkness.

Schmalsle continued his wild ride till his horse became completely exhausted and dropped dead on the road. The young scout then travelled on foot, and after two nights of continuous marching—he was compelled to hide during the day—finally reached Camp Supply, where he furnished information of the critical situation of the supply train.

Colonel Lewis at once sent Major Price with a battalion of the Eighth United States Cavalry to the relief. The appearance of this large force caused the Indians to raise the siege and disperse in all directions.

"The Indians," First Sergeant George K. Kitchen, of Troop I, Sixth United States Cavalry, relates, "concentrated their entire force, and made a vigorous and united charge on the train. This charge was repulsed after a hard fight, the Indians coming

SERGEANT NEILON CARRYING AMMUNITION TO THE BESIEGED TROOPERS

to within fifty yards of the train, and repeatedly attempting, after being beaten off, to overwhelm the troops by dint of superior numbers.

"The wagons were then, as it was impossible to advance, put into park as rapidly as possible, forming in an egg shape. The infantry was thrown out on a skirmish line round the hastily formed corral, some 25 yards from the wagons. When this movement was completed, the little band of cavalry found themselves, at the end of some hard fighting, about 500 yards away from the skirmish line, and surrounded by the enemy. To regain their comrades of the Fifth Infantry they had to charge through a mass of Indians, who concentrated themselves between them and the wagons. This was successfully done.

"On reaching the park we secured our horses inside the enclosure, and were then ordered out on the skirmish line.

"The hostiles now divided, and about 400 of them at this time made two unsuccessful charges on the right rear of the corral, defended by about one-half of the command. These charges were made in column of platoons, and the alignment was as precise and well maintained as regular troops could do it. Each time they came up to within forty yards of the line in admirable order, and only the perfect steadiness and continuous, well-directed fire of our troops prevented this well-conceived and daringly executed movement from being successful.

"By our heavy fire, however, we at last succeeded in repelling them in confusion from the very muzzles of our guns.

"The enemy then, unsuccessful in storming us, took up position on the numerous sand hills around, some as far away as 400 yards, others at about only 200 yards, surrounding us by a complete circle. As we lay beneath them we were exposed to a severe and vexatious fire from all points, and our return fire was comparatively harmless. When darkness arrived we were divided up into squads, and orders were given to dig rifle pits, from twenty to thirty yards distant, around the corral. The enemy followed our example and were occupied in entrenching themselves on the sand hills they held during the day. Their object now appeared to be to starve us out, as they knew we had no means of quenching our thirst.

"The Washita was one mile away, and the one water-hole near us had been inaccessible during the day, and our repeated attempts to get at it at night proved futile. Several details tried to reach the water, but the Indians placed a strong guard around it, and their fire was too well-directed to allow of our men getting near. They would permit us to get within fifty yards of the hole, in fancied security, before opening on us, and then poured in their fire, which balked every effort to reach the desired spot. In the meantime a desultory fire was kept up by them on all sides of us.

"Next day this fire became regular and continuous, and was returned by us from the rifle pits. We killed many a brave, but his place was taken at once by a comrade, after the dead body had been carried off. This was done always by two Indians, riding at full gallop, one on each side of the dead man, who was picked up by them without their making the slightest halt, and dragged into shelter.

"When we first went into corral the command had but very little water in the canteens, and this was saved for the use of the wounded. From the 9th to the morning of the 14th of September no one, except our wounded, had one drop of water. On the third day, when driven almost to despair by the torments of thirst, some men opened a barrel of vinegar, and undertook to drink it when sweetened somewhat by sugar. It was with difficulty that they were prevented from swallowing too much of the mixture. One of the ten men whom I had in my rifle pit drank, in spite of my efforts to prevent any excess, so much of the vinegar that he became delirious and very violent. We had to tie him hand and foot to keep him inside the pit; he frothed at the mouth, bit and fought, and exhibited every token of insanity. It was two days before he recovered from the effects.

"The fighting, until the night of the 13th of September, was continued in the same way, we staying in our rifle pits, exhausted by heat and thirst, and returning as best we could the fire of the Indians, who remained in possession of their sand hills.

"On the morning of the 14th we saw, with relief, the whole band of Indians pull out and move south. If we had had water, we could have lasted a long time. Without it, we could not have stood the siege for many more days."

A few days prior—on September 12th—another no less thrilling incident occurred at about the same place, the Washita River.

General Miles had sent a detachment of six men, Sergeant Z. T. Woodall, Company I; Privates Peter Roth, Company A, John Harrington, Company H, and George W. Smith, Company M, Sixth U. S. Cavalry, and Scouts Amos Chapman and William Dixon, to carry a dispatch to Camp Supply.

On the way this party was attacked by a force of warriors numbering about 125. Four of the six men were wounded at the beginning of the fight, Private Smith mortally, and the other three severely. Surrounded by a foe outnumbering them twenty-five to one, the men were facing almost certain death; yet they were determined to sell their lives as dearly as possible.

Private Harrington describes the fight as follows:

"Between us and the Indians was a good-sized ravine, to which we advanced and rode into. We had scarcely time to dismount and leave the horses in charge of Smith, before the Indians were on us from all sides. We hurriedly sought shelter on the sides of the ravine. Smith was shot through the arm and compelled to abandon the horses and join us. About twenty-five Indians then charged down the ravine and stampeded our horses, taking all but one. Concluding that things were getting too warm for us, and that we would have to find some better position, we formed a skirmish line and fell back, the one horse left by the Indians following us. An Indian attempted to capture it, when Sergeant Woodall turned and fired, and the Indian fell.

"We again retreated in skirmish line, receiving their fire from all directions. Whenever we attempted to secure a knoll or other vantage ground, the Indians would be ahead of us in such numbers as to make us change our direction. None of us expected to get out of the fray alive, with such fearful odds against us, but all determined to die hard and make the best fight possible. We continued our skirmishing, and whenever a shelter was secured, took what little rest we could until driven out by renewed attacks.

"At every halt the Indians, dismounted, would surround us, closing in from all sides. The medicine man, decorated with buffalo horns and an immense head dress of eagle feathers reaching to his horse's tail, looking like the devil himself, tried to force them to charge over us; each time, as they circled into within about twenty-five yards, we would jump up, yell, and run towards those in our rear. The Indians could not fire for fear of hitting their own party, but would open out and allow us to pass through their line, firing at us as we went through.

"It seems almost incredible that we should have received their fire as long as we did without serious injury; but it could not go on so forever. We kept up these tactics until about 4 o'clock in the afternoon. The medicine man, now the only mounted one of their party, kept riding around us all the time, getting bolder and firing his pistol when he came in range. Chapman, the scout, said, not to mind him, for he couldn't hit anything, but at last he came within about twenty yards, when Scout Dixon fired at him, after which we saw no more of the bold medicine man.

"By this time we were about done out, and our ammunition, of which we had 200 rounds per man in the morning, was nearly exhausted. Determining to make one last stand, we broke for a small knoll, on the top of which was a buffalo wallow. While attempting to gain this position, Smith was again shot and fell, mortally wounded. Woodall was shot in the groin, and I in the hip. All gained the knoll but Smith."

Sergeant Woodall adds the following:

"At this stage of the fight we were eye witnesses to some magnificent feats of horsemanship, that could not be equalled by any like number of men in the world—men rising readily from the stirrups while their horses were in rapid motion, and standing erect on the backs of their, animals while they delivered their fire, and then instantly dropping, as if shot, into the stirrups; swinging themselves rapidly under their horses bellies, in which position they could easily aim and fire. These tactics were continued by them for some time. There was one spot on the prairie where the grass stood over five feet high.

"Toward this place the Indians would ride as fast as their ponies could go, and I noticed every time any of the men fired at an Indian near this place the latter would drop as if hit, while his pony would continue on until finally caught by some of the squaws. Fully twenty of them dropped in this manner, leading us to believe that they were all hit. Nothing more was seen of them for about an hour, during which our attention was engaged in an opposite direction by another party of Indians, who repeatedly charged us, eventually forcing us from our position.

"In moving to higher ground we approached the bunch of tall grass before referred to, near which we had seen so many Indians drop. We got within fifty yards when a line of Indians sprang up, presenting as good a skirmish line as anybody of soldiers could form, and poured a murderous fire into our party, dropping Smith and severely wounding Amos Chapman, Harrington and myself."

Smith, who had fallen outside, was thought to be dead. In a little while, however, he was seen to move, and Chapman heroically volunteered to attempt to rescue him. Chapman tells the story of his noble act in the following words:

"'Now, boys,' said I to my comrades as I started out, 'keep those infernal redskins off me and I will run down and pick up Smith and bring him back before they can get at me.'

"I ran full speed to Smith and attempted to shoulder him, Smith was not a large man, but I declare that he seemed to weigh a ton. Finally I laid down and got his chest across my back, and his arms around my neck, and then got up with him. It was as much as I could do to stagger under him, for he couldn't help himself a bit. By the time I had got twenty or thirty yards, about fifteen Indians came for me at full speed on their ponies. They all knew me, and yelled, 'Amos! Amos!' we have got you now! I pulled my pistol, but I couldn't hold Smith on my back with one hand, so I let him drop. The boys in the buffalo wal-

Amos Chapman bringing in Smith

low opened on the Indians just at the right time, and I opened on them with my pistol. There was a tumbling of ponies and a scattering of Indians, and in a minute they were gone.

"I got Smith up again and made the best possible time, but before I could reach the wallow another gang came for me. I had only one or two shots in my pistol, so I didn't stop to fight, but ran for it. When I was within about twenty yards of the wallow a little old scoundrel that I had fed fifty times rode almost on to me and fired. I fell, with Smith on top of me, but as I didn't feel any pain I thought I had stepped into a hole. The Indians couldn't stay around there a minute—the boys kept it red hot—so I jumped up, picked up Smith, and got safe into the wallow. 'Amos,' said Dixon, 'you are badly hurt.'

"'No, I am not,' said I.

"'Why, look at your leg,' he said, and, sure enough, the leg was so badly shattered just above the ankle joint that I had been walking on the bone, dragging the foot behind me, and in the excitement I never knew it."

Night came, and with its merciful darkness an end was put to the unequal struggle. The bodies of more than twenty Indians lay stretched upon the ground.

The savages had no further desire to engage in a combat with that small but heroic band of soldiers and scouts and left the scene before the break of day.

Private Smith died early in the morning of September 13; Sergeant Woodall, Private Harrington and Scout Chapman were so severely wounded that they were unable to move, and Private Roth and Scout Dixon, though injured themselves, had to remain in the same small ditch to watch over the corpse of their dead comrade and comfort their wounded friends. The entire day passed before relief came. They were without food, and to quench their thirst were compelled to drink the filthy water that had collected in the trench and been mixed with their own blood.

At night Major Price, with a strong command, came and took them to Camp Supply.

In speaking of this affair General Miles says:

The simple recital of their deeds and the mention of the odds against which they fought; how the wounded defended the dying, and the dying aided the wounded by exposure to fresh wounds after the power of action was gone; these alone present a scene of cool courage, heroism and self-sacrifice which duty, as well as inclination, prompts us to recognize, but which we cannot fitly honour.

Hand-to-Hand Fights With Indians

Simultaneously with the operations of General Miles in Indian Territory were those conducted by Colonel R. S. Mackenzie, who was moving with his command, Troops A, D, E, F, H, I, K, Fourth Cavalry, towards the Red River, Texas, from the south.

The torrents which follow the dry season made the roadbeds almost impassable for wagons, and impeded the progress of this column seriously. In spite of the difficulties of the march and the many privations which resulted therefrom, the troops preserved a most excellent spirit, and easily repulsed two determined attacks made by the Indians. After crossing the head of the Tule Canyon Colonel Mackenzie located five camps of Southern Cheyennes and their allies at Canyon Blanco, a tributary of the Red River, and immediately proceeded to attack them.

In the subsequent fight, which lasted two days, September 26 and 27, 1874, the Indians were put to utter rout, leaving their entire camp outfits and their herds of ponies, some 1,400 animals, in the possession of the victors. The Indians lost four killed and several wounded, while of the troops but one was wounded, and he only slightly. Corporal Edwin Phoenix and Privates Gregory Mahoney and William McCabe, of Company E, were especially conspicuous for their gallantry in this conflict and received the Medal of Honour in consequence. A like honour was conferred upon Private Adam Paine, who as an Indian scout rendered invaluable services to Colonel Mackenzie.

After this victory the column continued its march and had

many other engagements with the redskins. In the fight on November 3rd Farrier Ernest Veuve, of Company A, had an interesting encounter with a hostile Indian who faced him at a most unexpected time and when he was completely separated from his comrades. The intrepid farrier, however, proved equal to the emergency, and after a brief hand-to-hand fight put the Indian to flight.

Private John W. Comfort, of the same company, two days later had a similar experience, but with a more fatal result, as far as the attacking savage was concerned. Comfort killed his adversary outright during the struggle.

The chase after the Indians continued all winter and lasted till the spring of the following year. The hostiles, wherever found, were attacked and driven back to their reservations.

At one time First Lieutenant Lewis Warrington, of the Fourth Cavalry, had been pursuing a small band of savages, when, on December 8th, at Muchague Valley, he found himself suddenly attacked by five Indians. In his ardour to get close to the warriors he had become separated from his detachment, and thus found himself face to face with five savages, who, with taunts and sneers in true Indian style, demanded his surrender. The lieutenant, however, was loath to part with his scalp, and he replied to their sneers by firing a shot, which disabled one of them; another shot and a second Indian was placed where he could do no harm. The Indians were no longer inclined to keep up an acquaintance with a soldier who could aim so accurately and shoot so rapidly, and rode away, taking their wounded with them.

Private Frederick Bergendahl, a member of the band, and John O Sullivan, of Company I, also had an encounter, on the same day, with a body of Indian braves whom they were pursuing, and desperately fought with them until the Indians retreated, leaving several of their dead and wounded to show the gallant work done by these two soldiers.

A successful chase under the direction of First Sergeant Dennis Ryan, of Company I, Sixth United States Cavalry, also belongs to this campaign. The sergeant, accompanied by a detachment of twenty men, discovered a large band of Indians on Gageby Creek, Indian Territory, December 2nd. Fully realizing the danger of attacking so large a force of savages, the sergeant, nevertheless, charged and chased them for ten miles, capturing some fifty ponies and destroying a large amount of property belonging to the hostiles.

Snatched From a Horrible Fate

If the stories of the encounters civil engineers and surveying parties had with the Indians in the wild, unsettled regions could be written they would be found replete with stirring incidents of adventure, of splendid courage and heroism. The trackless wastes, the rugged mountain fastnesses, the impressive stillness of nature, furnish each a scene for hostile action, and it was rare, indeed, that the white man did not encounter his natural foe, the Indian, before he was many days on the ground. At a time perhaps when least expected, a savage horde would appear on the brow of a mountain or its ambushed presence would be made known by the whizz of an arrow. There was no time for *parleying* or preparation; but, instantly put upon the defensive, the white man would take up his cause with his handy arms and a gallant fight was the result.

In the year 1874, when Lieutenant King, of the Fifth Cavalry, was detailed to make surveys of a military reservation in Arizona, he had an experience which, in thrilling adventure, might be taken as the original of a story one reads in a book for boys. There is much in the beauty and grandeur of the territory to attract the student of nature and the artist, and one may be allowed the liberty of believing that Lieutenant King and his party looked forward to enjoying themselves in a country where little is tame or common in its scenic character.

If the hope was indulged at all, it was dashed to pieces at the very outset. Their advent was marked by an unexpected uprising of the Apaches, who had resisted every effort to civilize them. They were not the only Indians in the territory, but none of the others could surpass them in relentless cruelty and savagery toward the white man. During the winter months, preceding the arrival of the surveyors, near Sunset Pass, Arizona, they accepted the bounty of the government, with the poorest grace, and with the coming of spring they threw off the clothes the government had provided them with, and, armed with the rifles the government had given them for purposes of hunting, went forth to kill the white invader. It was of small consequence that the troops pursued the savages. The latter knew the mountains and had a deadly mode of warfare in which they were masters. Gifted also with a cunning which seemed to anticipate every move of the military, the soldiers were obliged to meet the Apaches on their own terms.

The Indian fighter cheerfully accepts the fortunes of his lot, and seldom counts the cost; but a sturdy heart was needed to face the Apaches on their own stamping ground. This was what Lieutenant King did when he went forth to try conclusions with the savages, and had it not been for the remarkable coolness and courage of a sergeant at the first encounter, the day would doubtless have ended disastrously for the lieutenant. On the first of November, after days of hard riding, in the hope of administering a decisive blow to the Indians, Lieutenant King advanced some distance ahead of his command.

Suddenly he came upon a band of the enemy, ambushed and waiting for him. He turned into the underbrush, in order to flank his position, when an arrow whizzed past, almost striking him in the head. Then followed another, which cut the muscles at the corner of his eye, making an ugly wound, and in another moment a rifle ball pierced his arm. Lieutenant King's men, who were witnesses of how their officer was faring, hastened with all speed to his aid. King was exhausted from his wounds and only half conscious, and after a few steps his foot caught in the root of a tree and he fell to the ground.

An experienced Indian fighter, he knew what fate awaited him should he fall into the hands of the Apaches. There seemed no hope of rescue, and only a matter of choice as to the manner of death. Like the soldier he was, King drew his revolver, and but for the timely arrival of Sergeant Bernard Taylor would have taken his own life. Taylor, who had dashed out of the woods, was a big, strapping, powerful fellow, and taking his superior officer in his arms forged ahead of the Indians, stopping every few paces to send a bullet among them. Lieutenant King was no light burden, and under favourable conditions to carry him would have been less of a feat for a man like Taylor, but the Apaches, thoroughly roused, trained their arms upon the sergeant.

Arrows and bullets flew thick and fast, singing ominously as they passed him. But Taylor kept on, determined to save his lieutenant if he could, and to die hard if he must. King feared the worst for both, and told Taylor to leave him and save himself. Taylor believed that the circumstances justified him in disobeying orders, and one can almost hear his emphatic "No!" as he passed on resolutely with his burden. King implored, then ordered his subordinate to return to the troops; but Taylor refused, for well did he know that should the Indians once capture either of them death by means of torture too horrible even to contemplate would be the result.

Sergeant Taylor carried his wounded officer for nearly half a mile, under the constant fire of the savages, over rocks and ravines, until safe within the picket line, and for his heroic conduct he was awarded the Medal of Honour.

Chasing Indians by Railroad

MARCUS M. ROBBINS

The military operations against the hostile bands in the Indian Territory, were continued during the winter, and well into the spring of 1875, and at length, early in March, the Southern Cheyennes, completely broken down, gave up the contest, and under principal chief, Stone Calf, the whole body of that tribe, with a few trifling exceptions, surrendered themselves as prisoners of war, restoring at the same time the two elder Germaine girls, who had been captives among them for nearly eight months. Although the conditions of surrender required the Indians to deliver up their arms, only a few guns and a large quantity of bows and arrows were turned in, the greater part of their more valuable firearms being hidden away where no search by the troops would be likely to find them.

Orders were received, when the Indians began to surrender, to select from among them the principal ring leaders who had incited or led bands of hostiles in the recent outrages, to be sent to the sea coast, there to be kept in confinement, for a time at least. Seventy-five men were accordingly picked out from the several tribes. On April 6th, whilst shackling Black Horse, one of the Cheyennes who were thus to be disposed of, he broke from the guard and ran directly towards the camp of his people. He was pursued by Captain Bennett, Fifth Infantry, with the guard, who fired upon and killed Black Horse. The shots being in the direction of the Indian camp, several passed beyond the escaping prisoner and wounded some persons there.

After a volley of bullets and arrows upon the guard, about one-half of the tribe fled to the sand hills on the south side of the Canadian, opposite the agency. The troops under command of Lieutenant-Colonel T. H. Neill, Sixth Cavalry, followed, but the Indians, well supplied with firearms they had hidden in that vicinity, occupied a difficult hill and defended themselves against the troops for several hours until nightfall. By night the troops had forced their way nearly to the crest of the hill occupied by the Indians, but at daylight it was found the enemy had fled during the night. Eleven Indians were found dead, and nineteen soldiers were wounded. Troops from other posts in the vicinity were ordered to assist in the pursuit, and eventually most of the Cheyennes gave themselves up.

A party of about sixty or seventy, consisting of the worst criminals of the tribe, who had murdered the Germaine family and others, and being afraid on that account to surrender with the rest, crossed the Arkansas River west of Fort Dodge and attempted to make their way to the Sioux country, north of the Platte.

The commanders of the troops, however, were on the alert, and with quick wit they utilized the then partly completed railways running through Kansas. Lieutenant A. Henley was dispatched with forty men of the Sixth Cavalry to chase them by rail and then head them off. On the 23rd of April this was accomplished, on the North Fork of Sappa Creek, southeast of Fort Wallace, Kansas. It was during the severe action that followed, and, by conceiving and executing a dangerous movement with a small detail of men, turning the trend of the fight, that Private Marcus M. Bobbins and several others of Company H, Sixth Cavalry, won their Medal of Honour. A description of the affair is given by Robbins as follows:

"In the evening of April 21st a telegram was received by our commanding officer at Fort Lyon, Colorado, stating that the band of hostile Cheyennes, who had made good their escape, had been fording the Arkansas at the crossing of the Cimmaron, headed to the north, and directing him to send a detachment of cavalry in pursuit.

"A party of forty men was detailed under Lieutenant Henley, first lieutenant of Company H, with orders to take a special train from Las Animas, a small town five miles from the fort, to Fort Wallace, Kansas, there leaving the train and march in an attempt to head off the hostiles and punish them.

"In order that the plan may be understood, it is well to state that at this time there were two parallel lines of railroad crossing Kansas und Colorado, from east to west, the Atchison, Topeka and Santa Fé Railroad, following the Arkansas Valley, and the Kansas Pacific Railroad along the Smoky Hill River. There was also a branch line running diagonally from Las Animas on the Santa Fé to Kit Carson on the Kansas Pacific. And it was by means of this branch that we were expected to head off our foes.

"We were on board, horses and men, by 9 o'clock that evening, and, after a back-breaking ride over a new road for nearly 100 miles, we reached Fort Wallace early the next morning. Unloading our horses from the train, we stopped only long enough to feed them and then we started for the hunt.

"At about 10 o'clock the trail was discovered, leading across the railroad, almost due north, the hostiles having made over 100 miles on their ponies in 24 hours. We pushed along on this trail until dark, running across some buffalo hunters who were fleeing to the railroad, and learning that we were near the Indians camp, we accordingly laid down under arms. No noise or fires were allowed, and each man retained his horse's halter.

"At 3 o'clock in the morning we were silently aroused and ordered to creep cautiously forward to the valley where the camp was supposed to be. Crawling to the edge of the bluffs we were rewarded by a full view of their camp, with the entire herd of nearly 400 animals a half mile away and no one guarding. Ten

WE SPRANG UP THE BANK AND DIRECTLY INTO THE PIT

men were at once sent forward to capture the herd, and the rest charged down the slope through the creek and into the camp of the half-wakened and wholly bewildered Indians.

"It was a complete surprise, and all who were not killed at the first charge, or made their escape, took refuge in the natural rifle pits along the bank of the stream, made by the washouts at high water. In these pits the hostiles gave us a hot reception, the man who had the temerity to poke his head over the bank getting it literally in the neck. We lost two men in this manner in as many minutes.

" At this time I saw what I believed to be a fine chance to rout the rascals out of their holes, and communicated the plan to Lieutenant Henley, who approved it. Taking four or five men with me, we made a detour down the creek until out of sight of the hostiles; then getting into the creek, we waded in the mud and water back up the stream until directly behind the rifle pits, doing this without attracting the attention of the Indians. Then, making the signal agreed upon, we sprang up the bank and directly into the pit, while the rest charged from above at the same time.

"I had run my head into many a hornet's nest in my time, but they did not compare with that which buzzed around us for a while. I still have a hazy recollection of emptying my revolver into an Indian who sprang up in front of me, and of my 'bunkie' saying I had saved his life, but how I did it is impossible for me to tell, so frenzied in 'battle fever' was I at the time. The contest was all over, for there were no more foes to fight. We lost two men killed and one horse wounded. Nine teen Indians were killed in the fight, all bucks. We captured the entire camp, which was rich in buffalo robes, beaded *moccasins*, war bonnets and the different adornments of savage life, and also captured 367 horses, ponies and mules.

"On our return trip a dreadful blizzard—although it was the latter part of April—caught us on the prairie and we suffered terribly, nearly all of us going on the sick report when we arrived at Fort Wallace. After a sojourn of only two weeks here we were able to return to our proper station, where we were given a royal welcome, the band and all the garrison turning out to receive us."

Lieutenant Henley recommended not only Private Robbins for the Medal of Honour, but also Sergeants Richard L. Tea and Frederick Flatten, as well as Privates James Lowthers, Simpson Hornaday, Peter W. Gardiner of the same company and regiment, these being the men who were with Robbins during his desperate fight. Trumpeter Michael Dawson and Private James F. Ayers, also of Company H, received the Medal of Honour for their display of heroic courage in the same affair. Of both it is reported that their conduct was so exceptionally brave and inspiring that it challenged the admiration of all who participated in the dash upon the hostiles.

Adventures With Indians in 1875

By the treaty of 1869 the Indians were granted various reservations west of the Missouri River, and in addition to these they were allowed a large range of country as hunting grounds over which they were permitted to rove without molestation in the pursuit of game. But this treaty was not rigidly adhered to by either the Indians or the government, and as a result constant trouble was had with the various bands, especially the Sioux, during the year 1875.

While the great chiefs, Spotted Tail, Red Cloud and others, made strenuous efforts to keep their people on the reservations and carry out the terms of the treaty the younger element, emulating the spirit of Chief Crazy Horse, who was one of the younger chiefs, would organize raiding parties and go on long expeditions against other Indian nations, or, as was most frequently the case, against the white settlers. In many of these raids terrible atrocities were committed; surveyors, settlers and travellers were killed without warning, while women and children were carried into captivity to suffer untold horrors.

Again, some of the bands had never accepted the reservation system, would not recognize the authority of the government, and insisted upon remaining wild and perfectly free from control. Among these were the bands who followed Sitting Bull and Crazy Horse, who were, properly speaking, not chiefs, but headmen, and whose immediate following did not exceed 40 and 120 lodges, respectively. These unruly redskins roamed about the country striking terror to the hearts of all settlers with whom they came in contact for purposes of trading. They would go into a trading post, obtain their necessary supplies, chat in a cordial manner with the whites, and upon leaving the post in apparently the friendliest spirit they would suddenly turn about and fire volley after volley into the startled traders. Then before the whites could regain their composure the devils would stampede and run off their herds of stock.

During the summer of this year General Custer conducted an expedition into the Black Hills, and later an expedition under General Crook went out against this hostile element of the Sioux, in an endeavour to subjugate them. The expedition started out from Fort Laramie late in the fall and followed the Indians over the roughest kind of country, with great persistence, finally encountering the hostiles under Crazy Horse near the headwaters of the Tongue River, where a most spirited fight took place. When Crazy Horse saw that he could not cope with the well-armed and skilful white soldiers he turned heel and with his band escaped into the fastnesses of the mountains.

A portion of Crook's command under General Reynolds later surprised Crazy Horse and captured a herd of horses, thus depriving the wily chief of some valuable animals. Reynolds then started back to the main body of this command with his captured horses, followed by the Indians, who were awaiting an opportunity to recapture the beasts. This opportunity presented itself to the redskins a few days later when Reynolds was overtaken by a terrific snowstorm. The men plodded along through the snow unconscious of Crazy Horse's intention, and when they went into camp the Indians stealthily approached the troops, under cover of the blinding snow, and succeeded in stampeding the herd, thus recapturing them. Winter had by this time set in with all its hardships and further attempts to corral the hostiles were given up.

During the early part of the year campaigns were being prosecuted against the Indians in various parts of the western country also for the purpose of rounding up those who would not remain on their reservations.

The expedition against the Kiowas and Comanches, in the Department of Texas, under Colonels Mackenzie, Davidson and Buell, in co-operation with the column under Miles, was prosecuted with such energy that these two tribes gave up the unequal contest and went into Fort Sill, first in small parties and then in larger numbers, surrendering there, and by June the last of the bands absent from their agencies, the Quehada Comanches, also came into the fort and surrendered themselves, with large numbers of ponies and mules, to Colonel Mackenzie, commanding at that post. Colonel Davidson had in the meantime made an important capture on the Salt Fork of the Red River. He met a band of Kiowas at that place, and in a sharp fight with them he captured 65 warriors and 175 women and children, with 375 ponies and mules. The prisoners, including Lone Wolf, Red Otter and Lean Bull, three most dangerous characters, all surrendered unconditionally with their arms and ponies.

Many small engagements and skirmishes marked these expeditions, among the more important of which was the following:

Lieutenant Bullis with a detachment of three men of the Twenty-fourth Infantry was out scouting on the 26th of April and came upon a band of about twenty-five Indians, on the Pecos River, Texas. The lieutenant and his three men approached the Indians unseen, and when within close range they attacked the redskins, killing three and wounding one. This little quartet of soldiers fought bravely during the short time the engagement lasted and then retreated safely to their command. Sergeant John Ward, Trumpeter Isaac Payne and Private Pompey Factor, all Indian scouts of the Twenty-fourth Infantry, constituted Lieutenant Bullis's detachment, and they were rewarded with the Medal of Honour for their exceptional bravery in standing by their officer against those twenty-five Indians.

On May 5th, Sergeant Marshall, with a detachment of Troop A, Tenth Cavalry, attacked a band of Indians at Battle Point, Texas, and on June 3rd Lieutenant J. A. McKinney, with a detachment of the Fourth Cavalry, in pursuit of thieving Indians, overtook a band of Osages robbing a cattle herd on Hackberry Creek,

Troops in hot pursuit

Indian Territory. A corporal and two men in advance attempted to arrest the Indians, but the latter opened fire and a fight ensued in which one Osage was killed and several wounded.

The Sioux Indians in Dakota, however, were causing the most trouble, and on July 6th a band of about 200 of them attacked the Ponca Agency in that territory. As soon as the attack was made Sergeant Danvers was immediately posted at a point of vantage with a detachment of eleven men of Company G, First Infantry. This little band of eleven withstood the brunt of the attacking forces of Indians, and with an old cannon which they pressed into service fought them valiantly. Lacking regular shot and shell, the men loaded this piece with old scraps of iron, and with their improvised ammunition successfully drove off the attacking party in three assaults, whereupon the hostiles withdrew. The latter part of October Captain J. M. Hamilton, with Troop H, Fifth Cavalry, left Fort Wallace in quest of the Indians, and met a band of them near the Smoky Hill River, Kansas, where in the subsequent fight he routed them, killing two of their number and wounding many others.

In November the closing actions of this year took place in Texas, near the Pecos River, where Lieutenant A. Geddes, of the Twenty-fifth Infantry, with two troops of the Tenth Cavalry, attacked a large band of renegades, killing one and capturing five; and in Nebraska, near Antelope Station, where a detachment of Troop G, Third Cavalry, under Lieutenant E. Crawford, had a fight in which they drove the Indians before them for many miles.

During the entire campaign of 1875 the troops were kept busy pursuing the Indians, driving them into their respective agencies, and protecting the settlers and emigrants from frequent raiding, and although there were no large battles in accomplishing the tasks set before them they nevertheless acquitted themselves bravely in the many small encounters and suffered many privations during the excessively hot and cold seasons of this year.

The Little Big Horn

JEREMIAH J. MURPHY

Of all the Indians contesting the advance of the white man in the Northwest, the Dakotas, more commonly called Sioux, were by far the most warlike and powerful. They formed a federation of many related tribes, as for instance the Ogalallas, Uncpapas, Brules, Minneconjoux, Assiniboines, Santees, Yanctonnais, Cheyennes (partly), Tetons and Sans Arcs.

By treaty in 1868 the United States Government assigned to these Indians the vast tracts of land they claimed in what was then the Territory of Dakota. But when the discovery of gold in the Black Hills attracted white adventurers by the hundreds and thousands, the integrity of the treaty could no longer be strictly maintained. Crime followed crime on this frontier, and although the whites were by no means blameless, the savages finally showed such a ferocity, boldness and lawlessness that their subjugation became imperative. As late as 1876 the United States Government had no control over these savages, who roamed free and independent over an area more than 100,000 square miles in extent; the horrors and atrocities committed by their raiding parties along the frontier, and which culminated in the Little Big Horn massacre of June 25, 1876, actually beggar description.

The leading spirits among these savages were Sitting Bull, the powerful "head man" of the Uncpapas, the foremost figure in later Indian history, a man equally strong and unbending in character, resources and crime; Crazy Horse, Gall and Red Cloud, all three Ogalallas, and Rain-in-the-Face, an Uncpapa.

The task which confronted the troops was a most difficult one, as very little knowledge had been obtained about that particular stretch of the country and the number of the hostiles was problematical. A guess in that respect by the highest and best authorities in Washington fell far from the actual figures, so far indeed that to it was due in a measure the shocking catastrophe of the Little Big Horn.

After an exploring expedition by General Custer in the summer of 1875 and a fruitless expedition against Crazy Horse and his followers by General Reynolds in the spring of 1876, the main expedition was ordered out by General Sheridan in May of the latter year, with Generals Terry and Crook in charge.

General Sheridan was under the impression that the winter season was the most opportune time to "catch" the Indians, and three columns were consequently fitted out in all haste.

One was organized by General Gibbon, to start from Fort Ellis, on the Yellow stone, Montana; one at Fort Russell, under General Crook, and a third at Fort Lincoln, Dakota, by General Custer; but the latter having incurred the displeasure of President Grant, General Terry was ordered to accompany this column.

There was no reliable information at that time as to the whereabouts of the Sioux. Terry was under the impression that they had camped near the mouth of the Little Missouri; later he learned that they were some 200 miles farther west, near the Dry Fork of the Missouri.

The extremely cold weather in the early spring prevented the three main columns from starting. But the impatient General Crook sent out a reconnoitring party under Colonel I. I. Reynolds, which left Fort Fetterman early in March, working slowly towards the head waters of the Powder, the Tongue and the Rosebud Rivers. Old Chief Crazy Horse was reported camping in the vicinity of these streams with a numerous band of Sioux and Cheyennes.

The columns consisted of troops A, B, E, I and K of the Second and troops A, E, F and M of the Third Cavalry. These troops suffered terrible hardships on the march, the thermometer registering forty degrees below zero on March 17th. Notwithstanding, Reynolds succeeded in completely surprising the enemy, who was found in camp on the Powder River, at the mouth of Otter Creek. The squadrons rushed the village, the enemy fled and the troopers destroyed all the lodges, 105 in number, and captured 800 of the hostiles ponies.

But the success of the troops was only temporary. The Indians, soon perceiving their own great superiority in numbers, rallied, made a vigorous and desperate counter-attack and forced the command back. Although the troops kept perfect order in their retreat to Fort Fetterman, the rear-guard could not prevent the Indians from stampeding the captured ponies, which thus again fell into the hands of their former owners.

While the attack upon the village was in full swing an Indian band managed to sneak between the main forces of the troops and an outlying picket, consisting of a corporal and five men of Company M, Third Cavalry. The little squad fought with the courage of desperation to break through the lines of the redskins and reach their retreating comrades, but one after another they were shot down.

Finally, Private J. J. Murphy was the only one left not disabled. When one of the wounded called to him in a heartrending voice: "O, Murphy; for mercy's sake, do not leave me in their hands," Murphy fearlessly turned back, lifted the groaning man on his shoulders and tried to make his way through the advancing savages, who poured a rain of bullets at him. The wounded man was again hit, and Murphy's carbine-stock smashed by a rifle-ball. He managed to draw his pistol and fired until the last cartridge was spent; then, being without ammunition and seeing absolutely no chance of saving his comrade, he was compelled to abandon him and succeeded, to the surprise of his officers, who watched his movements, in reaching his comrades. His uniform was pierced by several bullets, but the brave man escaped unscathed. For his heroism, so gallantly displayed, he was awarded the Medal of Honour.

Among those men who covered the retreat and fought the attacking Indians with the utmost intrepidity, showing a seemingly reckless courage, was Blacksmith A. Glavinsky, of Company M, Third Cavalry, who had to be recalled several times by his officers from self-selected, exposed positions. He also earned the Medal of Honour.

The weather continued inclement during March and April, and the main body of the troops made preparations for the final start, as soon as the weather would permit.

At last, on May 29th, General Crook moved out from Fort Fetterman, with his column, consisting of rive troops, A, B, D, E and I, of the Second Cavalry, ten troops, A, B, C, D, E, F, H, I, L and M, of the Third Cavalry, and five companies of infantry, C, G, H, of the Ninth, and D and F, of the Fourth. They started for Goose Creek, where they established a supply camp on June 8th.

A peculiar incident happened here, which, though insignificant, in all likelihood saved Crook's command from the fate reserved for the unfortunate Custer.

General Crook had been expecting a large war-party of friendly Crow Indians, deadly enemies of the Sioux, which had promised to join his command. On one of the last days of May the general decided to send his best three scouts, Gruard, Pourrier and Richard, to the Crow Agency, some 300 miles away, in Montana, to bring the tardy Crow warriors in.

At 11 o'clock, on the night of June 8th, at the Goose Creek Camp, the sentries were stirred up by most extraordinary outcries like the howling of coyotes, but supposed to emanate from Indians. The general sent Scout Arnold down to the Tongue River to ascertain the cause of the shouting in that direction. Arnold hailed the mysterious shouter and thought he recognized the Crow dialect. "Any Crows in your camp?" asked the

Private Murphy was the only one left not disabled

unknown cautiously. Arnold, who suspected Sioux, replied in that language, and there was no further reply.

Afterwards it was learned that an advance party of the expected Crow scouts had hailed the command, but hearing the dreaded Sioux dialect, immediately withdrew.

General Crook, who had guessed the truth, was very angry that evening; the prolonged absence of the Crow re-enforcement caused delay. Yet Crook was thereby prevented from getting to the Rosebud River and into a trap which two weeks later sealed Custer's fate on the Little Big Horn.

Towards evening, on the 9th of June, a party of Sioux made the first attack on Crook's camp. They were easily repulsed, Colonel Mills attacking them with four dismounted troops and driving them from the bluffs whence they had been firing into the camp.

An Indian bullet pierced the pipe of the stove in Colonel Mills's tent, and a report sent to a newspaper stated that someone had sent a ball through the colonel's stove pipe; whereupon the editor could not refrain from criticising, in a scathing editorial, the recklessness of a colonel wearing a stove-pipe during battle.

On the evening of June 14th, to the joyful surprise of all, and not the least to the general commanding, the faithful scouts rode into camp with a following of some 200 Crow Indians, in war paint and full of eagerness to meet their deadly foe. General Crook learned from the Crow chiefs that the main force of the Sioux was encamped on the Rosebud, near the Yellowstone.

Early on the morning of the 16th the whole command started in that direction, leaving the wagon train, tents, etc., behind.

The following morning the column halted in a valley on the Rosebud, to give the tired mounts a rest, while the scouts were sent out to reconnoitre. They did not have to reconnoitre far. Shortly before 9 o'clock they rushed in with their reports that the Indians were at hand, and immediately after the latter came on furiously to the attack. "Heap Sioux!" yelled the panic-stricken Crows and Snake warriors, whom the appearance of their hated and dreaded enemy seemed to have completely upset.

In a few moments the battle raged all along the line. The

troops drove the enemy from one line of bluffs to the next, and then to one still farther back. The Indian allies aided by noisy and boisterous demonstrations rather than by active participation.

General Crook realized soon after the beginning of the fight that his opponents were not stray bands, but organized forces of unusual and unexpected numerical strength. But even his calculations did not approach the actual numbers. Afterwards it was ascertained that Crazy Horse's followers, many times multiplied by a constant stream of bucks from Sitting Bull's village and malcontents from the different agencies, had been the general's adversaries. There were between 2,000 and 2,500 of them, while the actual fighting force of Crook's command did not reach 1,000 men.

In the attack upon the third bluff the troops suffered severely, especially Company L, of the Third Cavalry, under Captain Vroom, who had ventured too far forward. It was only the skill of Captain G.V. Henry of Company D, Third Cavalry, and Colonel Royal, who brought up re-enforcements, which prevented the cutting off and, of course, consequent cutting up of this troop. In the *mêlée* Captain Henry was shot through the face. The gallant officer, with blood rushing from his mouth, kept on his horse, although for the time being completely blinded; finally he fell from the saddle fainting and exhausted. So close together were the contestants that a party of howling Sioux actually charged over the captain's prostrate body. But they were quickly repelled, as was the whole hostile line.

It was during this *mêlée* that First Sergeant J. H. Shingle, of Troop I, Third Cavalry, won his Medal of Honour. Shingle had been placed in command of the horses of a battalion of four dismounted troops, by Captain Henry. When the Indians swarmed around them, and Shingle saw some of the men waver, he left the horses in command of a sergeant, mounted his horse, rushed into the thickest of the fight and did exceedingly valuable service in rallying the breaking ranks, which finally enabled the hard-pressed battalion to keep the Indians at bay until the oncoming supports under Colonel Royal put the red skins to flight.

JOSEPH ROBINSON

Among the troopers engaged in this fight, whose bravery was rewarded by the Medal of Honour, were: First Sergeants John Henry, of Company I, Michael A. McGann, of Company F, Sergeant Joseph Robinson, of Company D, and Trumpeter Elmer A. Snow, of Company M, Third Cavalry; the last-named receiving wounds through both arms.

It was now late in the day. and the Indians retreated. The troops had forced them back in battle for about five miles, but the result of the encounter was far from satisfactory to General Crook's command. The Indians left behind thirteen Crow and Shoshone scalps, 150 dead horses and a few blankets. Eleven dead bodies of the enemy were counted on the field.

The command lost ten whites killed and twenty-three, including Captain Henry, wounded; and of the Crows and Shoshones two warriors were killed and eleven wounded.

As the rations were almost completely used up and 25,000 rounds of ammunition expended, the general considered it proper to fall back upon his base of supplies on Goose Creek, eighty miles to the rear. Again the Indians had, morally at least, been victorious.

While General Crook's column was supposed to act independently, General Terry was the assigned commander of the other two. That fitting out and starting from Fort Ellis was in command of Colonel Gibbon; he had four companies of cavalry and six companies of infantry, some 450 men in all, and marched out in April to unite finally with Terry, which junction was effected in the latter part of June, on the Yellowstone, at the mouth of the Rosebud River.

Custer had his troops ready at Fort Lincoln, Dakota, towards the middle of May. The command included the entire Seventh

Cavalry, 12 companies with 28 officers and about 700 men; two companies of the Seventh and one of the Sixth Infantry, 8 officers and 135 men, one battery of Gatling guns, manned by 2 officers and 32 men of the Twentieth Infantry, and forty Indian scouts.

On the 17th of May this expedition left Fort Lincoln for the Yellowstone, and on the 27th of May the troops crossed into the Bad Lands. The 30th found Custer on a reconnoissance with four troops, returning on the same day without having seen anything of hostile Indians. On the 1st and 2d of June the command was unable to proceed on account of a severe snowstorm.

By this time pack mules, eleven to each troop, were allotted to the Seventh Cavalry, and soon the rumour spread of a prospective scout of the regiment up the Powder River. All was bustle in the camp of the cavalry.

On the 10th of June, Major Reno, of Custer's regiment, was sent to reconnoitre up the Powder River, his detachment comprising six troops, with twelve days rations.

The rest of the column marched to the mouth of the Powder River, and, after a short delay, farther up to the mouth of the Tongue River, where it halted until the 19th in expectation of news from Reno's party. On this date rumours began to circulate that Reno had found a three-weeks-old Indian trail, indicating a party of not less than 350 lodges, which he had followed up the Rosebud for forty miles.

It was on the 17th, just while Crook was fighting his battle not forty miles away, that Reno decided to turn back. Both commands, of course, were unaware of each other's proximity, and in all probability the Indians had no knowledge of Reno's advance.

On the 21st Custer's column reached the mouth of the Rosebud. Here he found Terry, who had left the command to meet Gibbon, whose column had travelled from Montana. The three leaders had a conference, with the result that the Seventh Cavalry, in command of Custer, was ordered to proceed up the Rosebud in pursuit of the Indians whose trail was discovered by Major Reno a few days prior. The rest of the order of Terry to Custer, the regimental commander, left all further dispositions to the judgement of this experienced Indian fighter. The bugle sounded officers call as soon as the conference—which Custer had left seemingly excited—had ended.

The regiment was to take fifteen days' rations of hardtack, coffee and sugar, twelve days' rations of bacon, and fifty rounds of ammunition per man on the mule pack train; besides each man in the command was to carry 100 rounds carbine and 24 rounds pistol ammunition on his person or in the saddle-bags, and forage of twelve pounds of oats to be carried on the horse.

This meant a heavy pack for each charger some eighty pounds, besides the rider's average weight of 150 pounds and the saddle equipment.

At 12 o'clock noon, on the 22nd of June, the Seventh Cavalry marched out from the mouth of the Rosebud in column of fours, the band playing the commander's favourite battle tune, "Garry Owen." Every man, every officer, knew and felt that serious times were ahead. After a twelve miles march the regiment went into camp at four o'clock in the afternoon, and immediately the officers call wafted its well-known tune over the stirring rabble of men, horses and mules.

After they who were called had assembled in the cheerless tent of their leader, the latter announced that no more trumpet calls would be sounded except in case of emergency; that according to the reports of the Indian Office in Washington they might have to meet from 1,000 to 1,500 hostile Sioux; that the march would thenceforward begin at 5 o'clock in the morning; that only two things from now on would be regulated from headquarters: *viz.*, when to move out of and when to go into camp, and that for all the rest he would hold the company commanders responsible.

He also mentioned an offer by General Terry of a battalion of the Second Cavalry and of the Gatling detachment, but that he had declined, as he thought that if the Seventh could not meet emergencies successfully, the aid of a battalion would hardly turn the scales, and that the Gatlings might hamper quick movement in the difficult and unknown country to be traversed.

Officers who knew Custer well and were present at this conference were very much impressed with his manner, and one of them remarked to a comrade who was leaving the conference with him: "I believe Custer is going to be killed; I never heard him talk so seriously about a coming fight."

The 23rd and 24th of June were spent in marching, and brought the first fresh signs of Indians. On the latter date the command made a short halt near a large "sun-dance" lodge, in which was found the scalp of a white man, supposed to be one of Gibbon's force murdered a short time before.

Late in the evening on the 24th the general assembled his officers once more, telling them that the march would be continued at 11:30 that night; that the enemy were located by scouts over the divide, in the Little Big Horn Valley, and that he was anxious to get the troops as near this divide as possible before daylight, so that they could bear down upon the hostiles at sunrise, as he had done in his famous battle of the Washita.

After a march of ten miles, from 11:30 p. m. to 2:00 a. m., the column halted for six hours, most of the troops unsaddling their mounts to give them relief, for the animals were sorely used up. Towards 8 o'clock on the morning of the 25th the scouts came in and reported the Indians camping twelve or fourteen miles beyond the divide in the Little Big Horn Valley.

Promptly at 8 the march was again resumed and continued until half-past 10, when the whole command was brought to a halt in a ravine, evidently for the purpose of escaping detection by the enemy, if such were possible.

The Little Big Horn and the valley mentioned were now to the front and left of the force; towards the northwest was the river which is a rapid mountain stream twenty to forty yards wide, with steep, soft banks. The country north and east of the valley is a plateau, rough, broken ground with many steep hills and narrow, deep gulches. The "divide" mentioned above is formed by the Little Chetish mountains. In front of the command, where it now was, flowed a little creek, in a northwesterly direction, towards the bend of the Little Big Horn. At that time the creek was nearly dry, and the trail of the Indians followed its bed down into the valley.

JOHN H. SHINGLE

Custer had gone forward to where the scouts were to scan the valley and obtain, if possible, a view of the enemy. On account of a bluff cutting into the valley from the north it was impossible to see all parts from his place of observation, but what he saw strengthened his belief in the correctness of his calculation as to the enemy's number. But even had he then had a true conception of the real magnitude of his task he could not have withdrawn. With the hostiles before him, and the War Department behind him, there was only one way: forward.

There were then encamped in the valley some 15,000 redskins, counting between 2,000 and 3,000 warriors, with a pony herd of some 30,000 head, the order of the tribal villages being from south to north—the Uncpapas, Sans Arcs, Minneconjoux Ogalallas, Brules, Cheyennes and Arapahoes.

When the general had finished his scout he made up his mind to make the attack the next morning at daybreak. But on his return to camp he found from the observations of some of his officers that the Indians were well aware of his whereabouts; he thought they might possibly escape, and therefore ordered the attack to be made immediately.

The divide was crossed by the command a little before noon. The regiment, which had so far advanced as one body, was now divided into three battalions, as follows:

The advance battalion, under Major Reno, containing troops M, Captain French; A, Captain Moylan and Lieutenant De Rudio; G, Lieutenants McIntosh and Wallace; the Indian scouts and Interpreter Girard, under Lieutenants Varnum and Hare; Surgeons De Wolf and Porter, and Lieutenant Hodgson as acting-adjutant.

The battalion of Captain Benteen, containing troops H, Captain Benteen and Lieutenant Gibson; D, Captain Weir and Lieutenant Edgerly; and K, Lieutenant Godfrey.

The battalion under Custer himself, containing troops I, Captain Keogh and Lieutenant Porter; F, Captain Yates and Lieutenant Reily; C, Captain Tom Custer and Lieutenant Harrington; E, Lieutenants Smith and Sturgis; L, Lieutenants Calhoun and Crittenden; Dr. Lord as surgeon, and Lieutenant Cook, the regimental adjutant. The pack train, under Lieutenant Mathey, was escorted by Troop 13, Captain McDougall.

Reno's detachment advanced into the valley along the bed of the little creek, followed by Custer and the pack train; Benteen advanced farther to the left, towards a high bluff, from where he was to scan the front, and, in case he saw the enemy, to report immediately.

At the place where the regiment was divided nobody could anticipate the extremely difficult nature of the ground. After struggling over several lines of bluffs without seeing a sign of the enemy Benteen was forced to join the trail just in front of the pack train and follow the main body.

Reno's advance guard had in the meantime reached a burning *tepee*, chasing some Indians who had fired it. In the *tepee* was the body of a trooper killed in General Crook's battle at the Rosebud. Custer sent an order to Reno to hurry forward and charge the village, and the whole force would support him. Reno trotted ahead until he reached the river. Crossing it he sent word to Custer that the Indians were in front of him in large numbers. After moving forward about two miles Reno dismounted his men, advancing them as a line of skirmishers, with his Ree scouts to the left. Two horses ran away with their hapless riders, carrying them right into the hostiles lines, whence a demoniacal howl arose, leaving no doubt as to their fate.

Custer had in the meantime swerved to the right, thus putting the river and a line of high bluffs between his own and the other two battalions.

This was without doubt the fatal move which decided the

day. "Custer's mistake of his life," as one of the veteran company commanders of Reno's battalion put it.

Reno was by this time hotly engaged with the hostiles; he occupied a position across the valley about one mile south of the river bend. A mounted Indian force rushed against his line; the Ree scouts fled, and Reno, seeing no force coming up as a support, retreated to the river. His position was a strong one, as both his flanks were covered by the bends of the river, and the dry river bank, fringed with timber, protected his front. But for some unknown reason he concluded to retreat up the river to some high bluffs towards the southeast, on the other side of the stream. The order to mount created confusion; fifteen soldiers, the interpreter, Girard, two scouts, and also Lieutenant De Rudio, whom the order had not reached, were abandoned among the bushes.

Reno's retreat made the Indians bold, and they pressed the column hard. The major, who rode at the head of the retreating command, was aware that he could not reach the ford by which he had crossed when entering the valley; so he kept close to the river and was lucky to strike a pony trail that led him to a fordable place at the steep bank, just opposite a ravine in the bluffs. No evidence of an organized resistance on the part of the troops during this retreat was displayed, which, by the time they reached the river, apparently had degenerated into flight. Casualties became numerous as soon as the command got out of the timber.

Reno lost during this retreat, beside those abandoned in the timber, three officers and twenty-nine men and scouts killed, and seven men wounded. Lieutenant McIntosh was shot dead soon after leaving the second position at the river bank. Lieutenant Hodgson's horse received a bullet in the body; in its agony it jumped into the river, unseating its rider, whose right leg had been pierced by the same bullet. Hodgson shouted loudly for someone to help him. A comrade grabbed the wounded man, who, clinging to his rescuer's stirrup, was thus dragged through the stream to the opposite bank; but on reaching it a bullet crashed into his head, killing him instantly.

THE END OF CUSTER'S COMMAND

Dr. De Wolf fell dead while seeking a way up the ravine to the bluffs. Charley Reynolds, the famous scout, was killed while crossing the river.

When the battalion had finally reached and occupied its new position the Ree scouts were nowhere to be seen. In fact the cowards, when put to flight in the first clash with the enemy, never stopped until they reached the supply camp at the mouth of the Powder. The Crow scouts remained faithfully with the troops.

During the crisis of this retreating movement a deed of most gallant daring and loyalty came under the observation of many of the officers and men.

Benjamin Criswell, sergeant in Company B, was the man who had helped Lieutenant Hodgson out of the stream and to the other side. When Hodgson was killed the sergeant was so occupied with rallying the men that he could not take care of the body. But as soon as order was somewhat restored he turned his horse and rode fearlessly back, down the river bank, picked up the body, took the ammunition from the saddle-bags of several fallen horses and returned thus laden to his comrades under a most galling fire of the savages, who yelled fiendishly and seemed frantic that the sergeant's deed should deprive them of such a valued trophy.

Criswell was rewarded for his extraordinary exploit with the Medal of Honour.

Up to this time the Sioux were firmly convinced that they had fought and routed the whole body of troops under "Long Hair" Custer, they not having noticed the departure of the latter's battalion.

Custer had entered the valley about two miles east of the creek, from where he had started and rode in a north-westerly direction, slightly diverging from the general course of the river until he reached a high bluff, about three miles distant. While his column pushed down near the river the Indians discovered their new and unexpected foe, and from what they afterwards related the sight of this body of troops spread terror into their lines.

This happened just when Reno decided to abandon his second position and was retreating to the bluffs. Cunning Chief Gall, who anticipated Reno's intention, was already on the way with his numerous band to cut off Reno's line of retreat and trap him, when suddenly one of the Uncpapa lookouts came running after him, shouting with all his might, "More pony-soldiers; look!" and pointed to the bluff, where part of Custer's squadrons could be seen rapidly filing past.

Gall abandoned his plan immediately, rallied his band and rushed back to the river, crossing it at the mouth of what was afterwards called Reno's Creek.

By this time all the Indians were aware of the coming of Custer's troops and concentrated against him, abandoning gradually their position in front of Reno.

Custer had Calhoun and Keogh occupy the knoll mentioned by their two dismounted troops. Gall, who pressed with his Indians up the bed of a dried-up creek, observed their horses being led away. Immediately the redskins set out to stampede the excited animals, and were successful.

Meanwhile Custer had deployed his whole line along the ridge, Smith's company joining with its left wing Keogh's right, and with its right wing the troops of Yates and Tom Custer, who extended down to within half a mile of the river from another knoll, now known as Custer's Hill. Here the general, too, took his stand.

By this time a sergeant from Custer met Benteen and brought orders to hurry the pack train up. Shortly after another messenger, a trumpeter, met Benteen with the following message signed by Adjutant Crook: "Benteen, come on; big village; be quick; bring packs." Evidently the Custer battalion was in need of the reserve ammunition.

Benteen rushed forward, to comply with the order; his command was drawn out in line, with pistols in hand. Finally, the valley came into full sight; thick clouds of smoke rolled over the ground, cutting off the view. A great number of horsemen could be seen galloping to and fro through the clouds of smoke and dust. Away off, on a bluff to the right, a body of fighting troopers could be distinguished, and some Crow scouts hurried by, and, pointing to the troops on the bluffs, shouted that they were soldiers. Benteen followed their beckoning and turned to the right towards the bluffs, where he found Reno's command, which was still slightly engaged.

The Indians now commenced to withdraw from the attack. They were all massing against Custer, leaving just enough braves in front of Reno to keep him in check.

On the other side of the battlefield Keogh's and Calhoun's companies lost their saddlebag ammunition with their stampeded horses. Gall and his band kept the skirmishers firing until they calculated their ammunition well-nigh exhausted, when the Indians made a rush, on foot and on horseback, in overwhelming numbers. There was no standing up against this demoniacal wave, which swept over the brave little cluster of heroes, killing every one of them.

Crazy Horse, Crow King and several other Sioux chieftains had in the meanwhile gathered all their available forces in a ravine leading up to a ridge opposite Custer's Hill. They rushed up to this ravine and, spreading along the crest of the ridge, fell on Yates', Tom Custer's and Smith's rear and right flank. While they were pouring an overwhelming fire into the rapidly thinning lines, Gall's victorious hordes, blood thirsty and intoxicated with their recent success over Keogh and Calhoun, rushed up from the front and left flank.

In this onslaught the scanty remnants of the three troops were annihilated; while defending their honour and lives until the last drop of blood, the last cartridge was spent.

Thus died Custer and his 223 men, including 13 commissioned officers of the Seventh Cavalry.

In the meantime, the soldiers under Reno heard the distant firing. It was towards 3:30, when two heavy volleys were distinctly heard on the bluffs. Instinctively a sensation came over many that this was Custer's signal for help, and so it was, alas, the last signal which came from yonder side.

Captain Weir and Lieutenant Edgerly could no longer endure

the suspense of uncertainty, so they started with the troop down the ravine in the direction of the firing. Weir, who was ahead, reconnoitring, perceived in time the approach of a large band of Indians and warned Edgerly, who regained a safe position.

Captain McDougall joined Reno now with the pack train. Of those who had been left in the timber at the river bank thirteen men and a scout rejoined their commands at about this time; they had lain hidden in the brush until the departure of the Indians towards Custer's stand gave them an opportunity to escape.

Reno now made an attempt to push down the river and ascertain the whereabouts of Custer's command. The advanced troops reached the high bluff which rose in the direction of the junction of the Little Big Horn and a small creek where some of Reno's men said they had seen Custer waving his hat while he was fighting the oncoming Indians in the valley.

A haze of dust and smoke hanging over the valley rendered distinct observation impossible, but the groups of stationary or moving horsemen could be recognized as Indians. On the western slope the immense pony herd of the savages could be seen, but not a trace of Custer or any part of his command. The impression prevailed that the general had been repulsed and had very likely marched off to join the column under Terry and Gibbon; no anxiety whatever was felt.

Soon swarms of mounted Indians moved swiftly from all sides upon the position which Reno now held, and opened a heavy fire. Major Reno withdrew all the squadrons to the bluffs formerly occupied and installed himself there, as well as he could for the defence, where within a short time the soldiers were encircled by savages.

During the retreat to the bluffs Sergeant Richard P. Hanley, of Troop C, exhib-

RICHARD P. HANLEY

ited fearlessness and coolness of an unparalleled nature, which gained him the Medal of Honour. A pack mule, loaded with precious ammunition, had become frightened by the incessant whizzing of the bullets and broke away, making straight for the hostiles lines.

Hanley, seeing the runaway mule, mounted his horse and ran out to head him off. Instantly the Indians concentrated their fire upon the daring man. The mule had a good start, and its pursuer didn't overtake it until within dangerous proximity to the Indians. The latter immediately directed their fire towards the fearless trooper. Bullets fell like hailstones. Hanley seemed not to notice the bullets which by dozens splashed up the sand and dust around his horse's hoofs. The mule tried to evade its pursuer, who had succeeded in heading it off, and ran up and down the firing line; his comrades and the officers yelled and shouted to Hanley to let up and come in, but in vain. He was determined to capture this mule, and capture it he did, at last. During this twenty minutes chase Hanley had run the gauntlet of a perfect hail of bullets, but he escaped uninjured and brought his mule in with the ammunition. Loud cheers greeted him when he passed within the circle of his comrades.

When darkness began to set in the Indians dropped back from the firing line, and soon all shooting ceased. But silence was to be banished in the valley during this terrible fight. Down in the hostiles' camp all hell broke loose and lasted without intermission until daybreak. Evidently the red fiends were enjoying a scalp dance. The terrific yelling and howling, together with the incessant sound of the *tam-tams* and gun-firing, sent chills down the backs of that thirsty, wearied, hungry and discouraged handful of troopers upon the bluffs. All night the men worked with knives and whatever came handy, to dig pits for better shelter, as the crisis was to be expected with the break of day.

Some of the Indian scouts of the command went out to establish communication with Custer, but they soon returned with the news that the whole surroundings were thickly covered with Sioux.

HE WAS DETERMINED TO CAPTURE THE MULE

The attack was renewed early in the morning, before 3 o'clock. At sunrise the firing was general all around the position. The Indians did little damage, but still they succeeded in drawing the fire and thus forced the soldiers to spend their scant ammunition. Captain Benteen's troop suffered severely; his men occupied the south front, which was open to the long range fire of the Indians from the north bluffs. Many of his troopers had but three cartridges left. Benteen finally went to seek Reno, leaving to Lieutenant Gibson strict orders not to retreat from the position.

OTTO VOIT

On this side of the position, the Indians showed incredible daring and recklessness, partly, in all probability, on account of the scantiness of ammunition, which necessitated a slackening fire. A man in Benteen's line was shot and killed. The copper-coloured slayer dashed up into the line, touched the body with his "coup-stick" and tried then to run back into shelter. But he was felled by a dozen bullets ere he could run as many steps.

Benteen at last obtained Major Reno's consent to get Captain French's company, M, into the thinned line on the south front as a support. With the sharpened instinct of an old Indian campaigner, Benteen felt that the enemy knew the weakness of this part of the position and would ere long rush it with overwhelming forces. To discourage such a plan Benteen rallied all the available men in the lines and made a rush, out of the pits and down the slopes, at the astonished redskins. They had, in fact, already been gathering in a ravine for the final assault, which the gallant Benteen anticipated and frustrated so timely.

Many deeds of daring happened on the bluff during this

memorable day. Sergeant Thomas Murray, of Company B, brought the rations up to the command, passing to and fro several times through the terrific fire of the exasperated savages. He had already distinguished himself on the first day of the siege, bringing the pack train within the reach of the command and into a comparatively sheltered position.

Corporal Charles Cunningham, of Company B, had been shot through the neck during the fight of the 25th, and was ordered to retire, but he refused positively to leave the line, and held out bravely during the whole day of the 26th, saying that he could do better lying on his belly with gun in hand than on his back among the helpless in the rear.

Private Henry Holden, of Company D, repeatedly went for ammunition for his comrades, being exposed to the heaviest of fire. Again and again he sought his way through the storm of Indian bullets to keep his company's line supplied with food for the guns.

HENRY B. MECHLING

The worst thing was the lack of water, especially for the wounded. If the burning thirst was maddening to the uninjured, its quenching became a question of life and death with the injured. The situation was terrible and became more so the higher the sun rose. Towards noon something had to be done at all hazards, to obtain water.

Nineteen brave men volunteered to take their lives in their hands and try for it. Four of them, Sergeant George Geiger, Blacksmith Henry W. B. Mechling, Private Charles Windolph, and Saddler Otto Voit, of Troop H, were instructed by their captain to take an exposed position outside of the line and protect those soldiers who would go for water from the fire of the Indians. These four brave men kept in their dangerous position for nearly four hours, and it was due to their vigilance and reckless exposure that none of the water carriers were killed by the enemy.

THOMAS J. CALLAN

Sergeant Stanislaus Roy, Privates D. W. Harris and Neil Bancroft, of Troop A; Sergeants R. D. Hutchinson and C. H. Welch, and Privates Thomas Callan and James Pym, of Troop B; Privates Abram B. Brant, William M. Harris, Frederick Deetline, George Scott, T. W. Stevens, Frank Tolan, of Troop D; Private Peter Thompson, of Troop C, and T. W. Golden, of Troop G, reported themselves ready to fetch the water. They carried camp-kettles and singly they slipped out from the right wing of Benteen's line, making a dash for the river. A space of about eighty yards, which they rushed over, brought them into a deep ravine, which afforded shelter and led down to within fifteen yards of the river. The men would, upon reaching the ravine, rush over the remaining distance, dip their camp-kettles into the river and then return with them.

While they were dashing over the exposed spaces, Geiger, Voit, Mechling and Windolph kept their rifles cracking to check the enemy's fire. A group of Indians had concealed themselves in some bushes, from which their rifles had good command of the exposed stretches of the water carriers path, and they would, undoubtedly, have killed some of the carriers but for the vigilance and skill of the four sharpshooters. The result was that only one of the carriers, Peter Thompson, was wounded. He was shot through the head, but, notwithstanding, he made two more successful trips for the water, even though his sergeant ordered him to go to the rear.

Although the hostiles wounded only one man, there were nevertheless many narrow escapes, for several camp-kettles were smashed by bullets. The courageous and self-sacrificing men who had thus exposed themselves and risked their lives for their comrades were all awarded the Medal of Honour.

About 2 p. m. of the 26th the fire of the Indian line began to slacken. The fire against the water carriers, however, was kept up until 3 o'clock. Shortly thereafter the savages abandoned their position. They fired the grass, and under the screen of the smoke the village was abandoned. The besieged troops could see through the smoke the whole cavalcade moving briskly away, in almost military order, towards the Big Horn range.

It was now near 7 o'clock and sighs of relief went up from the exhausted and sorely-tried white warriors on the bluff. There was not the slightest doubt in their minds that Custer had by this time united with Terry and that aid was near. But the moving of the Indian village excited suspicion, and it was decided to move into a new position down the slope, in order to escape the stench of the decaying bodies of men and horses. The losses of the command during this day had been eighteen killed and forty-two wounded.

The evening of this never-to-be-forgotten day had a joyful surprise in store for the men; towards 9 o'clock Lieutenant De Rudio, Private O'Neal, Scout Jackson and Interpreter Girard, who had been left in the timber during the retreat from the second position in the valley, joined their comrades, hale and hearty, and the stories of their thrilling adventures were listened to in wonderment. De Rudio and O'Neal's escape was remarkable. On the 25th they concealed themselves in the bushes at the river-bank; they saw the squaws come out after the fight and mutilate the bodies of the fallen. De Rudio was once so overcome by the horrid sight that he cocked his revolver to shoot down some of these human hyenas. But O'Neal pointed out the inevitable result, and the officer prudently desisted.

Towards evening they saw what they in hopeful expectation took for Lieutenant Smith's gray horse squadron come trotting along. There could be no mistake, thought De Rudio; there were the campaign hats and the blue tunics; the horse men, then, must be American cavalry. De Rudio stepped out of shelter and shouted: "Ho, there, here we are, take us away from here." A fiendish yell from the personage supposed to be the lieutenant showed De Rudio his mistake, and a volley from the mounted band chased him and his companion back into the brush. Those men were Indians clad in soldiers uniforms, and riding soldiers horses. De Rudio and his companions outwitted the redskins and remained hidden in the brush until darkness set in, when they slipped away and joined their command.

When De Rudio told the command of the Indians wearing soldiers uniforms, some soldiers ventured the statement that they had seen Custer's cavalry guidons in the ranks of some of the beleaguering Indians, and gloom spread over the men on the bluff.

The night passed without further incident. The next morning, towards 10 o'clock, while preparing to resist any attack which might be attempted, the dust of a moving column was seen approaching in the distance. Soon it was discovered to be troops who were coming, and in a little while a scout arrived with a note from General Terry to Custer, saying that some Crow scouts had come to camp stating that Custer had been whipped, but that their story was not believed. About half-past 10 o'clock in the morning General Terry rode into Reno's lines and the fate of Custer was ascertained.

Precisely what was done by Custer's immediate command, subsequent to the moment when the rest of the regiment last saw them alive, has remained partly a matter of conjecture, no officer or soldier who rode with him into the valley of the Little Big Horn having lived to tell the tale.

The only person who came away with his life from Custer's command after firing began was the Crow scout, Curley. He managed to sneak through the Sioux lines by arranging his blanket in their fashion. His version throws no light upon the point mentioned. There is no good reason, however, why Custer should have been spared to the last; it was certainly not in his

Four brave men kept in their dangerous position

nature to go out of death's way, and the Indians said afterwards that they did not see him nor even know where his stand was.

The only real evidence of how the men of Custer's command came to meet their fate was the testimony of the field where it overtook them.

Custer's trail, from the point where Reno crossed the stream, passed along and in rear of the crest of the bluffs on the right bank, for nearly or quite three miles. Then it came down to the bank of the river, but at once diverged from it again, as though Custer had unsuccessfully attempted to cross; then turning upon itself and almost completing a circle, the trail ceased. It was marked by the remains of officers and men horribly mutilated, and the bodies of horses, some of them dotted along the path, others heaped in ravines and upon knolls where halts appeared to have been made. There was abundant evidence that a gallant resistance had been offered by Custer's troops, but that they were beset on all sides by overpowering numbers.

The officers known to be killed were General Custer, Captains Keogh, Yates and Custer, Lieutenants Cooke, Smith, McIntosh, Calhoun, Porter, Hodgson, Sturgis and Reily of the Seventh Cavalry, Lieutenant Crittenden of the Twentieth Infantry, and Acting Assistant Surgeon De Wolf; Lieutenant Harrington of the cavalry, and Assistant Surgeon Lord were missing. Mr. Boston Custer, a brother, and Mr. Reed, a nephew of General Custer, were with him and were killed.

Twenty-three bodies, among them those of Lieutenants Harrington and Porter, were never found; the fate of those who once animated them has remained a mystery; were they tortured, or did they sink and disappear in the quicksand of the Little Big Horn? It will never be known. The Indians claimed afterwards that they had no prisoners, and could consequently not have tortured any but who is to believe an Indian? On the other hand, according to all signs, Custer never came nearer than half a mile to the river. His men can therefore not have fallen into the quicksand.

What the outcome of the battle might have been if Reno's

command had firmly held on to its first position, or if it had come over the *plateau* later on from the bluffs and attacked the enemy in the rear, is not within our province to discuss here. Sioux who had fought in the battle said afterwards, when asked, that in both cases they would have fled.

When Reno was pressed back in his second position towards the river bank, Gall and his band, as has been mentioned, hastened to cut off his retreat to the bluffs and set a trap for him.

Had Custer appeared later so that Gall's band could have fallen upon the retreating Reno, bringing him thus between two fires, Reno's command would certainly have been annihilated. The Indians would then still have had time to deal with Custer alone, and, after they got through with him, to finish the small command of Benteen and the pack train.

The news of the disaster shook the country from end to end, but Sitting Bull's evil-bearing influence among the tribes on the warpath grew stronger than ever.

Agency Indians sneaked away by the hundreds to join the rebellious bands, and the War Department set all the necessary power in motion to stamp out the scandalous menace.

Three Daring Couriers

After the Battle of the Little Big Horn the relief column of General Terry and Colonel Gibbon's force took back the wounded and remnants of the Seventh Cavalry to the Rosebud Landing on the Yellowstone, where they remained for the time being, awaiting re-enforcements, just as General Crook did, farther down south, in his supply camp at Cloud Peak.

All kinds of rumours and reports reached both commanders as to the whereabouts of the hostile Indians. On July 9th General Terry found it desirable to impart certain weighty information to Crook, which had to be done by couriers. The task was an extremely dangerous, if not a hopeless one, as nobody exactly knew where the hostiles might have their scouting parties roaming. Two attempts to deliver the dispatches had been made and both failed, but a third succeeded. Three brave men volunteered to undertake this trip: Privates James Bell, Benjamin F. Stewart and William Evans, all three of Company E, Seventh Infantry. They reached General Crook's camp safely on July 14th and returned with dispatches from this officer. The Medal of Honour was their reward for this brave deed. On this trip they lay hidden during the daytime and travelled at night. Singular as it may seem, they did not come upon any Indian war-party or across any trail, which, of course, did not render the act less conspicuous as a heroic deed.

General Crook was to be joined by General Merritt's column, with the Fifth Cavalry, which force was delayed by Merritt's brilliant exploit against the Cheyennes under Yellow Hand.

As is well known, the Cheyennes were surprised and defeated at the War Bonnet Crossing, where their chief, Yellow Hand, was slain by Buffalo Bill in a single-handed duel. The two columns effected a junction on the 3rd of August at the Goose Creek. The combined column mustered now 2,000 fighting men, all tents and baggage having been sent back by order of General Crook, with the exception of the mule pack train carrying the reserve ammunition and rations for fifteen days.

Terry's column joined Crook's near the Yellowstone, bringing the expedition up to 4,000. As there was no chance that the Indians would stand up against such a force, Terry separated from Crook on the 24th of August to cross to the left bank of the Yellowstone.

Crook's command then started on an expedition which as to hardships and physical suffering, as well as determination and boldness of conception, has no equal in warfare against the Indians.

On the afternoon of September 4th the column in the truest sense of the word a "flying column," for no man, from the general down to the packer, had more clothing or package with him than what he could carry on his own or his animal's body crossed the Little Missouri. The command was then about 200 miles from the northern edge of the Black Hills and about 150 miles from Fort Lincoln, with rations sufficient for but two and a half days.

Here, in a wretched, rain-soaked camp, Crook decided on the 5th of September to push on to the Black Hills. "It's hard, I know it," said this indefatigable hunter of Indians, "but we'll live on our horses and half rations." Under continuous rain and hail-storms the column pushed on.

On the evening of the 7th a column of 150 men from several companies of the Third Cavalry was sent ahead under Captain Anson Mills to try and get some supplies from the Black Hills settlements.

After they started the men of the main force began to kill horses for food. They had had no shelter for several days from the ever-pouring rain, and no wood to build fires through nearly ninety miles of marching.

Early in the morning of September 9th a packer rode into camp with the announcement that Mills had met and surprised a party of Sioux at Slim Buttes that he had attacked, but was opposed by a superior force and needed re-enforcements without delay. General Crook started immediately himself with 100 men of the Third, 50 men from the Second, and the whole of the Fifth Cavalry.

Captain Mills had taken only fifty rounds for each man, in order to march light and swift. He came upon the Indian village of American Horse at Slim Buttes, Dakota, unexpectedly, and attacked without hesitation, capturing the entire village of about thirty-seven lodges, with quantities of supplies, arms and ammunition, and about 175 ponies. Among the articles taken from this village were a guidon of the Seventh Cavalry, a pair of gloves marked with the name of Colonel Keogh, Seventh Cavalry, who was killed with Custer, and many other things which were recognized as belonging to that command.

The battalion of Captain Mills suffered a loss of one enlisted man killed, six wounded, and Lieutenant A. H. von Luettwitz, Third Cavalry, so seriously wounded in the leg as to require amputation. The loss of the Indians was American Horse, mortally wounded, four Indians killed and about a dozen captured. The village of Crazy Horse was only a short distance away, and after the first flight from camp the Indians returned in increased numbers and attacked Mills's command, but, the main column of General Crook having arrived, the Indians were worsted in several encounters which took place.

The Indians would hover around the command, taking positions in ravines from which they had to be dislodged, and which they defended with desperate determination. In order to get a glimpse of their foe the soldiers had to expose themselves, and many acts of bravery were performed here. Scout Charley White was shot through the heart, Private John Wenzel, one of the best horsemen of Troop A, Third Cavalry, died from a bullet which passed through his head, Sergeant Edward Gloss of Troop E, same regiment, was wounded. Sergeant John A. Kirkwood and Private Robert Smith of Troop M, of this regiment, showed exceptional fearlessness, and gained for this fight the Medal of Honour.

The Indians under the mortally wounded chief, American Horse, finally surrendered. Several squaws and even a baby *papoose* had lost their lives in this most desperate fight, which abounded in revolting scenes characteristic of the border warfare of those times.

Battle of Wolf Mountain and Cedar Creek

JAMES S. CASEY

Preparatory to the winter campaign of 1876-77 against the Sioux and Northern Cheyennes, under Sitting Bull and Crazy Horse, in Montana, Colonel Nelson A. Miles equipped his command, the Fifth United States Infantry, as if he were organizing an expedition for the Arctic regions. His foresight was commendable, for frequently the thermometer registered as low as fifty degrees below zero. They were abundantly supplied with food and clothing, and every precaution was taken to protect both men and horses against the severity of this intense cold. The command, numbering about 400 men and one piece of artillery, when dressed in their blankets and furs, looked more like a large body of Esquimaux than like white men and United States troops, and when they wore their woollen masks over their heads it was impossible to distinguish one from the other. Thus equipped the men were well prepared to battle with both the elements and the Indians during this trying campaign, which opened early in October, 1876.

A cantonment had been established at the mouth of the

Tongue River by Colonel Miles, and on the 10th of October a train of ninety-four wagons started for it from Glendive Creek with supplies, but was attacked and driven back. With a new escort of 185 men of the Twenty-second Infantry, under Colonel E. S. Otis, the train again started out, but was a second time attacked by 700 Indians on Spring Creek. The train, however, formed in compact lines, pressed on, the infantry escort charging the Indians repeatedly and driving them back, while the wagons slowly advanced.

Three or four scouts from Colonel Miles's command were met here, having been attacked by Indians, and one of their party killed. The train proceeded, with the escort skirmishing, until Clear Creek was reached. Here the Indians made a most determined attack, firing the prairie, and the wagons were obliged to advance through the flames. Compactly arranged in four lines, the wagons proceeded, the entire escort being engaged in alternately charging the Indians, driving them back and then regaining the moving teams.

While the train was thus advancing, an Indian runner approached and left upon a hill the following communication:

Yellowstone
I want to know what you are doing travelling on this road. You scare all the buffalo away. I want to hunt in this place. I want you to turn back from here. If you don't, I will fight you again. I want you to leave what you have got here and turn back from here.
I am your friend,
Sitting Bull

I mean all the rations you have got and some powder. Wish you would write as soon as you can.

Colonel Otis sent out a scout, with a reply to Sitting Bull's note, stating that he intended to take the train through the Tongue River and would be pleased to accommodate the Indians with a fight at any time.

The train again proceeded, the Indians surrounding it and

keeping up firing at long range, but after a short time two Indians appeared with a flag of truce and communication was again opened with the hostiles, who stated they were hungry, tired of the war and wanted to make peace. Sitting Bull wanted to meet Colonel Otis outside of the lines of the escort, which invitation, however, Colonel Otis declined, though professing a willingness to meet Sitting Bull inside the lines of the troops. This the wary savage was afraid to do, but sent three chiefs to represent him. Colonel Otis made them a present of 150 pounds of hard bread and two sides of bacon, said that he had no authority to treat with them, but that the Indians could go to the Tongue River and there make known their wishes regarding surrender. The train moved on and the Indians fell to its rear, finally disappearing altogether.

On the night of the 18th of October Colonel Otis met Colonel Miles with his entire regiment, who, alarmed for the safety of the train, had advanced to meet it. The supplies were then taken to the cantonment at the Tongue, and the wagons returned in safety to Glendive.

Shortly after meeting Colonel Otis and learning from him the immediate situation, Colonel Miles, with the Fifth Infantry, started after Sitting Bull, overtaking him near Cedar Creek, Montana, north of the Yellowstone. Colonel Miles met Sitting Bull between the lines of the troops and of the Indians, the latter having sent a flag of truce to Miles, desiring to communicate.

After some conversation Sitting Bull desired to know what the troops were remaining in that country for, and why they did not go back to their posts or into winter quarters. He was informed by Miles that they were out to bring him and his Indians in, and that they did not wish to continue the war against them, but that if they forced the war it would end disastrously for the Indians. He was told that he could not be allowed to roam over the country, sending out war-parties to devastate the settlements.

Sitting Bull claimed that the country belonged to the Indians and not to the white men, and declared that he had

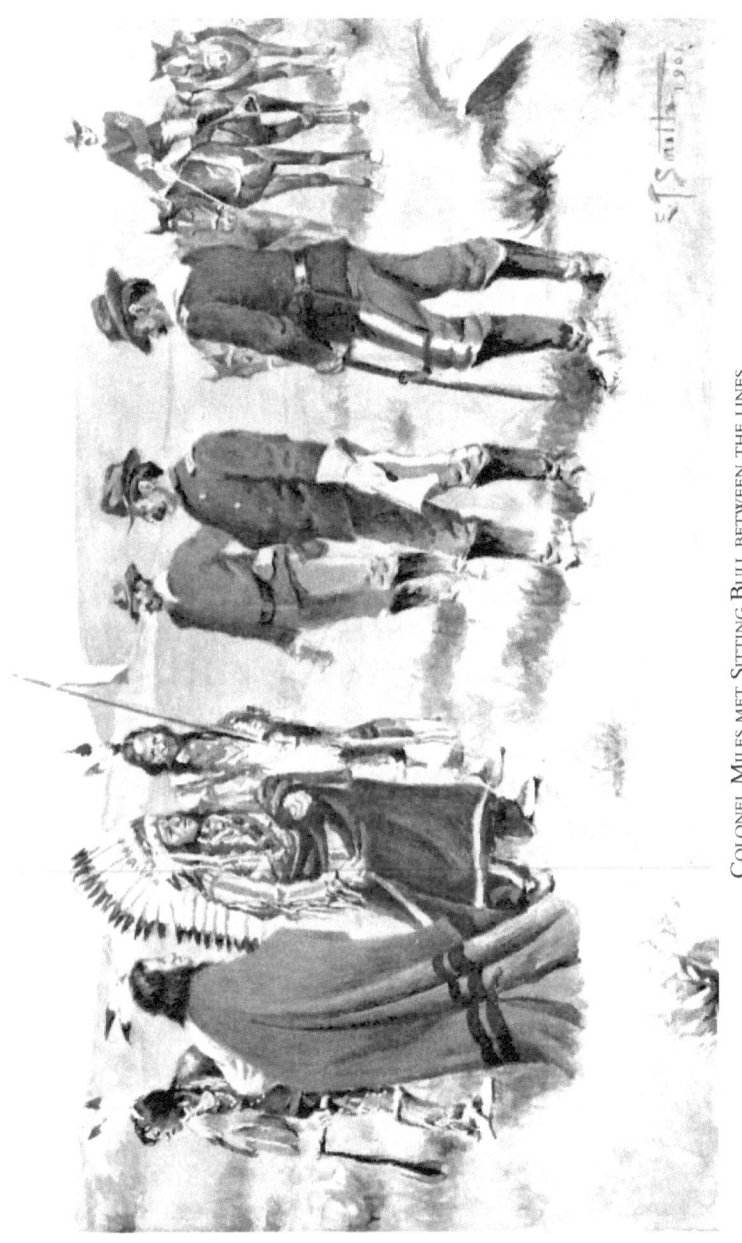

Colonel Miles met Sitting Bull between the lines

nothing to do with the white men and wanted them to leave that country entirely to the Indians. He said that the white man never lived who loved an Indian, and that no true Indian ever lived that did not hate the white man. He declared that God Almighty made him an Indian and did not make him an agency Indian either, and he did not intend to be one. After much talk the interview closed unsatisfactorily and Colonel Miles's column, numbering 398 rifles, moved and camped on Cedar Creek, so as to intercept the movement of the Indians, Sitting Bull being told to come again the next day.

While the command was moving north between the Indian camp and the Big Dry River, the Indians again appeared and desired to talk. Another council followed between the lines, October 21st, Sitting Bull and a number of principal men being present. Sitting Bull wanted peace, if he could have it upon his own terms. He was told the conditions of the government. He then said he would come in to trade for ammunition, but wanted no rations or annuities and desired to live free, as an Indian. He gave no assurance of good faith, and as the council broke up he was told that a non-acceptance of the terms of the government would be considered an act of hostility.

Sitting Bull and the men who accompanied him then returned with all speed toward their lines, calling out to the Indians to prepare for battle, and the scene was, for the next few minutes, one of the wildest excitement. The prairies were covered with savage warriors, dashing hither and thither, making ready for battle. At the end of the time mentioned, Miles ordered an advance of the entire body of troops, and immediately the Indians commenced setting fire to the dry prairie grass around the command, together with other acts of hostility. An engagement immediately followed, in which the Indians were driven out of their camp for several miles, and on the two following days were hotly pursued.

The Indians lost a few of their warriors and a large amount of property, both in their camp and on their retreat, including their horses, mules and ponies.

At one time the command was entirely surrounded by Indians, and the troops, although outnumbered three to one, were formed in a large hollow square in open order and deployed at five paces, with all the reserves brought into action; yet not a single man left his place or failed to do his full duty.

The energy and persistence with which the attack was made created such consternation in the Indian camp that after a pursuit of forty-two miles they sent out another flag of truce and again requested an interview. During this interview 2,000 of them agreed to go to their agencies and surrender, five chiefs giving themselves up as hostages for the delivery of men, women, children, ponies, arms and ammunition at the agencies.

Sitting Bull himself escaped northward with his own small band, and was joined later by Gall and other chiefs with their followers. Having returned to Tongue River Cantonment, Colonel Miles organized a force numbering 434 rifles and moved north in pursuit of Sitting Bull, but the trail was obliterated by the snow in the vicinity of the Big Dry River. A band of 119 lodges, under Iron Dog, crossed the Missouri in advance of the command and dissolved itself in the Yanktonnais camp, Sitting Bull continuing to hover about the neighbourhood of the Missouri River and its branches for some time afterwards.

On December 7th, First Lieutenant F. D. Baldwin, with Companies G, H and I, Fifth Infantry, numbering 100 officers and men, overtook Sitting Bull's camp of 190 lodges, followed and drove it south of the Missouri, near the mouth of Bark Creek. The Indians resisted Baldwin's crossing of the river for a short time and then retreated into the Bad Lands. Ten days later this same force, under Lieutenant Baldwin, surprised Sitting Bull's band of 122 lodges near the head of the Red Water, capturing the entire camp and its contents, together with about sixty horses, ponies and mules. The Indians escaped with little besides what they had upon their persons and scattered southward across the Yellowstone.

The large cantonment at the mouth of the Tongue River having been established, from this point as a base the pursuit of the remnants of the Sioux and Northern Cheyennes, with Sitting Bull and Crazy Horse, was energetically pressed by the troops under Colonel Miles. The low state of water in the river now gave the troops on the Yellowstone a three-fold task of great difficulty, to shelter themselves by building huts, to bring up their supplies by tedious hauling from the head of navigation, and to prosecute, simultaneously, in the midst of winter, vigorous field operations against the hostiles.

On the 29th of December, Colonel Miles, with Companies A, C, D, E and K, Fifth Infantry, and Companies E and F, Twenty-second Infantry, numbering 436 officers and men, with two pieces of artillery, moved out against the Sioux and Cheyennes under Crazy Horse, whose camp had been reported south of the Yellowstone, in the valley of Tongue River. As the column moved up the Tongue, the Indians abandoned their winter camps, consisting of about 600 lodges, and the column had two sharp skirmishes on the 1st and 3rd of January, driving the Indians up the valley of the Tongue, until the night of the 7th, when the advance captured a young warrior and seven Cheyenne women and children, who proved to be relatives of the headmen of the tribe. A determined attempt was made by the Indians to rescue the prisoners, and preparations were made for the severe fight to be expected next day. The next morning about 600 warriors appeared in front of the troops and an engagement followed, lasting about five hours. The fight took place in a canyon, the Indians occupying a spur of the Wolf Mountain range.

As the fight opened the two Napoleon guns exploded shells within the Indians lines, creating great consternation among the savages At one time they had completely surrounded the command, but the key of the position was a high bluff to the left of the line of troops, and the sharpest fighting was for the possession of this ground. The Indians who held it were led by Big Crow, a Medicine Man. He rushed out in front of the warriors, attired in a most gorgeous Indian battle costume of the brightest colours, and with a head-dress made of the waving plumes of the eagle falling down his back, jumped up and down, ran in a circle and whooped and yelled like a madman.

Then a charge was made by troops under Captains James S. Casey, Fifth Infantry, and Edmund Butler, Fourteenth Infantry, and Lieutenants Robert McDonald and Frank D. Baldwin, Fifth Infantry. It was done with splendid courage, vim and determination, although the men were so encumbered with their heavy winter clothing, and the snow was so deep, that it was impossible to move faster than a slow walk. They were conspicuous in this charge for their boldness and excellent judgement. In the very midst of their daring acts of bravado, Big Crow fell, pierced by a rifle shot, and his loss, together with the success of the charge that had been made and the important ground gained, seemed to cause a panic among the Indians, and they immediately turned in utter rout up the valley down which they had come a few hours before.

DAVID ROCHE

The ground was covered with ice and snow to a depth of from one to three feet, and the latter portion of the engagement was fought in a blinding snowstorm, the troops stumbling and falling in scaling the ice and snow-covered cliffs from which the Indians were driven, with serious loss in killed and wounded, through the Wolf Mountains and in the direction of the Big Horn range. For this gallant charge Captains Casey and Butler and Lieutenant McDonald received the Medal of Honour.

If the troops had met with disaster it would have been many weeks before any relieving command could have reached the ground from the nearest possible source of aid. Every officer and soldier knew this, and that a mistake meant disaster, and that disaster or defeat meant annihilation, and were therefore inspired to deeds of heroism and fortitude and a corresponding confidence. The lighting that occurred on the left of the line, as already described, was for a time very close and desperate, in which the troops lost three men killed and eight wounded. The column then returned to the cantonment at the mouth of the Tongue River.

The prisoners which Colonel Miles's command captured from Crazy Horse's village proved a valuable acquisition in communicating with the hostiles and in arranging for their surrender. On February 1st Miles sent out a scout with two of the captives, offering terms on which a surrender would be accepted, informing the hostiles that a non-compliance would result in a movement of the troops against them. Following up the trail from the scene of the engagement, near the Wolf Mountains, the Indians were found camped on a tributary of the Little Big Horn. The mission was successfully executed by the scout, and on February 19th he returned with nineteen Indians, mainly chiefs and leading warriors, who desired to learn the exact conditions upon which they could surrender. The terms were repeated, *viz*: unconditional surrender and compliance with such orders as might be received from higher authority.

The delegation returned to their village, the camps moved near the forks of the Powder River for a general council, and after another interview with Colonel Miles, Crazy Horse's uncle, named Little Hawk, with others, guaranteed to bring the Indian camp to the cantonment at Tongue River, or to take it to the lower agencies, leaving in Colonel Miles's hands, as a pledge of good faith, nine hostages, prominent men and head-warriors of both tribes. Three hundred Indians, led by Two Moons, Hump, and other chiefs, surrendered to Colonel Miles on April 22nd. The largest part of the bands, numbering more than 2,000, led by Crazy Horse, Little Hawk, and others, moved southward and surrendered at the Red Cloud and Spotted Tail Agencies in May.

Crazy Horse and his people were placed on the reservation near Camp Robinson, where, for a time, they appeared quiet and peaceable, but in a few months the restraints of this new position became so irksome to Crazy Horse that he began to concoct schemes again involving his people in war. It was determined, therefore, to arrest and confine him. While on his way to the guard-house he broke from those around him and attempted to escape by cutting his way, with a knife, through the circle of sentinels and bystanders. In the *mêlée* he was fatally wounded and died on the night of September 7th.

In the meantime Sitting Bull's camp had gathered near the Yellowstone, and when Crazy Horse and his confederates decided to place themselves under subjection to the government, Sitting Bull's band, in order to avoid surrendering and to escape further pursuit, retreated beyond the northern boundary and took refuge on Canadian soil, the party being in a very destitute condition, almost out of ammunition and having lost nearly everything excepting their guns and horses.

The campaign against these Indians, which brought about the preceding results, was carried on by the troops under the most unfavourable conditions and against greatly superior forces of Indians. The men not only withstood the rigors of the cold weather with great fortitude, but also fought the savages in the several engagements from Cedar Creek to Wolf Mountains with a vigour that challenged admiration.

Among these brave and hardy troopers were men who displayed exceptional acts of heroism and gallantry in these actions that won for them the coveted Medal of Honour.

They are as follows:

John Baker, Musician, Co. D, 5th U. S. Inf.

Richard Burke, Private, Co. G, 5th U. S. Inf.

Denis Byrne, Sergeant, Co. G, 5th U. S. Inf.

Joseph Cable, Private, Co. I, 5th U. S. Inf.

James S. Calvert, Private, Co. C, 6th U. S. Inf.

Aquilla Coonrod, Sergeant, Co. C, 5th U. S. Inf.

John S. Donelly, Private, Co. G, 5th U. S. Inf.

Christopher Freemeyer, Priv., Co. D, 5th U. S. Inf.

John Haddoo, Corporal, Co. B. 5th U. S. Inf.

Henry Hooan, Ist Sergeant, Co. G. 5th U. S. Inf.

David Holland, Corp., Co. A, U. S. Inf.
Fred O. Hunt, Private, Co. A, 5th U. S. Inf.
Edward Johnston, Corporal, Co. C, 5th U. S. Inf.
Philip Kennedy, Private, Co C, 5th U. S. Inf.
Wendelin Kreher, 1st Sergeant, Co. C, 5th U.S.Inf.
Bernard McCann, Private, Co. F, 22nd U S. Inf.
Michael McCormick, Private, Co. G, 5th U. S. Inf.
Owen McGar, Private, Co. C, 5th U. S. Inf.
John McHugh, Private, Co. A, 5th U. S. Inf.
Michael McLoughlin, Sergeant, Co. A, 5th U.S. Inf.
Robert McPhelan, Sergeant, Co. E, 5th U. S. Inf.
George Miller, Corporal, Co. H, 5th U. S. Inf.
Charles H. Montrose, Private, Co. H, 5th U.S. Inf.
David Roche, 1st Sergeant, Co. A, 5th U. S. Inf.
Henry Rodenburg, Private, Co. A, 5th U. S. Inf.
Edward Roonty, Private, Co. D, 5th U. S. Inf.
David Ryan, Private, Co. G, 5th U. S. Inf.
Charles Sheppard, Private, Co. A, 5th U. 8. Inf.
William Wallace, Sergeant, Co. C, 5th U. S. Inf.
Patton G. Whitehead, Private, Co. 0, 5th U. S. Inf.
Charles Wilson, Corporal, Co. H, 5th U. S. Inf.

Capture of Lame Deer's Village

After the surrender of the greater part of the Cheyennes under Crazy Horse and the escape of Sitting Bull's band into Canada, there still remained a band of renegades, chiefly Minneconjous, under Lame Deer, who had determined not to yield to Colonel Miles.

It was learned that these renegades had moved westward, and as soon as the necessary forage could be obtained Colonel Miles with a force consisting of four troops of the Second Cavalry, two companies of the Fifth and four of the Twenty-second Infantry, on the 5th of May started up the Tongue River in pursuit of them.

After a march of about sixty miles from the Yellowstone they crossed the trail of Lame Deer's camp, and after leaving the wagon-train with an escort of three infantry companies the rest of the command moved up the Rosebud River, they having scarcely halted at any time for rest until they reached a high divide between the Rosebud and the Big Horn Rivers, from the top of which could be discerned an Indian village some fifteen miles away as the crow flies, near the mouth of Muddy Creek, Montana. Having assured himself that it was Lame Deer's village, Miles moved his troops under cover of darkness within close proximity of the Indians, and at dawn of day on the 7th charged upon the village, the mounted infantry and scouts stampeding the Indian horses while the battalion of cavalry attacked the camp. The ponies, horses and mules were handsomely rounded up and brought to the rear of the fighting battalion. The Indians, after a short but sharp engagement, fled from their camp to the high hills in the vicinity.

Before the attack was made Colonel Miles called on the Indians to surrender; Lame Deer and Iron Star, his head warrior, appeared desirous of doing so, but after shaking hands with some of the officers the Indians, either meditating treachery or fearing it, again began firing. This ended peace-making and the fight was resumed, the hostiles being driven, in a running fight, eight miles, across the broken country. to the Rosebud. Fourteen Indians were killed, including Lame Deer and Iron Star, 450 horses, mules and ponies, and the entire Indian camp outfit were captured, including fifty-one lodges well stored with supplies. Lieutenant A. M. Fuller, Second Cavalry, was slightly wounded; four enlisted men were killed and six were wounded. The Indians who escaped subsequently moved eastward to the Little Missouri and the command returned to the cantonment.

Five men were awarded the Medal of Honour for distinguished gallantry in this action, they being: First Sergeant Henry Wilkens, Corporal H. Garland, Farrier William H. Jones, and Private William Leonard, of Troop L, and Private Samuel D. Phillips Troop H, of the Second U. S. Cavalry.

The following interesting episode relative to this action is told by General Miles in his *Personal Recollections*:

"When the Indians were attacked they fled from their camp, taking only what they carried in their hands, up among the high bluffs and rugged hills in that vicinity.

"In the surprise and excitement of the wild onset of the charge, a group of warriors was forced away from the others and became separated from the rest of the tribe. Before making the attack I had ordered our Sioux and Cheyenne Indians to. call out to the Lame Deer Indians that if they threw down their arms and surrendered we would spare their lives. I was anxious to capture some of them alive, as we hoped thereby to secure the surrender of all the Indians in the camp. As we galloped up to this group of warriors they apparently recognized the purport of the demand and dropped their arms upon the ground.

TROOPS ENCOUNTERING A WESTERN BLIZZARD

In order to assure them of our goodwill, I called out '*How-how-kola*' (meaning friend) and extended my hand to the chief, Lame Deer, which he grasped, and in a few seconds more I would have secured him and the others, as, although he was wild and trembling with excitement, my adjutant, George W. Baird, was doing the same with the head warrior, Iron Star.

"Unfortunately, just at that time one of our white scouts rode up and joined the group of officers and soldiers with me. He had more enthusiasm than discretion, and I presume desired to insure my safety, as he drew up his rifle and covered the Indian with it. Lame Deer saw this and evidently thought the young scout was going to shoot him. I know of no other motive for his subsequent act than the belief that he was to be killed whether he surrendered or not. As quick as thought, with one desperate, powerful effort, he wrenched his hand from mine, although I tried to hold it, and grasped his rifle from the ground, ran backward a few steps, raised his rifle to his eye and fired.

"Seeing his determined face, his set jaw, wild eye, and the open muzzle of his rifle, I realized my danger and instantly whirled my horse from him, and in this quick movement the horse slightly settled back upon his haunches; at that moment the rifle flashed within ten feet of me, the bullet whizzed past my breast leaving me unharmed, but unfortunately killing a brave soldier by my side. Iron Star broke away from Adjutant Baird at the same time. This instantly ended all efforts to secure their peaceful surrender and opened a hot fight that lasted but a few seconds. A dozen rifles and revolvers were opened on the scattered warriors who were fighting us, and all went down quickly beneath the accurate, close and deadly fire. The whole incident was over in a much less time than it takes to describe it.

"The main object of our expedition being now accomplished, and not desiring to risk more lives in an encounter than the circumstances absolutely demanded, we turned back and bivouacked at Lame Deer's camp, which was one of the richest I had ever seen. It was composed of fifty-one beautiful lodges, richly stored with robes, horse-equipments and every other species of Indian property. Whatever was desired by the troops was taken possession of and the remainder burned. The herd of horses were round, fat, sleek and in excellent condition.

"On the morning following commenced the greatest circus I have ever witnessed. Two hundred of the war and buffalo ponies were selected with which to mount our foot-troops. The Fifth Infantry was afterward completely equipped in this way, and on the frontier was sometimes known as the Eleventh Cavalry, there being then ten cavalry regiments in the army organization.

"Selecting the gentle and trained ponies from the vicious brutes was a difficult problem. The soldiers who were fortunate enough to select well-trained buffalo or war; ponies congratulated themselves in being able to put Indian bridles and saddles upon them, but even then they were not safe in mounting. Frequently it required the aid of two men to get one into the saddle. The ponies seemed as suspicious of the white man as the American horse is of the wild Indian.

"Still, many of the men succeeded in mounting, and in place of spurs used the Indian quirt, a stick about a foot long with a rawhide lash. These men were highly elated, and their derisive remarks to their more unfortunate comrades were equal to the best witticisms I have ever heard on the stump or under canvas. Some of the ponies would not allow a white man to go near them; others as fast as the scouts or Indians could rope them would submit to being bridled and saddled; in fact would look meek and calm, waiting for a good opportunity.

"With the help of one or two men the infantryman would mount, or at least reach his place above the saddle and beast for the time being, whereupon the pony would double up like a ball, make a bound into the air, coining down stiff-legged, jump about over the prairie, and repeating this exercise with lightning rapidity in almost every direction at the same time; then the soldier's hat would fall, and before many minutes he would follow suit, and frequently the pony would not stop until he had freed himself from the saddle; or, sometimes he would gallop around over the prairie and come back to the herd with the saddle underneath.

"Two hundred soldiers on the same field endeavouring to subdue the same number of wild horses created a scene of excitement which was not only humorous but also somewhat dangerous. Fortunately they did not have far to fall, and the ground was covered with a heavy crop of green grass. This scene continued until the command was completely mounted and the ponies and infantry had become better acquainted, and by that time we were ready to take up our return march to the cantonment.

Campaign Against the Nez Perces

WILLIAM R. FARNELL

The trouble with the Nez Perce Indians broke out early in the summer of 1877 and terminated in the fall of the same year. This tribe had lived in Idaho, and up to this time had always been at peace with the white population of the surrounding country. As a matter of fact the thrifty Nez Perce was regarded as one of the friendliest Indians of that section of the country, who had always treated the white traveller and explorer with hospitality and generosity. The same treatment was not accorded them by the white settlers, who from fear or general prejudice had always been more or less hostile. Nevertheless, these Indians remained quiet and peaceable, attending strictly to their own affairs and pleasures.

The direct cause of the trouble was a controversy for the possession of the Waliowa Valley. A band of white settlers claimed ownership of the land; the Indians pointed out that since the land had been given them by treaty as part of their reservation they were the rightful owners.

The result of the dispute was the Nez Perces were compelled to yield. The settlers succeeded in impressing the government at Washington with the importance of their claim for the possession of the valley, and to their intense satisfaction saw a military force moving to enforce their demands. This placed the Indians before the alternative of fighting for rights or abandoning their cherished land. The general sentiment seemed to favour the latter. Rather than begin hostilities they would emigrate. Looking Glass and Chief Joseph, the leading chiefs, prepared for the removal. Then an occurrence happened which changed the whole plan by which hostilities were forced upon the tribe. Some of the hot-headed settlers had become impatient, and, tired of waiting for the retirement of the Indians, began to annoy them.

One white man, more imprudent than the others, shot and killed a Nez Perce. With this one shot the discontent of the savages that had been smouldering for some time was now fanned into open rebellion. The quiet, undisturbing, harmless Nez Perce at once became as violent and valiant a foe as was ever encountered by the American soldier. And although the subsequent campaign was not of long duration, it was exciting while it lasted, full of thrilling episodes, included a number of sharp encounters, entailed a severe loss of life to the military forces and, when it finally ended, did not tend to decrease the respect which the civil and military authorities had always entertained for this savage tribe.

The first act of hostilities on the part of the Indians was the murder of a white settler. A brother of the Nez Perce who had been shot retaliated by taking the life of his brother's slayer. A hue and cry was raised among the white settlers, who feared a general massacre, and the military was urged to step in and prevent further outrages. On the other hand, the Indians were fully cognizant of what the result of the act of one of their tribesmen would be, and hastened to get away. They left their reservation and moved in a north-easterly direction toward Montana. They were pursued alternately by General Howard, Colonel Gibbon and Colonel Sturgis.

At the first sign of a disturbance General Howard sent an expedition under Captain David Perry and J. G. Trimble, consisting of Troops F and H, First United States Cavalry, to the scene of the disorder.

The impression prevailed in military circles that the uprising was not of a general character, especially since this Indian tribe was known to be very peacable and friendly.

The expedition then was intended by General Howard more in the nature of a demonstration rather than active hostilities. The sight of the troops was thought to be sufficient to restore peace and tranquillity. To this failure to comprehend the grievances of the Nez Perces and appreciate the seriousness of the situation was added another mistake. White settlers of the district of Idaho, threatened by the pillaging Indians, had grossly exaggerated the conduct of Chief Joseph and his tribesmen. "The Nez Perces are so loaded up with plunder and booty that they are hampered in their own progress and are able to proceed very slowly only," they said.

General Howard gave these stories more credence than the facts warranted and acted accordingly. His orders to Captain Perry were: "Get to the scene quickly, take away from the Indians their loot and chase them back to their reservation." The result was, that when the command moved on its mission—believed to be so simple and easy—it left Fort Lapwai poorly equipped and not even sufficiently provided with ammunition, Troop F having but forty rounds for carbine and twelve for pistol, Troop H not being much better off. The strength of the force did not exceed 90 men.

General Howard's first information about the trouble reached him June 15, 1877, and the next day found Captain Perry's expedition on the march. Prompt action had almost assumed the character of undue haste.

It was known that the Nez Perces were in camp in the White Bird Canyon, Idaho, and thither the command moved quickly, rapidly reaching its destination after an exacting and exhausting ride—wearing out the men and horses—of twenty-four hours. A surprise awaited the troops on their very appearance on the scene.

The Indians were occupying a strong position and had prepared themselves for a fray. Their attitude indicated plainly that they would not yield to a "demonstration," and that, if the soldiers wanted to recapture the plunder, they would have to fight for it. They then realized that they would have to fight anyway, since a retreat was impossible. And thus the battle of White Bird Canyon, which resulted in a very serious disaster for the cavalrymen, occurred on June 17, 1877.

Captain Trimble, who commanded Troop H, at the outset realized that as far as the command was concerned the fighting could be defensive only, the Indians out numbering the soldiers eight to one and being in an unassailable position.

MICHAEL MCCARTHY

To his right there was an elevation on rocky ground, which offered all the advantages of a strong defence. Accordingly, he at once placed there his first sergeant, Michael McCarthy, with a detail of six men, with orders to hold that point at all hazards.

Now the fight began. The Indians broke forth, yelling, screaming, filling the air with hideous howls and showers of bullets.

As soon as this rush was made—it looked as if hades itself had been turned loose—eight citizens, settlers who had been most loud in their denunciation of the Nez Perces and demands for vengeance, took to their heels and ran away as fast as they could. The soldiers, too, were not prepared to meet this furious and awe-inspiring onslaught and wavered. Soon most of the men of Troop F were hurrying to the rear. Captain Perry, doubting the advisability of a defence, ordered a general retreat. Captain Trimble did not lose his head in the general confusion. He galloped to the commanding officer and beseeched him to recall the order.

"What is to become of McCarthy and his men?" he said; "they are in a strong position. If we re-enforce him and hold the ground there, we shall check the attack."

Captain Perry saw that the proposition was plausible and consented to the plan.

Quickly Captain Trimble ordered the men to turn about and again face the savage foe, taking the lead himself, and thus by his personal example inspired the fear-stricken men to renewed confidence.

In the meantime the Indians had not been slow in taking advantage of the confusion within the ranks of the cavalry. They dashed forward with increased vigour and mingled shouts of triumph with their ugly war-cries.

From his elevated position Sergeant McCarthy with his small command was able to hold the advancing savages by sending into their ranks a hot and accurate fire.

He, too, observed the change of tactics, when the troops suddenly turned and formed for an attack, and hurriedly rode from his position to assist his captain in steadying the men. As soon as the attack was organized he joined his faithful six men at the former post.

However, Captain Trimble's well-conceived plan failed of success. It was simply impossible to withstand the onslaught of such an overwhelming force. Men fell wounded from their horses on all sides, and to maintain the fight much longer would have been like reckless slaughter. Once more the troops retreated before the exultant Nez Perces, galloping to some hills which promised protection about a mile away. Their retreat was much faster than the Indians were able to follow. This second retreat left McCarthy and his detail in a serious plight. Completely surrounded by savages, he nobly and heroically held his position against the storming foe.

The struggle was observed by his comrades on the hills, who followed every phase of it with anticipations of awe and terror. Closer and closer the Indians drew their circle around the gallant little band. One could now see them shoot, strike or club the foremost of the redskins. Now it was a hand-to-hand fight. Now they could no longer be seen. They seemed to have been swallowed up by the hundreds of the triumphant Nez Perces. Many of the soldiers turned away from the distant, sickening sight. But lo! Again the figure of McCarthy, still surrounded by his comrades, loomed up.

The gallant little band was cutting its way through the ranks of the hostiles. A detachment under First Lieutenant W. R. Parnell, Troop H, hastened to their help.

McCarthy was successful in escaping from the savages' grip and reaching the lieutenant's detail. But two of his six comrades fell into the hands of the foe during that brief but terrific ride.

Re-enforced by Lieutenant Parnell's detail McCarthy once more made a stand against the Indians, of which he at once assumed command, the lieutenant galloping to the rear to attempt to secure assistance.

McCarthy was truly omnipresent, now fighting, now helping a poor dismounting comrade from falling in the hands of the savage foe, now encouraging and steadying his men. He seemed to know of no danger and fought like a lion. One horse was shot from under him. He mounted another. Slowly he and his men retreated. Again his horse was killed and in the general *mêlée* that ensued the brave sergeant was separated from his comrades.

With great presence of mind and unabated energy he made a dash through the shouting and yelling Indians and made for a nearby clump of bushes in the bed of the creek, where he crawled as far as he possibly could and kept in hiding. He heard the shooting, saw the victorious savages ride by, observed the soldiers fleeing for their lives. He gnashed his teeth at the helplessness of his position, to be the eye-witness of sad defeat and not to be able to turn the tide and help his comrades. But his own situation was extremely perilous and common prudence dictated to him the necessity of remaining quietly in his place of concealment.

Nearby him lay a dead comrade—a dear comrade. Presently a number of squaws came up to rob and mutilate the dead hero.

HELD HIS POSITION AGAINST THE STORMING FOE

His own big cavalry boots stuck out of the bush. One of the women saw them and, concluding that they betrayed the presence of another soldier, called the attention of the other women to the boots. McCarthy, however, followed every move of the squaws and promptly anticipated their action. He slipped his feet out of the tell-tale boots and crawled still farther into the undergrowth. The squaws got the boots, but they failed to get their owner. Some soldier dropped them here in his hasty night, they thought, and desisted from further investigation.

After many hours of patient waiting McCarthy, bootless and with empty gun, made his escape by crawling down the bed of the creek and finally gaining the timbered mountains some miles away. From here he wandered over rough territory, hiding by day, marching by night, living on the scant rations he had with him, until after untold hardships he at last reached his camp at Mount Idaho, thoroughly exhausted, where his safe return caused great rejoicing, since every one of his comrades and superior officers had believed that he had suffered the horrible fate of a captive in the hands of the torturing redskins.

In this engagement the troops lost one commissioned officer and thirty-three men over one-third of the entire command. The Nez Perces, however, continued their march toward Montana.

Besides Parnell's heroic attempt to rescue McCarthy, he returned with a few men in the face of a heavy fire from the pursuing Indians, and at imminent peril rescued a soldier, whose horse had been killed, leaving his rider behind in the retreat.

Lieutenant Parnell and Sergeant McCarthy were awarded the Medal of Honour for the part they played in this action.

Battle of the Big Hole

The Nez Perces Indians were so elated over their success after repulsing Captain Perry's forces at the White Bird Canyon, Idaho, that they committed numerous crimes and outraged white women in a most brutal and fiendish manner.

These crimes were brought to the attention of General Howard, who at once took the field in person, determined to punish the savages who had committed them Detachments were sent out to scout the country and attack the Indians wherever they found them. These crimes must be stopped and drastic measures were a necessity.

One of the detachments encountered them at the Clear Water River, Idaho, and in this fight both the whites and the Indians losses were quite heavy. The Indians had succeeded in driving the soldiers away from a howitzer and two field guns, thus allowing them to fall into the Indians' hands. First Lieutenant Charles F. Humphrey, Fourth Artillery, upon seeing his men driven back and the guns abandoned at once called a few of his men together and voluntarily led them, in the face of a withering fire, to the abandoned guns, which were lying within a few yards of the hostiles. A most desperate fight ensued between him and the Indians for the possession of the guns, and in a short time he had them safely within the lines, hauling them by hand, as the horses had been shot down. Lieutenant Humphrey was warmly commended for this brave act and was awarded the Medal of Honour.

The troops were continually on the move in order to harass the Indians and intercept them whenever they attempted to leave Idaho, but notwithstanding their vigilance the hostiles broke up into several small bands and made for the "buffalo country" in Montana by way of the Lo-Lo trail.

General Howard at once notified General Gibbon, commanding the district of Montana, of the Nez Perces escape and the probable route they would pursue, whereupon General Gibbon dispatched Captain C. C. Rawn, commanding Fort Missoula, to look for the hostiles and head them off. Captain Rawn promptly threw a small force consisting of his company, Captain William Logan's and a few citizen volunteers, into the Lo-Lo Pass, where they intrenched themselves in the canyon and awaited the arrival of Chief Joseph and his Nez Perces into Montana. Small scouting parties were sent out to ascertain whether Joseph was coming on that trail, but they returned without seeing any signs of the approaching Indians. A few hours after their arrival, however, two of Joseph's Indian runners came through with messages stating that Joseph and his band wished to pass through the Bitter Root Valley on their way to the buffalo country, and that they would not molest the settlers if they were allowed to do so. Joseph's past record was such that the request could not be complied with and the two messengers were forthwith arrested. Captain Rawn then sought a conference with the Nez Perces, with the hope of detaining them until General Howard's troops, or expected assistance from Fort Shaw, under Gibbon, should arrive.

At this conference Joseph was informed that if his band would surrender their arms he would allow them to pass. This Joseph positively refused to do, and cunningly leaving a few Indians to make a feint, he at once climbed the hills and passed around Rawn's flank into the Bitter Root Valley. Rawn left a small force behind to guard the post and immediately gave chase, but when he overtook them it was found that most of the citizen volunteers had deserted him and that his remaining force of less than 100 was wholly inadequate to stand a fight with Joseph's braves, who outnumbered his men four to one. He therefore withdrew his command and returned to his post near Missoula.

General Gibbon in the meantime had collected from the several posts in Montana all the available troops and started out from Fort Shaw for Missoula, 150 miles away, and by making forced marches over a rough country accomplished the trip in seven days. Upon his arrival at Missoula, Gibbon's command was re-enforced by Rawn's company, thus bringing up his force to a total of 146 men, 17 officers, and some citizen volunteers. With this small force he set out in pursuit of Chief Joseph, who had on the 28th of July started up the Bitter Root. Joseph having a start of several days, moved slowly, believing that it would be some time before his pursuit would be resumed, but after five days of terrible climbing over the rugged and broken country the Nez Perce village was sighted by the troops on the evening of August 8th in the Big Hole Basin, Montana.

About 10 o'clock that night General Gibbon moved his command stealthily down to within a few hundred yards of the sleeping Nez Perce warriors, and as day began to break, the troops in perfect silence, moved to their positions for attack, being compelled to cross a slough with water waist deep before reaching the Indian camp. Captains Logan, Williams and Rawn were sent with their companies to the extreme right to cross and attack the camp near a small creek, while Lieutenant Bradley with a small force went farther down the stream to attack.

After proceeding some distance Bradley's men encountered a mounted Indian who was on his way to the pony herd. He was immediately shot down. This shot was quickly followed by others, and the line of men sprang forward to the charge. A heavy fire was at once opened along the entire length of the Indian tepees, the startled Nez Perces rushing from their lodges in every direction, many taking refuge in the brush behind the bank of the creek, along which the village lay.

For a few minutes no effective fire was returned, but soon the hostiles recovered somewhat from their surprise, and, getting under cover of the brush, they opened a destructive fire on the troops as the latter came into the open ground. The fire was particularly destructive on the right end of the line where Logan was sweeping forward. He and his men—Company A, Seventh Infantry—were in the rear of the hidden Indians who turned, as the soldiers came along, and fired into them with terrible effect. The greatest slaughter of the day took place here, Logan and others of the brave men laying down their lives.

In less than twenty minutes from the time the charge was begun the soldiers were in full possession of the camp and orders were given for its destruction. While part of the men were engaged in burning the lodges, the Indians kept up a fire from their sheltered positions, officers and men falling rapidly under these well-directed shots, until General Gibbon reluctantly withdrew his men from the village and took shelter in the timber.

Although the Indians were driven from their caimp, they were, however, not beaten, and as the troops sought shelter in the timber the Indians became more confident of themselves and came out from their shelter into the camp again. Another charge was ordered and the troops dashed back into the camp, engaging in a hand-to-hand fight. This deadly encounter lasted but a few minutes, when the Indians again retired to their shelter, all the while firing into the brave little band of soldiers.

General Gibbon now ordered a charge in opposite directions for the purpose of driving out the Indians who were in the woods, but as the soldiers advanced the Indians retreated still farther into the dense underbrush. When it became evident to General Gibbon that it would be unwise to hold his position in the valley, he ordered the men to retire up the hill and again take shelter in the timber. This movement was successfully accomplished, the troops carrying off with them such of their wounded as could be found, the Nez Perces following closely and keeping up a constant fire. Fighting continued all day, the Indians several times attempt ing to burn out the troops by setting fire to the grass and woods, and during the night shots were occasionally discharged into the position of the troops and in the evening of the 10th the Indians gave them a parting volley and disappeared.

The losses on both sides were very heavy, those of the troops being sixty-nine killed and wounded out of a strength of 191. The number of wounded among the Indians could not be ascertained, but their killed number eighty-nine.

Among this band of soldiers, every one of whom fought heroically, were five whose actions were of such a conspicuous nature that they were awarded the Medal of Honour.

These men were: First Sergeant; Wm. D. Edwards, Sergeant Patrick Rogan, Private Lorenzo D. Brown, Musician John McLennan, all of Co. A, 7th Infantry and Private Wilfred Clark, Troop L, Second Cavalry,

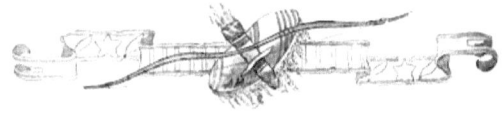

Chief Joseph's Camp Surprised

After the Battle of the Big Hole, the famous pursuit of Chief Joseph and the Nez Perces was begun. They proceeded south, murdering settlers and stealng stock as they went. They crossed the Rocky Mountains into Idaho and back again, moving rapidly to the Geyser Basin, and through that to the Yellowstone, which they crossed, and thence on to the junction of Clark's Fork and the Yellow stone, hotly pursued by General Howard's wearied troops and a detachment of Colonel Gibbon's command.

On the morning of August 20th the Nez Perces succeeded in capturing about 100 mules from General Howard's troops. Major Sanford, with two troops of the First Cavalry, one of them in command of Captain James Jackson, hotly pursued the Indians, overtaking them at Camas Meadows, Idaho, when after a sharp fight the troops recaptured about fifty of the animals. In this action several troopers had been wounded, among them a trumpeter. Captain Jackson saw him fall from his horse, and immediately he dismounted and went to his side.

In the face of a desperate fire from the yelling Indians he called upon one or two men, who quickly responded, and together they carried to a place of safety, out of the reach of the savages, the body of the trumpeter who had been shot and killed. For his heroic action while thus exposed to the Indians severe fire, Captain Jackson was warmly commended, and he was rewarded by the Medal of Honour.

Hither and thither the escaping hostile Nez Perces proceeded through Northern Idaho and Montana, in the vicinity of the

Yellowstone, leading the troops in a hot chase, in which the latter lost their trail. This, however, was again picked up early in September by the Seventh Cavalry, under Colonel Sturgis, and by forced marches of fifty and sixty miles a day the Indians were pursued until the 14th, their rear frequently attacking the troops. For days at a time the latter were wholly without rations, and the limit of endurance having been reached by both men and animals Colonel Sturgis gave up the chase and awaited the arrival of General Howard's forces.

On the evening of September 17th Colonel Miles was informed that the Nez Perces were beyond the reach of their pursuers and was requested to join in the chase, especially since the colonel, who with his forces was stationed at the junction of the Yellowstone and Tongue Rivers, was believed to be in a position to intercept the Indians by a much more direct and consequently shorter route.

The request was acted on immediately. That same night the troops were taken across the Yellowstone and early the following morning Colonel Miles started in pursuit of the warriors. His command consisted of a detachment of guides and scouts and thirty friendly Cheyenne Indians under the command of Lieutenant P. M. Maus, First United States Infantry, Troops F, G and H, Second United States Cavalry, Troops A, D and K, Seventh United States Cavalry, Companies B, F, G, I and K, Fifth United States Infantry, one Hotchkiss breech-loading and one twelve-pounder Napoleon gun. The command took a north-westerly direction toward the Missouri River, which was reached early on the morning of September 24th.

Colonel Miles pressed a passing Missouri steamer into service and ferried his force, except one small detachment, across the stream. This was fairly accomplished when he was informed that the Nez Perces were on the other side of the river and the boat, which had already steamed away, had to be recalled at once to take the force back. According to the information, the Indians were in the vicinity of the Bear Paw Mountains, a range of mountains connected by a low divide with the Little Rocky Mountains.

On September 30th, after a forced march through a difficult country, the trail of the long-looked-for savages was discovered at last and followed with much caution and great secrecy, the whole command marching stealthily along the base of hills and mountains. Colonel Miles had given strict orders that not a shot be fired, and that the numerous buffalo, deer and elk be left unmolested and undisturbed—an order which led many a hunter among the soldiery into dire temptation. The colonel himself recounts a unique incident.

Lieutenant Maus, who commanded the scouts, came across a grizzly or silver-tip bear. The animal raised upon its hind legs and was ready for a "scrap." Lieutenant Maus's sporting blood was aroused in a second, and he ached for the possession of such costly trophy. He brought his rifle to the shoulder, aimed—and one second more and a shot would have, in all probability, put a quietus on Mr. Bear's pugilistic ambitions. But there was the order not to fire a shot! Slowly the rifle sank from its raised position; the captain remembered the order, and his sense of duty conquered over his desires as a hunter.

The Nez Perces were located within the curve of a crescent-shaped cut bank in the valley of Snake Creek and also in the ravines leading into that valley.

The Indians seemed perfectly unconscious of the approaching danger, scouts failed to detect the troops, the buffalo grazed quietly, the elk, the deer moved about without show of fear or fright. What, then, was there to alarm the camping braves?

The last eight miles along the trail were covered in almost spectacular: the whole command riding and marching to the impending fray as on pleasure bent. The soldiers laughed, joked, hummed the popular tunes of the day—in fact the finest of military spirit prevailed.

Captain Tyler was ordered to take the Second United States Cavalry on a slight detour, attack in the rear and capture the herd, so as to render an escape of the Indians impossible.

This order was executed with great zest and dash and proved a complete success, Captain Tyler capturing about 800 ponies.

The Seventh United States Cavalry and Fifth United States Infantry then charged directly upon the village. The surprise of the Indians, however profound, was not complete, nevertheless. The tramp of the horses had given them warning and when the troops came upon the village they were met with a hot and deadly accurate fire. This was a somewhat unexpected reception, and for a minute checked the advance. But for a minute only. Again the troops charged ahead, and soon had; portion of the Indians driven from the camp into the ravines. The combat raged fiercely, the Indians putting up and maintaining a stout resistance. Colonel Miles, however, arranged his force in such a manner as to completely encircle the camp, first in a wide and large circle, but gradually tightening his grip and slowly driving the Indian force into the ravines.

This was not easily accomplished, and resulted in a great loss of life to the troopers. The Nez Perce proved to be a perfect marksman. Moreover, he knew how to select his victims and used his rifle with telling discrimination. He seemed to pick out the officers.

A few minutes stopped the advance of the Seventh. In the meantime White Bird and several other warriors rushed out from their camp, mounted their horses and made for the hills. The Second Cavalry had become widely scattered over the valley. Captain Tyler had captured more than 800 Indian ponies; Lieutenant Jerome had also secured a large number. Lieutenant E. J. McClernand, with but a few men, had moved far down the valley, where he had captured several hundred ponies. While he was driving them back he encountered the Indians who made their escape from the camp and they made a vicious effort to regain possession of the horses. In the sharp fight that followed Lieutenant McClernand successfully beat off the enemy and got his men and horses back to an opening in the hills in safety.

By this time the troops had completely encircled the Indian camp, but it had been done at awful cost. Captain Hale and Lieutenant Biddle of the Seventh Cavalry were lifeless upon the ground; Captain E. S. Godfrey and Captain Myles Moylan, who had led their troops at full gallop against the Indians, were severely wounded; Assistant Adjutant-General George W. Baird was shot through the arm and had one ear carried away while bringing orders to different parts of the battle field.

HENRY ROMEYN

Four of the five officers of the Seventh Cavalry battalion had been killed or wounded in the first charge, and Lieutenant Henry Romeyn, of Company G, Fifth Infantry, mounted on a captured Indian horse, was put in command also of troops A and H. With his own company and the cavalry Romeyn charged down the steep bank to cut the enemy off from water. He had scarcely got the men moving when he was struck by a bullet in the right breast, breaking a rib where it entered, and another where it passed out near the spine.

Another bullet pierced his belt, the handle of his hunting knife was shot away, his field-glass case was shattered and a ball had gone through his ear after grazing his shoulder. He was carried off the field by four of his men, who risked their lives in the act, but his wounds were considered mortal and he was left to die, something being given him to ease his pain. Lieutenant Mason Carter, of the Fifth Infantry, had continued the charge after Romeyn's injury, and succeeded in dislodging the Indians, inflicting heavy loss upon them.

Lieutenant Oscar F. Long had been directed by Colonel Miles to order one of the cavalry troops to advance. Finding both of its officers wounded, Lieutenant Long voluntarily assumed command and took the troop forward under a heavy fire. While the men were falling rapidly, Major and Surgeon Henry R. Tilton seemed everywhere among them giving them his best aid, notwithstanding the rain of bullets about him. He

HE WAS CARRIED OUT OF THE FIELD BY FOUR OF HIS MEN

rescued by admirable courage quite a number of fallen soldiers who would have received finishing bullets by the Indians had they not been taken care of by him.

Two officers and twenty-two soldiers had been killed; half a dozen officers and thirty-eight soldiers had been wounded. Colonel Miles had now to fear that the Indians who had escaped would bring the hostile Sioux to the assistance of the Nez Perces. The wounded were too many to be properly cared for, and he dared not risk another assault upon the Indian camp, knowing that a siege would be the safer though slower method of bringing the enemy to time. To make matters worse snow began to fall, and the suffering of the soldiers was intense. The next day, however, a flag of truce was sent out from the Indian camp and a *parley* followed, which resulted three days later in the complete surrender of the Indians.

Strange to say, Lieutenant Romeyn survived his wounds, although he had been prepared for burial. The next morning it was found that life was not extinct, and shortly after he regained consciousness. Seven days later he was placed in an army wagon filled with brush and grass, and after seven days of this sort of travel arrived at the Missouri River, where with the rest of the wounded he was put on board a steamer and taken down the river.

For gallantry in this engagement Medals of Honour were given to Captains Edward S. Godfrey and Myles Moylan; Lieutenants Henry Romeyn. Mason Carter, George W. Baird, Oscar F. Long, Edward J. McClernand and Major Henry R. Tilton.

OSCAR F. LONG

The Battle of Milk River

EDWARD P. GRIMES

During the latter part of August and the early part of September, 1879, frequent reports came in to General Pope, commanding the Department of Missouri, that the White River Utes had started several extensive fires in the mountains west of Hot Sulphur Springs, Colorado, that they had fired on an agency employee, attacked his house, driving him out and injuring him, and that the lives of the people at the agency were in great danger.

Satisfying himself that the reports were true, General Pope informed the War Department of the state of affairs, and orders were at once received for the nearest military commander to send a force to the White River Agency to protect the agent and arrest the ringleaders in the outrages reported. Accordingly General Crook, commanding the Department of the Platte, sent Troops D and F, Fifth Cavalry; E, Third Cavalry, and Company E, Fourth Infantry, under command of Major Thornburgh, to the scene of the trouble.

This force, numbering about 200 officers and men, left Fort Steele, in Southern Wyoming, on the 21st of September, and by rapid marches through rugged mountain passes and over barren plains, reached Fortification Creek, in Upper Colorado, where the infantry company was left to establish a supply camp, while the cavalry pushed on to Bear Creek. On the afternoon of the 26th, while the command was at Bear Creek, several prominent Ute Indians came into the camp and talked with Major Thornburgh about the troops coming to the agency, and being assured of the mission of the troops the Indians left in apparent good humour. This conference, however, did not satisfy the Indians at the agency, and the next day several other prominent Indians carried a letter to Major Thornburgh from the Indian agent, to the effect that the Indians at the agency were greatly excited and begging that the troops advance no farther, but that the major and five soldiers should come to the agency for consultation.

Major Thornburgh replied that he would meet the agent and five chiefs on the road some distance from the agency, after he had marched his command to a suit able camping place.

Two days later, on the 29th, a courier brought a letter from the agent saying he would leave the agency with several chiefs on the morning of the 80th, to meet Major Thornburgh.

It looked now as if the difficulties could be amicably settled and Major Thorn burgh, who had by this time reached Milk River, left Troop D to continue the march along the road with the wagons, while he with the rest of the troops turned off from the road and took up a trail leading to his left.

The troops with Major Thornburgh had gone scarcely a mile when, in crossing a high bridge, they came suddenly upon the Indians in large force.

This was less of a surprise to the troops than their hostile attitude, in view of the proposed meeting between the major and the Indian agent on the morrow. Major Thornburgh immediately dismounted and deployed his men, at the same time endeavouring to open communication with the Indians. His efforts were in vain and drew forth a volley from the redskins, whereupon a hot engagement began, in which the Indians had the advantage in both position and numbers. Slowly did they drive the troopers back toward the wagon train, which had "parked" near the Milk River, the soldiers leading their horses and tiring back into the Indians with deadly aim.

Again and again the Indians attempted to break the skirmish line, but each time they were driven to cover, and only when they realized that the troops were not in precipitate rout did they attempt to get between them and the wagon train. They succeeded in gaining a strong position on a knoll commanding Thornburgh's line of retreat, but a desperate charge by about twenty men under Captain Payne routed the Indians and opened the way to the wagon train.

Sergeant Edward P. Grimes, of Troop F, Fifth Cavalry, had covered the left flank of the troops with a party consisting of two non-commissioned officers, one trumpeter and seven men. Grimes's company commander ordered his troop to mount and charge. While the men ran to their horses Major Thornburgh came riding along, countermanding the order and directing Grimes to keep his position of defence on the bluffs. Grimes could only get the trumpeter and two men, as the others had already mounted and followed the rest of the troop. These few men defended their position with the greatest bravery until ordered by their company commander to mount and withdraw to the wagon train.

About the same time Lieutenant Cherry, Fifth Cavalry, called for volunteers to cover the retreat of the command to the wagon train, Grimes was again the first one to follow the summons of the lieutenant. With him Corporal Edward F. Murphy and Blacksmith Wilhelm O. Philipsen, of Troop D, Fifth Cavalry, jumped off their horses, and other men of both the Third and Fifth Cavalry followed their gallant example. The heroic band fought with unflinching devotion; their ammunition was running short, the Indians had them nearly surrounded, and some of these brave volunteers were already wounded—Lieutenant Cherry immediately saw that their position was becoming desperate, and that their chances of escaping were growing less, with all the wounded to care for and protect.

The officer called for a volunteer to make his way to the wagon-train for ammunition and support. Grimes realized that the effort was well-nigh hopeless, but fearlessly informed the lieutenant that he would attempt it. He mounted his horse, for what he fully believed to be the last time, and started on his mission. The Indians seemed to divine his purpose, and at once started in pursuit. His horse being stronger and speedier than the ponies of his pursuers, carried him safely to the wagon-train, where the desired ammunition and support were obtained.

The daring ride was made in full view of all the Indians and soldiers, and the encouraging shouts of the latter cheered the intrepid rider on his daring and dangerous mission.

In the meantime Major Thornburgh, trying to supervise the arrangements for protecting the wagon train, had himself started for it, but was shot and instantly killed when within 500 yards of it. The wagons were formed into an elliptical corral, about 200 yards from the river, the side towards the stream being ex posed to a furious fire from the Indians, who were now making determined efforts to capture or destroy the train. The horses were rapidly falling under the unerring tire of the hostiles. The wounded were quickly laid in sheltered places within the corral, while the wounded horses were led to the exposed side of the huddled group of men, wagons and horses and shot there, to form a defence for some of the men who were acting as sharpshooters.

The contents of the wagons were then quickly piled on top of the horses and behind this meagre shelter the troopers kept up their lire; but against one more deadly from the screeching, half-frantic redskins. Not content with the advantage they had over the small corral, the wily Indians set fire to the tall grass and sage brush down the valley. The flames, fanned by the high wind, spread rapidly towards the troops, igniting bundles, grain-sacks, wagon-covers and other combustible material, adding the horrors of fire to the rain of lead and arrows. The entire train was threatened with destruction. The troopers, besides being compelled to withstand a fusillade of bullets from the hostiles, were

His horse carried him safely to the wagon-train

obliged to cease firing and exert their energies to extinguish the flames and care for their wounded, whose cries and meanings added to the weirdness of the scene.

The sun was rapidly sinking behind the mountains and as twilight set in the Indians redoubled their efforts to dislodge the men, but the troopers took courage in the thought of approaching darkness and fought with renewed vigour, picking off a redskin every time he silhouetted his head and shoulders against the deepening gloam. Thus the fight was kept up from 3 o'clock in the afternoon until darkness put an end to the desperate struggle. In a final effort a large party of the reds had charged down upon the corral, firing volley after volley into the huddled-up mass of men, horses, wagons and debris.

With the cessation of hostilities a new difficulty presented itself. Water and ammunition were needed. The command was surrounded by the enemy on three sides, making it almost suicidal to attempt to leave the entrenchment. The command was not to be left in this predicament, however, without an attempt, at least, to obtain water and ammunition, and Sergeant E. P. Grimes and Corporal H. M. Roach volunteered to make the effort. They stealthily crept out of the intrenchments toward the river, and at almost point blank range secured water, going back and forth until a sufficient supply had been obtained. Grimes then crept to a supply wagon some distance away from the corral and secured enough ammunition to last another day. Roach bravely repeated his mission on the two succeeding nights, and luckily escaped the vigilance of the wary hostile guards.

During the first night of their camp, while Grimes and Roach were obtaining water and ammunition, those of the troopers who were not wounded dug better intrenchments, cared for the wounded, dragged away the dead animals and ate lightly of their rations, and at midnight couriers, among them Sergeant John S. Lawton and First Sergeant Jacob Widmer, of Company D, slipped away toward the railroad with dispatches reporting what had occurred and asking for aid.

On the following day, September 30th, the Indians kept up

an incessant fire, killing all of the remaining animals excepting fourteen mules. The troopers, being comparatively well protected now by their intrenchments, held their fire except when a good opportunity presented itself to pick off an unwary Indian. At night fall the Indians again gave the weary troopers a rest, but after that they worried them unceasingly with all the tricks known to them, all the time firing with a seemingly inexhaustible supply of ammunition.

The couriers who had slipped away travelled through a region infested with hostiles until they met Captain Dodge and Lieutenant Hughes with Troop D, Ninth Cavalry, late in the afternoon of the 1st of October, who were scouting in that section of the country. Captain Dodge immediately went into camp for the purpose of deceiving any Indians who might be in the vicinity, issued 225 rounds of ammunition and three days rations. Then, under cover of darkness, he broke camp and pushed to the relief of the men at Milk River, with his two officers, thirty-five men and four citizens.

The beleaguered troopers in the trench, waking from their restless slumbers on the morning of the 2nd, were greeted with the sight of advancing cavalrymen, who with some difficulty made their way between the Indians and joined the almost en circled men. It was Captain Dodge's command; and immediately after they entered the trenches the Indians opened fire. With these re-enforcements the troops kept up a vigorous attack, and the battle waged for the next three days. The troopers never lagged or flinched under the terrific fire of the Indians, who were now infuriated by the renewed vigour with which the troops fought.

Many a brave fellow seemingly exposed himself needlessly in his ardour to get a better shot at the red man, many helped the wounded to places of safety, but among those whose daring, almost sheer recklessness, was most conspicuous in the narrow confines of the corral were Sergeant John Merrill, who, though severely wounded, remained on duty and rendered gallant and valuable service; Corporal George Moquin, Corporal Edward

Henry Johnson

Murphy, and Sergeant John A. Poppe. Sergeant Henry Johnson, on the night of the 2nd, voluntarily left a sheltered position and under heavy fire at close range made the rounds of the pits to instruct the guards; and also, on the next night fought his way to the river and back to bring water to the wounded.

The couriers who went out on the night of the 29th, after meeting and informing Captain Dodge of the trouble at Milk River, pushed on and succeeded after many hairbreadth escapes in reaching headquarters with their requests for aid. Colonel Wesley Merritt with Troops A, B, D and M, Fifth Cavalry, was immediately dispatched from Fort D. A. Russell to the relief and in a short time was on a special train for Rawlins, a few miles west of Fort Steele, Major Thornburgh's starting point when he went to the relief of the White River Agency. From Rawlins the remainder of the distance had to be made over the mountains, and by a march of almost unparalled rapidity, in something over forty-eight hours Colonel Merritt's column, consisting of 850 men, one half of whom were infantry following in wagons, marched 170 miles over an almost impassable road and reached the command at Milk River at 6 o'clock on the morning of the 5th of October.

Upon the arrival of Colonel Merritt's column at Milk River the crippled and exhausted command gave as hearty a cheer as they could muster in their pitiful condition, after which they were tenderly cared for, given rations and then sent back to the railroad at Rawlins. The Indians retired from their concealed places when the relief column came within sight, but were followed by Colonel Merritt's command, which had been re-enforced by other troops. Merritt pushed on to the White River Agency, the Indians having all disappeared before him, and upon his arrival there he found that they had burned and utterly destroyed the agency, had killed the employees and agent, and had carried off all the females. The bodies were buried and preparations made for the continuance of the pursuit when orders were received to suspend operations at the request of the Indian Department, which was negotiating with the Utes for the release of the captive females and the surrender of the ringleaders in these outrages.

During the cessation of hostilities various reconnoitring parties were sent out from Colonel Merritt's command, and one of these on the 20th, consisting of five men under Lieutenant Wm. P. Hall, Fifth Cavalry, was attacked by thirty-five Indians about twenty miles from the White River. They defended themselves behind some sheltering rocks, Lieutenant Hall several times exposing himself to draw the fire of the enemy, thereby giving his small party an opportunity to respond with telling effect. They kept up the unequal fight until night, when they succeeded in returning to camp with the loss of Lieutenant W. B. Weir, of the ordnance department, and Chief Scout Humme, both of whom were killed.

The loss sustained by the command at the Milk River fight from September 29th to October 5th, when it was relieved by Colonel Merritt, was Major Thornburgh, Fourth Infantry, and nine enlisted men, Wagonmaster McKinstry, Guide Lowry and one teamster, killed; Captain Payne and Second Lieutenant Paddock, Fifth Cavalry, Sergeant Grimes, forty enlisted men and two teamsters wounded.

The Indians who numbered 350 and were well supplied with ammunition, admitted a loss of thirty-seven killed. The number of wounded, which must have been large, was never known.

All the non-commissioned officers and enlisted men, herein mentioned for conspicuous acts of courage and gallantry were awarded the Medal of Honour.

Hunting Indians in the Snowdrifts of Montana

T. B. GLOVER

Smoke from the *tepees* of the "friendlies" curled lazily up, then floated into straight lines, as the sun went down on a day shut in and blasted with the death of a Montana winter, but far out and beyond the sheltering hills of Fort Keogh there was murder in the chill air. That afternoon, February 8, 1880, word had come to the headquarters of the Second United States Cavalry that the treacherous Sioux were again riding with death; that a man had been murdered on Mizpah Creek, and his mutilated body with that of another, fatally wounded, had been found. "Spotted-Tail's work," commented the scouts, from experience.

The bearer of the ghastly news and his horse were exhausted from fatigue and exposure to the biting cold in their race across the white wastes. There were fifteen of the murdering reds, the rider stated. The sun had gone down bleak and cheerless, and over the endless waste of snow the midwinter night fell quickly, on the porch of the mess the thermometer read fifty-six degrees below zero. The prospect was not inviting, but every man knew that before sunrise troops would be in pursuit; that this roving band of renegade Sioux must be caught and punished, and the women and children in their white-roofed homes protected from the deadliest peril.

"Leave before daylight, with a detachment," was the order given to Sergeant Thaddeus B. Glover, of Troop B. "Ride to the scene of the depredations, pursue and capture the band of wandering Sioux."

Fifteen in number, the little party floundered through the deep drifts at the post gate, then out along those desolate wastes and on through the gray dawn, where finally the rising sun threw a cold, cheerless light on the crackling, snapping snow, beneath the horses feet. The cold cut into the very bodies of man and beast, and the vapour from their breath froze upon moustache and nostril, as they rode on under the command of Sergeant Glover. All that day over the bleak, drift-covered prairie, the men and horses pushed their way, struggling against the gnawing pain produced by a temperature unknown until experienced. Dragging and hauling, now up, now down, they pushed on in the face of the rising storm.

At 7 o'clock that night, hours after darkness had again come upon them, they came suddenly upon the tracks of the Indians. It was pitch dark, and the cold was intense; the country was strange and nothing could be done except wait for daylight; so there among the snowdrifts the little detachment spent the long winter night, stamping a path about the horses to keep the blood in circulation, and to fight off the deadly stupor which the cold brought, benumbing to the senses.

In the gray dawn they remounted their horses, just as a scout came creeping up to report the dead body of an Indian, covered with withered frozen leaves, at the foot of a nearby tree. From this tree led a trail, barely perceptible, but sufficient. It was quickly taken by the Indian scouts, and on again went the little band, through the drift and the maddening cold. After three hours of heart-breaking march, the men stiffened and rigid in their saddles, another halt was made.

The Indian scouts, treacherous and bold in this extremity, came back to the column and grunted that they could go no farther. Their horses, they said, were exhausted and useless from the work of breaking through the snowdrifts. They would do no more.

Sergeant Glover gave a hurried order. The troopers fell from their saddles and disarmed the Indians, taking them captive to the rear. This action of the scouts was evidence that they were hard upon the trail of the band of Spotted-Tail. Then forward again, another hour, with no word spoken, and each man suffering in silence. Sergeant Glover stopped upon the summit of a snow-covered hillock. Dismounting, he went on a little farther until the troop was brought to a sudden halt, huddled together in a valley, wind-swept and filled with whirling, stinging snow. The smell of smoke had come down on the wind to the quick sense of the sergeant. He crept on alone through the snow-banks and, peering over the icy ledge, he saw below him, on the plain, the band of murdering Sioux—the warriors of Spotted-Tail.

Orders were at once given to corral the pack train, which done, the men, be numbed and stiff, slid from their saddles. One half of the detachment, under Corporal Edwards, was sent by a circuitous route to a deep ravine far on the left. The rest, under the sergeant, moved to the right, where in whispers they received their instructions. They were to separate, converge upon the Indians, and at a given signal fire simultaneously upon the band, still unconscious of their presence.

"We had been creeping and floundering through the drifts for some time," said Sergeant Glover, "keeping as quiet as possible and taking every precaution to screen ourselves from the watchful eyes of the Indians in the hollow below. Suddenly a shot rang out, sharp and clear in the desert stillness. A private of the troop, in the other wing, had pushed too far forward in his eagerness to get a shot, and exposed his body to view over the snow-covered ridge for an instant. A puff of smoke from the camp below, followed by the crack of a rifle, and Private Douglass pitched for ward over the ridge, shot through the head. Further concealment was useless and both divisions of the little command opened fire simultaneously.

I STATIONED MY MEN ON ALL THE ELEVATED POINTS

"I stationed my men on all the elevated points about the rude fortifications the Indians had hurriedly thrown up. We kept up a heavy fire until dark, when I saw that such methods would prove futile. The Indians were too securely intrenched; they must be either shelled or starved out. Under cover of darkness I sent a courier back to Colonel Miles, asking for a Gatling gun, then disposed my men around the hostile camp, forming a chain guard. In that way there could be no reliefs, and during the long hours of that bitter night we suffered intensely.

"When daylight again straggled slowly over the bleak hills, I examined more carefully the position taken by the hostiles. They were actually inside of a great hollow rock, the most remarkable natural fortification I had ever seen. With provisions, water and good weather, six men could have held a regiment off for a month. Shortly after I withdrew a part of my force, ordering the rest to keep up a vigorous fire.

"At that moment, however, a scout rode out to me and reported that the Indians wished to surrender. I knew that some change of conditions, which had so far escaped us, must have forced the hostiles to this decision. Glancing over the dazzling horizon I saw, far to the west, mere specks on the waste of snow, a body of horsemen approaching. I determined to postpone the surrender of the Indians until the identity of the riders should reveal itself. On they came, their horses throwing up clouds of snow as they galloped toward us.

"Could they be hostiles? No; the sharp eyes of the Indians had seen them first, and they were willing to give up a practically impregnable position. Finally, we saw them rise in their stirrups, and a cheer—a very faint one, but no less a good trooper cheer—came down on the wind. We leaped to our feet and cheered back. It was Captain Snyder, now Colonel Snyder, with re-enforcements. After acquainting himself with the situation Captain Snyder ordered me to accept the surrender of the hostiles, and with them we returned that night to the post."

In that engagement in the snowdrifts, sixty miles from Fort Keogh, with the thermometer showing fifty-six degrees below zero, Private Douglass, of Company E, Second Cavalry, lost his life, and Private Guernsey, Company B, was severely wounded. The Indian scouts rode on to the post, and from their saddle-bows dangled the scalps of two Sioux. For this "gallantry and vigour" General Miles excused Sergeant Glover and his men from all post duty for a period of one month, and Glover was furthermore rewarded with the Medal of Honour.

This was not the only bold capture of murderous redskins in which Sergeant Glover figured prominently. In the Mizpah Creek expedition of April, 1879, a party of Indians, members of the same band that massacred Custer in that awful slaughter of the Little Big Horn, had terrorized the Creek. Sergeant Glover was ordered to pursue and capture them. They had murdered a telegraph operator at the Powder River Station.

For three days he followed, stalking them night and day. With all the wiles of their cunning they attempted to throw him from their trail, but the avenger was an old and resourceful Indian fighter. On the morning of the third day Sergeant Glover and his men came up with the Indians. The command was at once deployed for advance.

We were then in the Little Big Horn Mountains," said Sergeant Glover. "I advanced but a short distance, when I saw two Indians standing on a rock silhouetted against the background of sky, signalling with the white flag. I advanced and accepted their surrender. Turning, I heard the sound of furious firing in the rear. The two Indians had been joined by others and treacherously opened an attack as my men were leaning quietly on their arms. Not an Indian got away. We captured them all, and under a strong guard I took them back to the post. They were tried and convicted of murder, but cheated the executioner, for, Indian-like, they all hanged themselves in the jail at Miles City."

Thus ended the last chapter in the history of Little Wolf's band of Cheyennes.

The Surrender of Rain-in-the-Face

ELI L. HUGGINS

A number of Indian Chiefs, among others Broad Tail, Kicking Bear, Spotted Eagle and the noted Rain-in-the-Face, surrendered to the military authorities in 1880. The subjugation of these notables and their tribesmen was accomplished by a series of successful military operations in conjunction with the telegraph and telephone. The soldier and his rifle caused fear and respect; the appliance of modern invention awakened awe and reverence, mingled with terror, in the Indian.

The use of the telephone and telegraph to bewilder the simple-minded savages was a clever piece of strategy on the part of the military authorities at Fort Keogh, Montana, and the manner in which it was accomplished forms the text of a rather amusing story.

A number of Indians had been rounded up and captured, and messengers were sent to their tribes to notify them of the capture and demand the surrender of the remainder of their people.

In reply to this summons a delegation of eighty big, burly

warriors came from Sitting Bull's camp to Fort Keogh under a flag of truce to learn the conditions of the proposed surrender. At that time the military post and adjoining village were quite up-to-date in the way of modern conveniences. There was a telegraph station at the fort and a telephone plant in the village.

When the Indian delegation arrived it was treated with exquisite civility and politeness, but back of this show of deference was the determination of the military authorities to show these Indians something they had never seen before.

The Indian is always boastful when referring to his own deeds of valour. On this occasion the soldiers were equally as ostentatious with the display of their power and resources, and very soon had their unsophisticated visitors at their mercy.

Colonel Miles took the braves into the room where the telegraph clicker was in operation.

"With this here," he said, pointing to the instrument, "we can talk to the Great White Father in Washington."

The Indians examined the mysterious contrivance, listened to its incomprehensible click, click, but the significance of it all was beyond their understanding.

"How can you make this thing talk to the Great Father?" one of the old warriors asked.

"By means of electricity," was the reply.

"And what is electricity?" they questioned.

Colonel Miles, in narrating this incident, confessed his discomfiture. He could not find a definition which suited the mental horizon of his guests, but with the ready wit for which he is noted he replied: "The Great Spirit has loaned the white man His lightning," and to still more clearly demonstrate his unique definition he darkened the room and set the instruments at work. The blue little electric sparks set the Indian to serious thinking.

The demonstration with the telephone had still more startling results.

The Indians were divided into two groups, and separated from each other for quite a distance. One Indian was placed at each end of the line.

The oldest of the delegation was told to place the receiver against his ear. Presently he heard his own native Dakota tongue. He recognized the voice. He knew who was speaking to him. He knew he was far away. He looked into the instrument and could not see him. His hand trembled; he shook from head to foot and dropped the receiver.

"The Whispering Spirit has spoken to me," he said with an expression of awe, and ever since that is the name by which the telephone has been known among these Indians.

Colonel Miles dismissed the delegation in the kindest possible manner. What was said and told about the white man's strange powers in the Indian villages nobody knows, but the results proved that the plan was a complete success. The Indians had no desire to oppose a foe who had borrowed the lightning from the heavens and was in league with the "Whispering Spirit," and they surrendered to the number of fully 2,000.

As has been previously stated, the military operations which preceded and led up to the incident at the fort were equally successful. They were undertaken primarily to stop the Sioux from stealing horses. As a horse thief the Indian has no superior. To him stealing a horse is a sport he has developed to the degree of a fine art. To make it more exciting the horse must belong to another tribe; to steal it from a fellow-tribesman would be a crime punishable with death. Without going into details of the Indian's manner of stealing, it may safely be asserted that upon the planning and execution of a horse-stealing raid as much care, cunning and intelligence are bestowed as upon any enterprise in which the warrior interests himself.

In summer the young brave who is about to pay a visit to a hostile camp garbs himself green, paints himself green, and rides a roan pony, so as to make himself less conspicuous on the grass-covered prairie. In the winter, when snow covers the ground, his face is white, his dress is white, and his mount is white. He sneaks and moves stealthily and cautiously, watches and observes, and finally at the opportune time, mostly at midnight, when sleep prevails in the hostile camp, dashes into the village, gath-

THEY THREW THEMSELVES FLAT ON THE GROUND AND OPENED FIRE

ers the ponies and makes his escape. Then begins a mad race for home and safety, and triumph and joy reign when he reaches the tents of his tribe and boastingly exhibits his stolen animals as evidence of his prowess.

Sitting Bull and his band, after the massacre of General Custer, had taken refuge on Canadian territory just north of the boundary line.

For a time he and his followers kept quiet, though they steadfastly refused to accept the terms of the United States Government and return to their reservation. By-and-by his camp was increased by new accessions from Sioux tribes, until he had gathered about himself a force of several thousand warriors. Then trouble began. The Sioux could not resist engaging in the racial sport—horse-stealing—and small bands crossed the border continually to raid. Horses were stolen from the Crows, friendly, unoffending Indians, later from farmers and settlers, and finally even from the military posts.

In 1880 these expeditions occurred with such frequency and annoyance that Colonel Miles resolved to put an end to them.

The immediate cause was the theft of a herd of fifty ponies from the Crow scouts at Fort Custer, on March 24th.

The next day at sunrise Captain E. L. Huggins, Sixth Cavalry, with 32 men, six Cheyenne scouts and twenty pack mules left Fort Keogh in pursuit of the marauding Sioux. The first day the command rode seventy-five miles through rain and mud toward the Rosebud River without finding any trace of the Indians. The troops marched up the river and finally struck the trail, which was several days old and frequently obliterated by rain and snow storms. But Captain Huggins stuck to his task with wonderful tenacity. As soon as the trail was lost he called his scouts and would not yield until it was again located. This kind of marching was wearisome in the extreme, tiring and exhausting for men and beasts, especially since the rations were not plentiful, and the food, toward the last, consisted only of coffee and hard bread.

The trail led the command by a circuitous route through the Bad Lands and across the Tongue and Pawnee Rivers.

Finally on April 1st the scouts reported the presence of a Sioux camp at the head of O'Fallon's Creek. The stolen pony-herd was grazing a few hundred yards away.

Captain Huggins decided upon immediate action, Lieutenant L. M. Brett with ten men was directed to make a dash for the ponies and capture the whole herd. Another officer was given a sufficient number of men to make a detour and cut off the retreat of the Indians. The captain himself moved to attack the camp.

Lieutenant Brett executed his part of the program with singular success. The ponies were in his possession before the Sioux braves had time to think. When the whole band of warriors made a dash for their horses it was too late, and they were forced to run back. Five of them became separated and were taken prisoners, one was killed. The others took refuge in a slight fringe of cottonwood trees, threw themselves flat on the ground and opened a heavy fire on the troops, now advancing for an attack. A sergeant was shot through the head and one of the horses disabled. For a short time the charge was checked.

The Sioux took advantage of the situation by retiring to a position in a washout, which was admirably suited for defensive purposes. They were now completely surrounded, although it was not considered feasible to attack them in their stronghold. Night was coming on. The troops were exhausted, chilled, and in much need of rest. But long before midnight it was discovered that the wily Indians had made their escape, leaving no trail with their *moccasined* feet on the frozen ground.

Satisfied with having recaptured the entire herd, Captain Huggins and Lieutenant Brett returned with their prisoners to the fort, having made a complete circuit and averaged about sixty miles a day since the pursuit began.

The capture of the five Indians, however, proved to be of great importance, as it let up to the surrender previously mentioned, of over 2,000, and put an end to the horse-stealing along the Canadian border.

Captain Huggins as well as Lieutenant Brett were rewarded with the Medal of Honour.

Pursuit of Chief Victoria

In September 1879, the notorious Chief Victoria with his murdering and thieving band of Indians held New Mexico in a state of terror by his raids and outrages on the settlers. Coming out of Old Mexico these marauders practically swept over the whole territory of New Mexico, and so rapidly were their movements that the military had great difficulty in following them up.

The first attack made by the hostiles was upon the herd guard of Troop E, Ninth Cavalry, near Ojo Caliente and the attack was so well conducted by them that no less than eight men were killed in the short struggle. Victoria's band which had been re-enforced by Mescaleros and some Chiricahuas prior to this attack, then made for the hills, and although pursued by the troops they succeeded in carrying off with them about fifty horses. With this attack began a series of fierce and murderous raids, which struck terror to the hearts of the people throughout the territory for it was evident that the few troops alone could not check these marauding Indians. Citizens at once organized themselves into quasi-military companies and volunteered to aid in checking and subduing these savages.

Near Hillsboro a party of these citizens encountered about 100 of Victoria's followers and in the ensuing engagement they displayed great courage but were unable to inflict much damage on the redskins whose spirits were buoyed up by reason of their successful escape from the troops and the fact that they were fighting with armed citizens and not trained soldiers. The Indians therefore brought into play their worst traits of savagery

HIGHWAYMEN OF THE PRAIRIE

with the result that the whites were driven back with a loss of ten killed, a number wounded and scalped and all their stock captured. This occurred on the 17th of September and on the 18th another fierce battle took place at the head of Las Animas River, this time with the troops.

Captain Dawson of the Ninth Cavalry in his pursuit of Victoria was attacked at this place by the Indians who held an impregnable position from which it was impossible to drive them, and were after being re-enforced by two troops under Captain Beyer of the same regiment the hostiles still had the advantage. The concerted efforts of the troops proved unavailing and that night, after fighting the wily redman in his stronghold all day, it was found necessary to withdraw the troops, whose losses were considerable, five soldiers, two Navajo scouts and one citizen having been killed, many wounded and thirty-two horses lost.

Victoria then proceeded north, with the troops in hot pursuit, and on the 29th was overtaken and again attacked by Major Morrow near Ojo Caliente with a force of 200 men. Two days of fierce fighting ensued in which the soldiers succeeded in stampeding the Indian herds and recapturing sixty horses and mules, among them a number of those captured from Troop K on September 4th. On the second day of the fight the Indians killed and wounded several of Morrow's men and then retreated, successfully covering their trail. From a squaw prisoner who was captured on October 1st, Morrow learned the position of the Indians, and by a rapid night-march Victoria's strongly fortified camp was captured and destroyed, the Indians, however, escaping in the dark.

During these three days and nights Morrow's command was without water, and as their rations and ammunition were nearly exhausted, the men and animals were utterly worn out.

Morrow's force, now reduced to less than 100 available men, continued in pursuit of the fleeing Indians, following them by very hard marches over the mountains, through swollen streams and canyons, dragging their well-nigh exhausted horses after them in a tough foot-climb up the mountain side, or down through the dark ravines, and on October 27th again overtook Victoria about twelve miles from the Corralitos River, Mexico. Taking about forty men with him, Morrow charged down upon the Indian breastworks in the moonlight, and drove the Indians from them, with a loss of but one scout killed and two wounded.

The soldiers presented a picturesque appearance as they quietly rode toward the breastworks, their felt *sombreros* with upturned brims, their erect forms and their carbines being sharply outlined in the bright moonlight, and in regular order the men approached the hostiles camp. When within a short distance of the Indians the order to charge was given and away went horses and men with a dash, completely surprising the startled redskins. For a short time the fight was fast and furious, the Indians gradually backing off until they could make a dash for the dark ravines, where they secreted themselves. Work was then begun on the destruction of the camp and in a short time the sky was lighted up by the burning debris of what was a few minutes before Victoria's stronghold.

Further pursuit of the Indians was abandoned and the troops returned to Fort Bayard, New Mexico, reaching there November 3rd.

Tularosa Saved by Twenty-Five Cavalrymen

On the second day of January, 1880, Victoria and his band of Indians were reported raiding and murdering in Southern New Mexico, whereupon all the cavalry in that section of the country were sent out at once to round up this noted chief and his thieving band.

The Mescalero Agency at the Fort Stanton Reservation had largely served as a base of supplies and recruits for the raiding parties of Victoria, and it was determined to disarm and dismount the Indians then on the reservation and thus cut off the supplies of the raiders. Generals Pope and Ord, commanding the Departments of the Missouri and Texas, arranged that a force under Colonel E. Hatch, Ninth Cavalry, numbering 400 cavalry, 60 infantry and 75 Indian scouts, should arrive at the Mescalero Agency simultaneously with Colonel Grierson and a force of the Tenth Cavalry and Twenty-fifth Infantry. These two forces set out early in January and marched toward each other, each having, on the way, several encounters with the Indians.

While Grierson was moving north and engaging the hostiles Hatch's force was driving Victoria south toward the Mescalero Agency. In this manner both forces worked ahead over a rough country until they met at the Mescalero Agency, where, on the 16th of April, Colonels Hatch and Grierson made the attempt to disarm and dismount the Indians, but they put up a brave fight and made a desperate effort to escape. This effort, however, proved futile and the hostiles, numbering about 250, were captured, only about forty escaping. The captured Indians were disarmed and dismounted and taken into the agency.

Major Morrow, with a portion of Colonel Hatch's force, then pursued the escaping Indians and overtook them in Dog Canyon, where he killed three warriors and captured twenty-five head of stock.

After disarming and dismounting the Indians at the agency Colonel Hatch began again the pursuit of Victoria, assisted by troops from the Department of Arizona, but the campaign resolved itself into a chase of the hostiles from one range of mountains to another, with frequent skirmishes but no decisive fights, until the Indians again escaped into Old Mexico. One fight took place at Tularosa on the 14th of May which is described by Sergeant George Jordan, Troop K, Ninth Cavalry, as follows:

"On the 11th of May I was ordered to Old Fort Tularosa with a detachment of twenty-five men of the Ninth Cavalry for the purpose of protecting the town of Tularosa, just outside the fort. Besides our own rations we had extra rations for the rest of the regiment which was pursuing Victoria's band of Apaches. On the second day out we struck the foothills of the mountains, where our advance guard met two troops of Mexican cavalry. The captain of one of them told me that it would be impossible for me to get through with the small body of men I had, and advised me to return to the regiment. I replied that my orders were to go through and that I intended to do so, notwithstanding the fact that large bodies of hostiles were still roaming about outside the Mescalero Agency.

"After leaving our Mexican friends we pushed along with our wagon-train bringing up the rear, until that evening we struck the Barlow and Sanders stage station, where we went into camp. At the station all was excitement. The people were throwing up breastworks and digging trenches in the expectation of an attack by the Indians. My command, being dismounted cavalry, was pretty well exhausted from our day's march over the mountains and we were all ready for a good night's rest; but within an hour after our arrival at the station, and just before sundown, a rider from Tularosa came in and wanted to see the commander of the soldiers. He told me that the Indians were in the town and that he wanted me to march the men the remainder of the distance to save the women and children from a horrible fate.

"My men were in bad condition for a march, but I explained to them the situation as the rider had put it before me, and that I would leave it to them whether they wanted to continue the march that night or not They all said that they would go on as far as they could. We then had supper, after which each man bathed his feet so as to refresh himself, and at about 8 o'clock we started to the rescue. But our progress was slow. Besides the poor condition of the men we were hampered by our wagon train in that rough country. Once one of the wagons was upset as the train was coming down a steep hill and we lost valuable time righting it.

"About 6 o'clock in the morning we came in sight of the town, and I deployed the men and advanced quickly toward it, believing that the Indians were already there. We stealthily approached the town and had gotten to within a half mile of it before the people discovered us. When they recognized us as troops they came out of their houses waving towels and handkerchiefs for joy.

"Upon our arrival in the town we found that only a few straggling Indians had gotten there ahead of us and had killed an old man in a cornfield. The people gave us shelter, and after we had rested up a bit we began making a stockade out of an old corral, and also a temporary fort close to the timber.

"On the evening of the 14th, while I was standing outside the fort conversing with one of the citizens, the Indians came upon us unexpectedly and attacked. This citizen was telling me that the Indians had killed his brother that very morning and wanted me to go out and attack them. I could not do this, as my orders were to protect the people in the town. It was then that the Indians surprised and fired fully 100 shots into us before we could gain the shelter of the fort.

THE INDIANS SURPRISED US AND FIRED ONE HUNDRED SHOTS

"As the Indians rifles began to crack the people rushed to the fort and stockade, all reaching it in safety except our teamsters and two soldiers who were herding the mules and about 500 head of cattle. The bloodthirsty savages tried time and again to enter our works, but we repulsed them each time, and when they finally saw that we were masters of the situation they turned their attention to the stock and tried to run it off. Realising that they would be likely to kill the herders I sent out a detail of ten men to their assistance. Keeping under cover of the timber, the men quickly made their way to the herders and drove the Indians away, thus saving the men and stock. The whole action was short but exciting while it lasted, and after it was all over the townspeople congratulated us for having repulsed a band of more than 100 redskins.

"Our little detachment was somewhat of a surprise to the Indians, for they did not expect to see any troops in the town, and when we repulsed them they made up their minds that the main body of the troops was in the vicinity and would pursue them as soon as they heard of the encounter. The remainder of the regiment did arrive the next morning, and two squadrons at once went in pursuit, but the wily redskins did not stop until they reached the mountains. There they had encounters with the troops and were finally driven into Old Mexico."

Two other important fights took place in this chase of the hostiles after the engagement at Tularosa, one of them on the 24th of May at the head of the Polomas River, New Mexico, where fifty-five Indians were killed in one of the hardest fought battles of the pursuit. The other took place on June 5th. In this action Major Morrow, with four troops of the Ninth Cavalry, struck the hostiles at Cook's Canyon killing ten and wounding three of them Among those killed was the son of the fleeing chief, Victoria.

In August of the following year Sergeant Jordan was commanding the right of a detachment of nineteen men at Carrizo Canyon, New Mexico, in an action with the Indians. He stubbornly held his ground in an extremely exposed position and gallantly forced back a much superior number of the enemy, thus preventing them from surrounding the command. His bravery in this action and his skilful handling of the detachment and also his fearlessness in the engagement at Tularosa won for Sergeant Jordan his Medal of Honour.

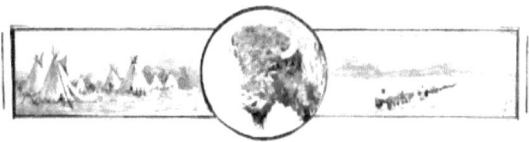

Saved From Annihilation

Geo. R. Burnett

A band of Indians under the notorious Chief Nana in the month of July, 1881, had committed a number of outrages, killed several women and children and stolen considerable property along the San Andreas Mountains in New Mexico, and Colonel E. Hatch with eight troops of the Ninth Cavalry and eight companies of infantry was sent to punish the savages and recapture the plunder. The command started in pursuit at once and in a number of encounters drove the hostiles persistently from one point to another.

A notable engagement occurred on August 12th near Carrizo Canyon, in New Mexico. Nana's band was struck by a detachment of nineteen men under Captain Parker. In the ensuing fight the troopers were outnumbered three to one by the hostiles and lost one killed and three wounded, while one soldier was captured. The Indians, however, also lost heavily and were finally forced to withdraw. That the affair had such a successful ending and was not turned into a serious defeat was due largely to the extraordinary courage of Sergeant Thomas Shaw, of Company K, Ninth Cavalry, who with his few men stubbornly held the most advanced position and refused to yield an inch of ground. He was an excellent shot, his bravery so dismayed the Indians that they gave up the attack and retreated. A still larger engagement followed a few days later.

On August 16th, Troop I, Ninth Cavalry, First Lieutenant Gustavus Valois in command, and Second Lieutenant George R. Burnett on duty with same, was lying in Camp Canada Alamosa, New Mexico, recuperating from an arduous campaign in quest of hostile Apaches, when about 9:30 or 10 o'clock in the morning a Mexican whose ranch was a few miles down the canyon came charging into the town shrieking at the top of his voice that the Indians had murdered his wife and children, and were coming up the canyon to attack the town; in an instant all was excitement, men, women and children ran hither and thither screaming, crying, cursing and piteously calling on the "Good Father" to have mercy on them and save them.

In the cavalry camp orders were at once given to "saddle up," and in an incredible short time this was accomplished. Lieutenant Burnett requested and received permission to take the first attachment ready and proceed toward the scene of trouble. The ranch referred to was soon reached and the ranchman's story corroborated in the finding of his dead wife and a number of small children all horribly mutilated.

The trail was taken up and followed across the creek and up over the "*mesa*," where the Indians were sighted about a mile off, heading toward the Cuchilla Negra Mountains, about ten miles distant. They were heavily encumbered with a large quantity of stolen stock and other plunder that they were endeavouring to get away with.

At the ranch Lieutenant Burnett had been joined by a number of mounted Mexicans, bringing his force up to about fifty men. The Indians, as nearly as could be estimated, numbered between eighty and one hundred. Immediately on sighting the Indians Lieutenant Burnett deployed his command, placing his First Sergeant, Moses Williams, in command on the right and one of the Mexicans on the left, remaining in the centre himself. As soon as the advance was begun the Indians dismounted to make a stand, and commenced firing.

Favoured by the rolling country, the fire of the Indians soon became so warm that Lieutenant Burnett was obliged to dismount his command and to send a part of it under Sergeant Williams to flank the Indians from their position. This the sergeant succeeded in doing, and as soon as he signalled that the Indians had broken and were on the run Lieutenant Burnett mounted the balance of his command and charged them, keeping up a running fight until the Indians came to the next ridge, when they dismounted again, compelling the command to do likewise and to repeat the former tactics of flanking them out of position and then charging.

The fight was so continued for several hours, the Indians fighting hard and con testing every foot of the ground in order to save as much of their stock and plunder as possible, but so closely were they pressed that they lost a number in killed and wounded, were obliged to abandon a large quantity of their stuff and a number of their ponies and shoot others to prevent their capture.

Finally the foothills of the Cuchilla Negra Mountains were reached, and here the Indians made a determined stand. Being unable to flank them on their right as usual, Lieutenant Burnett decided to make an effort to get around their left flank and if possible keep them out of the mountains. In working this detour he was ac companied by only about fifteen soldiers. The Indians observing his movements and apparent purpose, and his small force, offered no opposition for some time, when suddenly they found themselves in a pocket and surrounded on three sides by a heavy tire, and to make matters worse the Mexicans in the rear were firing into the bank against which the men were seeking to shelter themselves.

Fortunately the pocket of basin-shaped formation was so deep that all shots passed just overhead and among the rocks and did no harm except to wound some of the horses. The Indians kept crawling nearer, their shots striking dangerously close, and the situation was growing desperate for the little detachment, unless they could get relief. Orders were given to reserve their revolver fire and fight to the last man.

The Indians kept up a concemtrated fire on Lieutenant Burnett

It was at this juncture that Trumpeter John Rogers, at the suggestion of Lieutenant Burnett, volunteered to carry a message to Lieutenant Valois, whom he knew must be somewhere in the vicinity. Rogers endeavoured to crawl out, but getting discouraged with his progress ran to where his horse was picketed and quickly mounting him rode to the rear amid a hailstorm of bullets, miraculously escaping harm, although his horse was wounded.

Rogers found Lieutenant Valois and delivered Lieutenant Burnett's message, which was to take a large hill to the right which commanded the position. Lieutenant Valois endeavoured to comply with the request, but the Indians anticipated his purpose, and leaving Lieutenant Burnett's position got their first, greeting him with a volley that dismounted ten men, Valois among their number. From Lieutenant Burnett's position the Indians could be seen rallying from all points toward the hill, and divining the cause he proceeded to withdraw for the purpose of re-enforcing Valois Mounting his men and taking about thirty Mexicans who had then joined him, he started to the right and rear.

On coming up over the little rise he saw Lieutenant Valois's entire command on a slight ridge about a quarter of a mile distant, dismounted and seeking shelter behind some prairie dog mounds, about the only thing in sight, and it looked as if the Indians, only a few hundred yards off, were just about to charge them. Without halting an instant, the command being deployed and at a gallop, Lieutenant Burnett ordered it to charge. This was done in a magnificent manner, the command charging splendidly up to and beyond Lieutenant Valois's line; and, dismounting, held the Indians in check until Lieutenant Valois was enabled to get his wounded and disabled men to the rear, when the whole line was ordered to fall back, as its position was untenable.

Lieutenant Valois had commenced the backward movement before the charge was made, and in doing so had left four of his men behind unobserved, in places of comparative shelter.

When the general order to fall back was given, one of the men called out: "For God's sake, lieutenant don't leave us; our lives depend on it."

At this time Lieutenant Valois and most of his command was well to the rear and apparently did not hear the cry. Lieutenant Burnett seeing the position these men were in called for volunteers to go to their rescue. Two men only, First Sergeant Moses Williams and Private Augustus Walley, responded to the call. Lieutenant Burnett directed his men to crawl to the rear while he, with Williams and Walley, behind such shelter as they could find, would try to stand off the Indians, who, emboldened by the troops falling back, were making a desperate effort to kill or capture those remaining behind.

The marksmanship of the trio, all being good shots, caused the Indians to pause, and two of the soldiers were enabled to get to a place of safety, a third, who made no effort to escape was apparently wounded. This man was Walley's "bunky", so he asked for permission to go to his assistance. Going back to where his horse was picketed he mounted, rode rapidly up to where the man was lying, assisted him in the saddle, got up behind him and galloped safely to the rear.

Strange as it may appear, the Indians made no apparent effort to get Walley, but seemed to concentrate their efforts on Lieutenant Burnett whom they readily recognized as an officer among the coloured troopers, and his solitary companion First Sergeant Williams. Finally the fourth man who was left behind was seen wandering off in the direction of the enemy, or rather away from his own lines, and acting very strangely. He was apparently badly rattled. Indians could be distinctly seen making an effort to cut him off.

Lieutenant Burnett, realizing that if this man was to be saved no time must be lost, ran to his horse, mounted him, and galloping toward the soldier managed to place himself between him and the Indians and finally drove him to the rear. All the while the Indians kept up a concentrated fire on Lieutenant Burnett, to which he replied with his revolver, but in their excitement they shot wildly and only succeeded in recording two hits, both on his horse,

Lieutenant Valois had in the meantime taken up a new position and assisted by some Mexicans the fight was continued until nightfall. Many horses were recaptured or prevented from falling into the hands of the Indians. The ammunition being about exhausted the command fell back to camp, and at daybreak started on the trail again and followed it until obliged to turn back at the Mexican border.

Medals of Honour were awarded to Lieutenant Burnett and his coloured troopers, Williams and Walley, for their courageous conduct and rescue of life under such perilous circumstances.

Lieutenant Valois reported to the district commander that "Lieutenant Burnett's heroic charge had undoubtedly saved from annihilation his entire detachment."

Following this battle an engagement occurred August 19th about fifteen miles from McEver's ranch, New Mexico.

Lieutenant Smith with a detachment of twenty men, after a severe fight, defeated the hostiles, but the lieutenant and four of his men were killed. At the most critical moment of the combat a party of citizens joined the military forces and rendered valuable services. In this encounter Sergeant Brent Woods of Company B, Ninth Infantry, distinguished himself not alone as a brave and gallant fighter, but also the heroic manner in which he went to the succour of his wounded comrades and injured citizens saving them from falling into the hands of the savages. Nana's band was finally driven across the Mexican border, when the chase, under orders from the government, was abandoned.

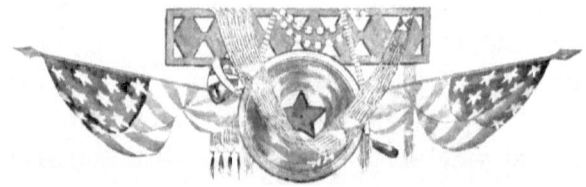

The Treachery at Cibicu Creek

WILLIAM H. CARTER

During the summer of 1881 there appeared among the White Mountain Apaches in Arizona a rising star in the guise of a Medicine Man named Nockay det Klinne. This oracle gradually inflamed the minds of the Indians and became so infatuated by his success that he doubtless believed the truth of his own weird dreams. So long as he confined himself to ordinary incantations there was no special cause for anxiety. In common with more civilized charlatans, however, he had gradually mulcted the faithful believers of much of their limited wealth, and it became necessary for him to make a bold stroke to conceal the falseness of his prophecies.

Considering the length of time the White Mountain Indians had been associated with the whites and their intelligence, it is inexplicable how this fanatic imposed upon the tribe so seriously as to make large numbers of them believe that if they would rise and murder the whites he would restore to life all their ancestors. He had been promising to raise the dead for some time, and he was growing rich through the bounty of his foolish patrons. When he announced that all the dead Apaches were risen, except that their feet were held down waiting for the whites to be driven from the Indian country, the time for interference had arrived.

Fort Apache is an isolated post in the midst of the White Mountain Reservation. Colonel E. A. Carr, of the Sixth Cavalry, had been ordered there for temporary duty during the early part of the summer, when there was no indication of Indian trouble. As dissatisfaction among the Indians became daily more apparent, its source was located and Colonel Carr had an interview with the Medicine Man and several chiefs, in which he explained how futile would be their efforts to rise successfully against the white race. Nockay det Klinne was repeatedly summoned to report to Agent Tiffany at San Carlos, but ignored all orders and retired to his camp on Cibicu Creek about forty miles from Fort Apache. Agent Tiffany's police having failed, he requested Colonel Carr to arrest the Medicine Man.

Recognizing this very serious turn of affairs, Colonel Carr telegraphed the department commander recommending that additional troops be sent at once to Fort Apache to overawe the Indians and prevent an outbreak, by convincing them of the folly of an uprising. Troops were not sent, but Colonel Carr temporized with the Indians, who were growing more bold and insolent day by day, hoping to impress upon the authorities the absolute necessity of re-enforcements to prevent an Indian war, expensive alike in blood and treasure.

Orders were ultimately issued for more troops to proceed to Fort Apache, but through some strange mischance, or ill advice, they were not allowed to proceed over the mountains from the Gila River, seventy miles away from the scene where soldierly diplomacy was arrayed against Indian fanaticism and wily cunning. The hours for parleying reached their limit when the agent made a formal demand that the military arm should be set in motion and the recalcitrant Medicine Man be brought before him dead or alive.

During the excitement of the dances inaugurated by the Indian Messiah, the craze became widespread and involved the Apaches in nearly all the camps in the White Mountain Reservation. The Indians brewed "*tizwin*," a frightful intoxicant made from corn, which added to their weird madness.

As soon as the department commander telegraphed the order for Colonel Carr to comply with the agent's request, the Indians cut the line and occupied the only practicable road and mountain trails, thus completely isolating the garrison. Warning had been received that the scouts, hitherto of unblemished character for fidelity, were strongly fascinated with the uncanny doctrines of the plausible and silver-tongued medicine man.

Upon receipt of his orders to arrest or kill Nockay det Klinne, Colonel Carr sent a runner to his camp with a message that no harm was intended toward him, but he must come in and report as desired by the agent. An evasive answer was received. It was learned he was to visit the camps adjacent to the post for another big dance and arrangements were made to secure him, but he grew suspicious and failed to put in an appearance.

On Monday, August 29th, Colonel Carr paraded his little command, consisting of two troops of his regiment, D and E, with a total strength of seventy-nine men and twenty-three Indian scouts, and marched on the trail to Cibicu Creek. There was but one officer for duty with each organization. One small infantry company was left for the protection of the garrison. The command moved leisurely and camped in a deep gorge at the crossing of Carizo Creek.

Some days prior to this time it had been deemed advisable to withdraw the ammunition in the hands of the scouts. Colonel Carr now thought that it was more judicious to have a plain talk with them, and assume an air of confidence. No overt act had been committed by any of them, and in past years they had accompanied the troops on innumerable scouts, exhibiting at all times courage, untiring energy and vigilance. The object of the expedition was explained and the ammunition restored to all the scouts.

Sergeant Mose was selected to precede the command and notify the Indians that no hostile action was contemplated, and that the only purpose was to have Nockay dot Klinne come to the post. Mose carried out his instructions faithfully.

Next morning the command toiled slowly up the narrow trail on the top of the canyon and crossed the divide. Upon arriving in the valley of the Cibicu the scouts took the trail leading along the creek, but Colonel Carr chose the fork along the high open ground. While still several miles from the Medicine Man's camp, Sanchez, a well-known chief, rode out of the creek bottom, shook hands with the officers at the head of the column and then calmly and deliberately rode down the line counting the men. He then turned his pony and galloped back to the creek which, at this point, ran between low bluffs and hills. This was the first and only suspicious act noticed by anyone.

The column marched steadily forward and turned into the bottom, crossing the stream not far from the Medicine Man's "*wicky-up.*" Officers and men had all been cautioned to be in readiness for treachery, but the Medicine Man surrendered so readily that the warning seemed unnecessary. Colonel Carr directed the interpreter to state plainly that Nockay det Klinne and his family would be taken to the post and no harm was intended to them, but if any attempt at rescue was made the Medicine Man would be killed.

Lieutenant Thomas Cruse, who commanded the scouts, was directed to take charge of the prisoners with the guard, and follow in the column between Troops D and E. Colonel Carr, with his staff, then led the way across the creek by a different trail from the one used in going over. This trail led through high willows and underbrush, and it was not discovered, until too late to rectify the mistake, that Lieutenant Cruse had missed the entrance to the crossing and was going down the opposite side of the lower crossing, followed by Troop E.

THE WOUNDED MEN WERE RESCUED BY LIEUTENANT CARTER

Colonel Carr selected an excellent camp sight and the packs were taken off, the horses of Troop D were turned out under the herd guard and the usual preparations made for camping in a country where tents were seldom used.

At this time it was observed that mounted Indians were coming up the creek from the gulches which the column had avoided, and that they were collecting around the Medicine Man's guard. When the guard crossed the creek and was about entering the limits of the camp, Colonel Carr told Captain E. C. Hentig to quietly warn the Indians away from the camp, and directed Lieutenant W. H. Carter, regimental quartermaster, to separate the scouts and put them in camp. These two officers walked only a few paces to where the Indians were.

Lieutenant Carter called the scouts and directed Sergeant "Dead Shot" to put them in camp. The scouts left the other Indians, but appeared uneasy and demurred about camping because of numerous hills of large red ants, common to all parts of Arizona. The scouts arranged themselves at intervals along the crest of the "*mesa*," or tableland, which had been selected as a camp ground.

Captain Hentig passed a few yards beyond the scouts and called out to the Indians, to all of whom he was well known through his five years of service at Camp Apache, "*Ukashe*," which means "Go away." As he raised his hand to motion to them, a half-witted young buck fired and gave the war cry. The long-delayed explosion took place at the moment when the men on foot had been warned not to show any signs of expecting a fight.

Captain Hentig and his orderly, who was between him and Lieutenant Carter, fell at the first volley, but the bodies of the wounded men were rescued by Lieutenant Carter and carried to the rear. The dismounted men of Troop D seized their arms; the small headquarters guard, engaged in putting up a tent for Colonel Carr, advanced on the scouts with brave Sergeant Alonzo Bowman in the lead, and opened fire. At this time there were more than 100 Indians besides the scouts in camp, and less than forty dismounted men engaged in a hand-to-hand conflict.

Colonel Carr walked calmly towards the position just vacated by the mutinous scouts and called firmly to the guard. "Kill the Medicine Man!" Sergeant McDonald, who was in charge of the guard, fired, wounding Nockay det Klinne through both thighs, but the sergeant was immediately shot by the scouts. The Medicine Man and his squaw endeavoured to reach the scouts, the Messiah calling loudly to the Indians to fight, for if he was killed he would come to life again.

Lieutenant Carter's orderly trumpeter was going towards the guard with a saddle kit, and when Colonel Carr called he drew his revolver, thrusting the muzzle into the mouth of the yelling Medicine Man, and fired. The squaw was allowed to pass out of the camp chanting a weird death song in her flight.

The scouts and other Indians were promptly driven from the immediate vicinity. Lieutenant Stanton, whose troop had been at the rear of the column, was just forming line mounted, when the fight began, and as the scouts drew off into the underbrush the troop was dismounted and charged through the bottom, driving the Indians out at the other side of the creek.

Sanchez and a few followers shot the herder nearest the stream, and with wild yells stampeded such horses as had been turned loose. The mules still had on their *aparajos* and remained quietly standing in the midst of all the turmoil around them until the packers were ordered by the quartermaster to take them to the bottom for protection.

There was but a moment's respite during the retreat of the Indians to the neighboring hills. The command was immediately disposed to resist the attack, which commenced as soon as the Indians had gotten to cover in their new positions.

Colonel Carr had but three officers, Lieutenants Stanton, Carter and Cruse, and the small size of the command required everyone on the firing line. Assistant Surgeon McCreery was kept busy with the wounded, whom he attended under fire with perfect composure and courage. The loss in this fight was Captain Hentig and six men killed. That the loss was no more was due in a great measure to the coolness and courage of Colonel Carr.

A situation better calculated to try the mettle of a command could scarcely be imagined. Having effected the object of the march—the arrest of a notorious and mischief-making Medicine Man—without difficulty, and with no resistance on the part of his people, the troops had set about making ramp for the night, when suddenly they were fired upon, not alone by the friends of the Medicine Man, but by their own allies, the Indian scouts, who had hitherto been loyal. The confusion and dismay which such an attack at such a time necessarily caused might well have resulted in the annihilation of the entire force, and constituted a situation from which nothing but the most consummate skill and bravery could pluck safety.

When darkness settled over the field the dead were buried in a single grave prepared inside of Colonel Carr's tent. The burial party and a few men who could be spared from the firing line stood about the grave with bared heads while Colonel Carr recited the burial service. As the last sad notes of "taps" died away the column prepared to return to the post, toward which small parties of Indians had been seen going all through the afternoon.

Before leaving the field Colonel Carr sent Lieutenant Carter to examine the body of the Medicine Man and determine if life was extinct. Strange to say, notwithstanding his wounds, he was still alive. The recovery of this Indian, if left in the hands of his friends, would have given him a commanding influence over these superstitious people, which would have resulted in endless war. Colonel Carr then repeated the order for his death, specifying that no more shots should be fired. Guide Burns was directed to carry out the order with the understanding that a knife was to be used. Burns, fearing failure, took an axe and crushed the forehead of the deluded fanatic, and from this time forward every person murdered by these Apaches was treated in a similar manner.

The column then started and inarched all night, arriving at the post during the next afternoon. Many of the Indians had preceded the command, and all night they were haranguing in the vicinity. They covered the roads and trails, and killed a number of citizens, besides the mail carrier and three soldiers coming from duty at the ferry on Black River.

On the following morning, September 1st, the Indians burned some buildings in the vicinity, and in the afternoon attacked the post, but were driven off. Captain Gordon was wounded during this attack while at the corner of the main parade.

There was much in the situation to produce gloomy forebodings, not for the safety of the post, but for that of the scattered settlers. There were not enough troops in Arizona to handle a general outbreak, and it could not be determined just what tribes were implicated in the revolt. The first thing necessary was to open communication. This was accomplished by sending Lieutenant Stanton, with thirty-three men, to Fort Thomas. That part of the road which was in the mountains was covered in the night, and the balance of the seventy miles was made during the following day. Colonel Carr's command had been reported for several days as massacred, and the papers of the entire country were filled with dire forebodings as to the results of this outbreak. The news carried by Lieutenant Stanton was the first to lift the clouds from the grief-stricken relatives and friends of the Fort Apache garrison.

First Lieutenant, William H. Carter, Sergeant Alonzo Bowman and Private Richard Heartery were awarded the Medal of Honour.

Treachery of the Scouts Avenged

THOMAS CRUSE

There was great rejoicing when the report, spread by the treacherous Apaches, that they had killed the entire command of Colonel E. A. Carr was contradicted, yet the loss was severe enough to keep public indignation alive and arouse a demand from all parts of the country that the traitors and their allies be punished. This caused the expedition of 1882, of which Second Lieutenant Thomas Cruse, Sixth United States Cavalry, gives a full and graphic narration in the following:

"The spring of '82 saw us still out in the field after the hostiles. But in June they all appeared to have gone into the deep recesses of the mountains of Old Mexico, many miles below the line; so that the Fourth of July was spent at our post, Fort Apache, and was celebrated in befitting style with horse racing, wrestling, running, target matches, etc. The morning of the 9th of July, however, brought a telegram stating that a band of hostiles had dashed into San Carlos, killed the chief of scouts, several Indian policemen, friendly Indians and all the white people that could be found in that vicinity, except the agent.

"The telegram also stated that the hostiles had started toward Tonto Basin, and directed us to march toward Cibicu

Creek and try to intercept them when they crossed the Black River. We were further notified that two companies of the Third Cavalry, from Fort Thomas, were after them, and that one troop of the Sixth, with a company of Indian scouts from Fort McDowell, under Captain Chaffee, had been ordered to watch them from the west and intercept them, if possible. The command, consisting of Troops E and I of the Third, and Troops E and K of the Sixth U. S. Cavalry, under Major Evans of the Third Cavalry, left the post that day.

"On the morning of the 16th, on one of the small branches of the Black River, fresh signs of the Indians were found, and that night, about 8 o'clock, while we were encamped, we were much surprised to hear that Captain Chaffee with his troop from McDowell was only about a mile away. Word was sent to him and he came and had a consultation with Major Evans. It was decided that it was highly probable that the Indians would be overtaken the next day, and would probably tight. Chaffee was ordered to break camp, at his own suggestion, very early in the morning and attempt to climb the precipitous bluffs which surround the country, called Tonto Basin, and the main command was to follow on, after he found the Indians.

"This program was carried out, and about 11 o'clock word was sent back that the Indians had been located and were evidently waiting for us. We were much amazed to hear this, because the Apaches never fight unless they have every advantage on their side, and then they become the most dangerous foe of any of the Indians. A year or two later this was explained to me by one of the men who was in the fight by saying that their scouts, whom they had left in the rear on the trail, had seen Chaffee's troop, which was mounted on white horses, and had determined to prepare an ambuscade for it, knowing full well the small number of men he had, but being in ignorance of the fact that re-enforcements were in the vicinity, as they had never seen Major Evans's command.

"Five troops now moved forward at a gallop and soon came up to the spot where the Indians were waiting. Their place was certainly well chosen, it being where the trail which led from the Apache Reservation to the Navajo Reservation crossed over a deep crack in the earth—a branch of the celebrated Canyon Diablo. This country is near the celebrated Colorado Canyon, and abounds in cracks and ravines of volcanic origin, which are absolutely impassable for men. The troops were ordered to advance as quietly as possible within about a mile of the canyon and dismount.

"One troop, I, Third Cavalry, commanded by Lieutenant Converse, was deployed along the bank to fire at the Indians and attract their attention, while two troops were sent around to either flank, with the idea of getting on the other side of the canyon and capturing the redskins, or at least holding them so that they could not get away. This arrangement brought Troops E and I of the Sixth Cavalry together on the right flank, and Troop D of the Third and K of the Sixth on the left.

"E was my own troop, commanded by Captain Adam Kramer, an officer of the War of the Rebellion and hero of many an Indian fight. Major Evans now turned the actual command of the forces over to Captain Chaffee, who certainly was the right man in the right place. The Indians opened fire at about 3:30 o'clock in the afternoon. Troop I lined the edge of the canyon and replied, and the other four troops moved off quietly and rapidly to get across the numerous obstacles in their way, one of which was the canyon, apparently a stone's throw across, but about 300 or 400 feet deep.

"I remember as we crossed it we found a nice stream of water, and someone glanced up and remarked that the stars were shining, although it was still early in the afternoon. The task that was set before us was one that taxed our energies to the utmost, but finally, about 5 o'clock, we succeeded in getting across this canyon and to the right and rear of the Indians; and then the fun began. Troop I ran into their pony herd, killed the herders and captured the entire lot. Up to this time the Indians apparently were not aware of our presence, and had started in to make a counter attack on Troop I, but our fire on

I TOLD HIM TO LIE QUIET

their flanks soon brought to their mind the fact that there was somebody else there, and they began to fight for some way to get out and escape.

"Troop E was deployed near the edge of the canyon, and it was my good luck to have command of the left wing and to fall in with Al Seiber, one of the most noted scouts and guides in Arizona and New Mexico. I had been in several fights before this, but never found them very exciting affairs, as the Apache is not given to exposing himself for theatrical effect like the Sioux and the Cheyenne, but merely keeps behind a rock, well hidden, waiting a chance to kill without taking any chance whatever himself.

"On this occasion, however, as we advanced it became absolutely necessary for them to get out of the entrenchments they had hastily prepared and run, and for the first time I had a chance to shoot at something as well as to be shot at, Seiber, who was on my immediate left, would call out once in a while: 'There he goes!' and would raise his rifle and shoot, and sure enough, an Indian would jump up from behind a rock, not more than 150 yards away, and, with a shriek, throw up his hands and fall. Directly they began running in bunches and things became highly exciting. I called on my men to advance, saying that some of these Indians were my scouts and now was our chance to get even with them for their treachery of the year before. With this idea in mind, I, with eight or ten men, started across a small ravine, beyond which we could see the main camp of the Indians.

"As I started through the forest, which was park like and with no undergrowth, I was very much amazed at hearing Seiber call out after me: 'Lieutenant, don't go through there; that place is full of Indians!' But it was too late; I thought all the Indians in that part of the field had been killed, so we went—Sergeant Horan, Blacksmith Martin and six or eight privates of troop E, right after me.

"We got into their camp after firing several shots, and saw some of them run; when suddenly, about ten feet away, two Indians raised up slightly above the level of the ground and shot at me. I thought at the time I was hit, and Captain Kramer called out: 'I am afraid they have got Cruse.' So I judge from that, I must have dropped pretty quickly. At the same time Private McClellan, who was about two feet from me, went down in a heap also. The Indians dropped back behind a rocky ledge and were pretty well concealed. I called out to McClellan: 'Are you hurt?', and he answered—'Yes, I think my arm is broken.' I told him to lie quiet so that the Indians could not get another shot at him and that I would watch them.

"I got in a shot or two, then Blacksmith Martin came to my assistance and we succeeded in getting McClellan out of way of the Indians. In the meantime they had apparently sprung up on three or four sides of us, and things were very lively in that vicinity for the next five or ten minutes. During that time Sergeant Conn, of our troop, was shot through the neck and several other casualties occurred. As nearly as could be it was a hand-to-hand conflict all around, and when the melee was ended it was dark and I did not see any more Indians and began to think about getting across the Canyon to our pack-train.

"Private McClellan proved to be worse hurt than we supposed, for the bullet, in addition to breaking his arm, had gone through his chest, and he died about 11 o'clock that night.

"We squared up with those treacherous Apache scouts however. Four of them were hung at Fort Grant, Arizona; four more were sent to Alcratraz Island and five or six were killed in the fight I speak of."

During the attack First Sergeant Charles Taylor, Troop D. Third United States Cavalry, displayed the most wonderful bravery. He advanced far ahead of his comrades and in a cool and deliberate manner picked out one brave after another, killing them by his unfailing accuracy as he advanced amidst howls and shrieks.

Troop I, Sixth United States Cavalry, at one time of the fight was in a threatening position. It had crossed a deep canyon and was crawling up a steep cliff on the northern side, when

FRANK WEST

bands of Indians suddenly appeared on all sides. The men were retreating toward the bottom of the canyon, when First Lieutenant Frank West rallied them and successfully outflanked the Indians.

During this movement an interesting incident occurred, which Second Lieutenant George H. Morgan, of the Third Cavalry, who volunteered to go with the detachment of Lieutenant West, tells interestingly as follows:

"By crossing the canyon it was a hard, dangerous climb both down and up, and when at the top we found that the mesa ended at the side of the canyon by a ledge of rock, probably six feet high. The top was defended by a small force of renegade Apache skirmishers.

"Forming our men below the ledge, they were ordered to jump over and take to the nearest tree. After seeing all the men move forward I followed and dropped down behind my tree, selected before I started. By a natural and excusable mistake six of my men had chosen the same tree. It was not the largest there, but we were all safe, as owing to the disinclination of the men to expose themselves the Indians could not hit us, their bullets hitting the tree about three feet above the ground.

"The men, however, were uneasy, there being so little tree and so much of a crowd, and without a word all jumped up and ran back, fortunately without loss. As it was safer, and a good place, I crawled up to my vacated tree. A chief just in front of and very close to me—thirty feet—thinking the entire party had gone, sprang out from his cover and commenced a war dance. After stopping his play in short order, I became anxious to know how far back my party had gone, and went back with much haste and little dignity. I was glad

SIX OF MY MEN HAD CHOSEN THE SAME TREE

to find the men under the ledge cool enough and wondering where I was. We tried the advance again and in better form, and gained the top."

The chase after these Indians had been so energetically conducted that during the night following and the next morning there were twelve cavalry troops assembled on the scene from four posts—a remarkable concentration of scouting columns all in search of the same marauders.

The scouts crossed the canyon and found the hostiles had fled, abandoning everything and leaving six prisoners in the hands of the troops and sixteen dead bodies upon the field. A severe hail-storm set in, lasting four hours, which covered the trail so completely as to prevent pursuit. The troops remained two days near the scene of the fight. Litters were made and the wounded transported by hand eight miles back to the open country, where ambulances could reach them.

Seventy horses and much camp plunder were captured. Among the dead were two of the renegade scouts who mutinied in the Cibicu fight. The troops lost one man killed, seven wounded, and two officers of the Third Cavalry, Lieutenants Converse and Morgan, wounded. The rugged nature of this part of the Mongollon Mountains prevented the hostiles from being again brought to bay, and they escaped to the various Indian camps about the reservations where they were secreted by their kindred.

Chasing Geronimo and Natchez

The surrender of Geronimo and Natchez, the leading chiefs of the Apaches, concluded the campaign of 1886. It marked the closing of a long and tedious war with the Apaches who had terrorized the whole southern part of Arizona and northern part of Mexico and restored peace and prosperity to the inhabitants of a vast stretch of territory of two republics. Of all Indian savages the Apache is known to be the most brutal, unruly and barbarous. His treachery is proverbial, his cruelty notorious.

The young Apache warrior could not hope to command the respect of his tribe unless he had accomplished a "heroic" deed. This consisted of an outrage upon some hostile Indian, an American or Mexican ranchman, or a lone traveller. The more cruel the act, the greater the "heroism"; the more "heroic" deeds, the greater the honour and respect among his own people. This principle inculcated in the child, actuated the youthful warrior and was practiced by the old and experienced. It made the Apaches the most dreaded and feared of all Indian races.

In 1886 General Miles was called upon to subdue these turbulent and desperate bands and restore order in the territory mentioned.

The mountainous character of the country furnished these murderous savages with innumerable places of hiding and refuge and rendered them extremely difficult to get at. Many expeditions and campaigns had been previously under taken and failed before the seemingly insurmountable obstacles. In preparing for his campaign General Miles was determined to chase and hound these hostiles and keep chasing and hounding them and not let up on them until sheer exhaustion should force them into final subjection.

It was to be a war to the finish between the white man's perseverance and endurance and the same qualities of the redskin, the outcome of which, General Miles figured, would inevitably be in favour of the better equipped and infinitely more intelligent white man.

There was not the slightest doubt in General Miles's mind that the Apaches could be subdued, and in assuming the command of the Department of Arizona he selected such officers for the discharge of important missions and duties as agreed with him on the general proposition and were sufficiently energetic to carry out the common idea.

Then the general formulated a definite and systematic plan of campaign, re organized the troops, restored the confidence of the men, infused new hope into the minds of the timid ranchers and brought order out of the chaos.

For the first time in the history of American military operations General Miles during this year made use of the heliostat and adopted the system of heliographic messages—signalling by mirrors—for the transmission of orders and reports of the movements of the hostile Indians.

Experiments with this system, invented by an English officer some twenty years before, had been previously made by American generals, but it was not finally adopted and practically used until General Miles conducted his Apache campaign in 1886. Stations were established on the highest peaks of the mountains all over the country. Thus the movements of the savages were kept under constant observation, and much time, money and labour were saved in unnecessary and long and tedious marches in search of the elusive enemy. One more word about the Apaches.

General Miles described them as follows:

They were vicious and outlaws of the worst class. They were clad in such a way as to disguise themselves as much as possible.

Masses of grass, bunches of weeds, twigs or small boughs were fastened under their hat bands very profusely, and also upon their shoulders and backs. Their clothing was trimmed in such a way that when lying upon the ground in a bunch of grass or at the head of a ravine, it was almost impossible to discover them. It was in this way that they were wont to commit their worst crimes. An unsuspecting ranchman or miner going along a road or trail would pass within a few feet of these concealed Apaches, and the first intimation he would have of their presence would be a bullet through his heart or brain.

The campaign began in the latter part of April. The Apaches themselves made the first move. They boldly left the mountain fastnesses in the Sierra Madres and came clown upon the terror-stricken people of Northern Mexico. Among the first outrages committed was that of which the Peck family became victims. The sad story is told by Captain Leonard Wood, assistant surgeon, United States Army, in short but graphic words as follows:

Peck's ranch was surrounded by Indians, the entire family was captured, and several of the farmhands were killed. The husband was tied up and compelled to witness indescribable tortures inflicted upon his wife until she died. The terrible ordeal rendered him temporarily insane and as the Apaches, like most Indians, stand in great awe of an insane person, they set him free as soon as they discovered his mental condition; but otherwise he would never have been allowed to live. He was afterward found by his friends wandering about the place.

The family had two daughters, one of whom was outraged and shared the fate of her mother; the other, a little girl of ten years, was dragged upon the back of a horse and carried away into captivity. She was recaptured. On their flight through Mexican territory the Apaches met a force of seventy Mexicans. A volley was fired, killing an Indian woman, and the Indian who carried the child was wounded. This Indian's horse was shot at the same time. The little girl bravely ran away from her savage captor and was picked up by the jubilant Mexicans. The Indian retreated towards the rocks and there stood off the entire Mexican force, killing seven of them, each of whom was shot through the head. He then made his escape. On another occasion the hordes rode through a wood choppers camp and killed seven white men. Another time they crept stealthily into a small creek and murdered five Mexican placer miners.

Many other instances of the most reckless brutality and cruelty marked the opening of the campaign.

The command which was selected by General Miles for the expedition was placed in charge of Captain Henry W. Lawton, Fourth United States Cavalry, and composed of the best officers and men available. Troops were frequently changed and pro visions made for fresh transports to replace the tired and worn-out horses and pack-mules.

The pursuit of the Indians was now taken up and continued with untiring per severance. Over prairies, mountains, through valleys, across streams and thundering rapids, now about the peaks of giant mountains, now way down through canyons deep and narrow, wherever the trail of the Indians led the command fo lowed. The Indians would pass straight over the highest ranges of the roughest mountains, abandon their horses and descend to the valleys below, where they would supply themselves with fresh animals by stealing them; the soldiers would send their horses around the impassable heights, climb the ascent on foot and slide down the descent.

They would suffer from cold on the peaks and from an almost intolerable heat in the depths of the canyons. On one occasion the command marched twenty-six hours without a halt and was without water for eighteen hours in the intense heat of that season. The Indians were driven from one place to another, from Arizona to Mexico, with the tenacious troops clinging to their heels.

There was an agreement with the Mexican Republic and the government at Washington by virtue of which United States troops could enter Mexican territory when in pursuit of hostile Indians, so that in this campaign the boundary line between the two republics created no obstacles.

LIEUTENANT CLARK DASHED AMONG THE HOWLING APACHES

Several times the Indians were brought to bay and forced to fight, for example, in the Finite Mountains, in Sonora, Mexico, May 3, 1886, where in the midst of the battle Lieutenant Powhatan H. Clark, Tenth United States Cavalry, dashed among the howling Apaches and at the peril of his own young life snatched from them a corporal who had been wounded and fallen into their hands.

The dash was made well in advance of his troopers, who were themselves so busily engaged in keeping the hostiles at bay that they had not noticed the absence of their comrade. Clark's intrepidity and exceptional courage displayed by dashing among the savages, firing as he advanced and killing several of the hostiles before he reached the place where the corporal was lying, prevented the massacre of the man before the eyes of his own comrades.

The hostiles were badly defeated. Again twelve days later at Santa Cruz, Sonora, another engagement took place in which Sergeant Samuel H. Craig, of the Fourth United States Cavalry, was severely wounded, but nevertheless fought in the front ranks of the troops and with blood-covered face led a most gallant charge. The Indians were compelled to flee for their lives and leave the entire camp in the hands of the troops.

For three long months this inexorable chase was kept up until on July 13th the last and decisive blow was struck on the Yaqui River in Sonora in a section of the country that was almost impassable for man or beast.

Geronimo and Natchez evidently considered themselves safe from all attack, but Captain Lawton, by skilful manoeuvring, managed to surprise the whole camp and seize everything in sight, the Indians themselves having a very narrow escape from capture.

The savages now were tired of being the hunted game of the United States soldiers and yearned for peace. Geronimo especially was willing to submit to the inevitable and sent two of his women to open negotiations. He agreed to an unconditional surrender, begging only that he and his followers lives be spared.

This was promised. And thus Geronimo, the dreaded Apache chief, became a prisoner. He remained loyal, too, for when on the return march the command met a large Mexican force, which assumed a threatening attitude, and could have rendered the situation critical enough to make the outcome doubtful, Geronimo and his Apaches stuck to the command, and so eager were they to assist those to whom they had surrendered only a short time before that a clash between them and the Mexicans was narrowly avoided.

On September 3rd Geronimo surrendered to General Miles in person at Skeleton Canyon, whither the commander had journeyed to join Captain Lawton's camp.

Natchez still refused to come in, but General Miles brought about his surrender by a stroke of clever diplomacy, which had worked wonders on a former occasion.

He overawed Geronimo with the marvels of the white man's civilization. Among other things he showed him the heliostat and explained to him that by means of the instrument he could talk and receive information hundreds of miles away.

At the request of the superstitious Indian warrior the general inquired concerning the health of a brother of Geronimo, who was held a captive at a distant military post.

When the young chief had received the news he had asked for he was more terror-stricken than surprised, and sent a messenger to Natchez urging him to surrender, "as the white man was in league with powers strange and weird, and which he was not able to understand."

Natchez, perhaps glad to have a pretext to give up the hopeless and unequal struggle, followed the advice and surrendered on the same terms as Geronimo. His capture ended the Apache war.

Hazardous, But Successful

MARION P. MAUS

An interesting account of the hardships and ad ventures which our troops had to contend with during the memorable campaign of 1886 against, the hostile Apaches under Geronimo and Natchez is vividly described by Lieutenant-Colonel Marion P. Maus, then a first lieutenant of the First United States Infantry.

His excellent soldierly qualities were instrumental in several instances during this campaign in extricating the troops to which he was attached from dangerous positions in which they, owing to the nature of the extremely mountainous country, had fallen, and the undaunted courage and heroism which he displayed won for him the Medal of Honour.

Lieutenant-Colonel Maus narrates:

"Our command, fully equipped for field-service, left Apache, Arizona, on November 11, 1885, for Fort Here it was inspected by Lieutenant-General Sheridan and Brigadier-General Crook, and with words of encouragement from these officers the command started south by way of the Dragoon Mountains, endeavouring to find the trail of a band of Indians who were returning to Mexico after a raid into the United States.

"Thoroughly scouting through these mountains without finding the trail, we went on to the border and crossed into Mexico twenty miles north of the town of Fronteras, with the object of pursuing the renegades to their haunts in southern Sonora. We believed that if we could trace this band we could find the entire hostile camp under Geronimo and Natchez. Under instructions from Captain Crawford, I preceded the command to the town of Fronteras to notify the *presidente* of the town of our approach, of our object in coming, and to gain information. It was a small place, composed of the usual adobe buildings, and its people lived in a constant state of alarm about the movements of the hostiles. The command arriving, we proceeded to Nocarasi, a small mining town in the Madre Mountains. On account of the roughness of these mountains we found great difficulty in crossing them with the pack-train. We found one horse which had evidently been abandoned by the hostiles, but no distinct trail.

"In marching the command it was interesting to notice the methods adopted by our Indians in scouting the country to gain information and prevent surprise. It illustrated to us very clearly what we must expect from the hostiles, who would employ the same methods. It was impossible to march these scouts as soldiers, or to control them as such, nor was it deemed advisable to attempt it. Among them were many who had bloody records; one named Dutchy had killed, in cold blood, a white man near Fort Thomas, and for this murder the civil authorities were at this time seeking to arrest him.

"Their system of advance guards and flankers was perfect, and as soon as the command went into camp, outposts were at once put out, guarding every approach. All this was done noiselessly and in secret, and without giving a single order. As scouts for a command in time of war they would be ideal. Small of stature, and apparently no match physically for the white man, yet when it came to climbing mountains or making long marches, they were swift and tireless. The little clothing they wore consisted of a soldier's blouse, discarded in time of action, light undergarments and a waist cloth, and on the march the blouse was often turned inside out to show only the gray lining.

"Nothing escaped their watchful eyes as they marched silently in their *moccasined* feet. By day small fires were built of dry wood to avoid smoke, and at night they were made in hidden places so as to be invisible. If a high point was in view, you could be sure that a scout had crawled to the summit and, himself unseen, with a glass or his keen eyes had searched the country around. At night only was the watch relaxed, for these savages dread the night with a superstitious fear.

"It was necessary to allow them their way, and we followed, preserving order as best we could by exercising tact and a careful study of their habits. Under the influence of mescal, which is a liquor made in all parts of Mexico and easily procured, they often became violent and troublesome, and we could not help realizing how perfectly we were in their power. However, no distrust of them was shown. One of my Indians, a sergeant named Rubie, followed me one day while I was hunting. I thought his actions were curious, but they were explained when he suddenly came from the front and told me to go back. He had seen the footprints of hostiles nearby. In the action which followed later he came to me and warned me to cover. There was, however, very little evidence of affection or gratitude in them as a class.

"Continuing the march, we reached the town of Huasavas, in the valley of the Bavispe. Orange and lemon trees were filled with golden fruit, although it was now the 22nd of December. This valley, surrounded by high mountains, was fertile, though but little cultivated. The only vehicles in use were carts, the wheels of which were sections sawed from logs. The ploughs were pieces of pointed wood. The people were devoid of all the comforts of life. Corn flour was obtained by pounding the grains on stones. They were a most desolate people, and completely terrorized by the Apaches, who were a constant menace to them, as they were to the inhabitants of all these towns.

"Here occurred the first serious trouble with the Indian scouts. One of them, who was drunk but unarmed, was shot by a Mexican policeman. At the time I was on my way to the town and met the Indian, who was running down the road towards me, followed by two policemen or guards firing rapidly. One ball passed through his head, coming out through the jaw. The other Indian scouts were much incensed, and at once began to prepare for an attack on the town, giving us much trouble before we were able to stop them.

"The officers were unable to sleep that night, as many of the Indians had been drinking and continued to be so angry that they fired off their rifles in the camp. The next day I released one of them from prison, and subsequently had to pay a fine of five dollars for him. It was claimed by the Mexicans that the Indians had committed some breach of the peace.

"Here we got the first reliable news of the hostiles who were murdering people and killing cattle to the south. Crossing the mountains we passed the towns of Granadas and Bacedahuachi, the latter being the site of one of the fine old missions built by the daring priests who had sought to plant their religion among the natives many years before.

"Proceeding on our way over a mountainous country, we finally came to the town of Nacori. This place was in a continual state of alarm, a wall having been built around it as a protection against the Apaches, the very name of whom was a terror. From our camp, sixteen miles south of this town, two of our pack-trains were sent back to Lang's Ranch, New Mexico, for supplies. To our surprise a Deputy United States Marshal from Tombstone came here to arrest Dutchy.

"Captain Crawford declined to permit the arrest, and in a letter to the marshal asked him to delay the arrest till I may be near the border where protection for myself, officers and white men, with my pack-trains, may be afforded by United States troops other than Indians, offering to return if desired. The scouts were intensely excited, and under the circumstances the marshal did not wish to attempt to arrest Dutchy, and returned without delay.

"We had now penetrated over 200 miles into the mountains of Mexico, and we were sure the hostiles were near. It was decided to move immediately in pursuit of them. In this wild and unknown land even our Indians looked more stolid and serious. One by one they gathered together for a medicine dance. The Medicine Man, Noh-wah-zhe-tah, unrolled the sacred buckskin he had worn since he left Fort Apache. There was something very solemn in all this. The dance, the marching, the kneeling before the sacred buckskin as each pressed his lips to it and the old man blessed him. impressed us too, as we looked on in silence.

"Afterward the Indians held a council. They said they meant to do their duty, and would prove that they would fight to those who said they would not, and they seemed very much in earnest. I am satisfied that they desired to get the hostiles to surrender, but do not believe they intended or desired to kill them—their own people. In view of their relations it was little wonder that they felt in this way.

"It was decided that all must go on foot, and that officer and scout alike must carry his own blanket, all else being left behind. Leaving a few scouts (the weakest and the sick) to guard the camp, a force of seventy-nine was equipped with twelve days rations, carried on three or four of the toughest mules best suited for the purpose, and we started forward. We marched to the Haros River, which we forded, and then ascending the high hills beyond discovered first a small trail, then a large well-beaten one, evidently that of the entire band of hostiles.

"The trail was about six days old, and as we passed over it, here and there, the carcasses of cattle only partially used, were found. The hostiles had but a short time previously moved their camp from the junction of the Haros and Yaqui Rivers, a few miles to the west, and were going to the east to the fastnesses of some extremely rugged mountains, the Espinosa del Diablo, or the Devil's Backbone—a most appropriate name, as the country was broken and rough beyond description. The march was now conducted mostly by night. We suffered much from the cold, and the one blanket to each man used when we slept was scanty covering.

"Often it was impossible to sleep at all. At times we made our coffee and cooked our food in the daytime, choosing points where the light could not be seen, and using dry wood to avoid smoke. Our *moccasins* were thin and the rocks were hard on the feet. Shoes had been abandoned, as the noise made by them could be heard a long distance. The advance scouts kept far ahead.

"Several abandoned camps of the hostiles were found, the selection of which showed their constant care. They were placed on high points, to which the hostiles ascended in such a way that it was impossible for them to be seen; while in descending, any pursuing party would have to appear in full view of the lookout they always kept in the rear. The labour of the Indian women in bringing the water and wood to these points was no apparent objection.

"Crossing the Haros River the trail led direct to the Devil's Backbone, situated between the Haros and Satachi Rivers. The difficulties of marching over a country like this by night, where it was necessary to climb over rocks and to descend into deep and dark canyons, can hardly be imagined. When we halted, which was sometimes not until midnight, we were sore and tired. We could never move until late in the day, as it was necessary to examine the country a long distance ahead before we started. No human being seemed ever to have been here. Deer were plentiful, but we dared not shoot them. Once I saw a leopard that bounded away with a shriek. It was spotted and seemed as large as a tiger.

"At last, after a weary march, at sunset, on the 9th of January, 1886, Noche, our Indian sergeant-major and guide, sent word that the hostile camp was located twelve miles away.

"The command was halted, and as the hostiles were reported camped on a high point, well protected and apparently showing great caution on their part, it was decided to make a night march and attack them at daylight. A short halt of about twenty minutes was made. We did not kindle a fire, and about the only food we had was some hard bread and raw bacon. The medical officer, Dr. Davis, was worn out, and the interpreter also, unfortunately, could go no farther.

"We had already marched continuously for about six hours and were very much worn out and foot sore, even the scouts showing the fatigue of the hard service. These night marches, when we followed a trail purposely made over the worst country possible, and crossing and re-crossing the turbulent river, which we had to ford, were very trying. But the news of the camp being so close at hand gave us new strength and hope, and we hastened on to cover the ten or twelve miles between us and the hostiles. I cannot easily forget that night's march.

"All night long we toiled on, feeling our way. It was a dark and moonless night. For much of the distance the way led over solid rock, over mountains, down canyons so dark they seemed bottomless. It was a wonder the scouts could find the trail. Sometimes the descent became so steep that we could not go forward, but would have to wearily climb back and find another way. I marched by poor Captain Crawford, who was badly worn out; often he stopped and leaned heavily on his rifle for support, and again he used it for a cane to assist him. He had, however, an unconquerable will, and kept slowly on.

"At last, when it was nearly daylight, we could see in the distance the dim outlines of the rocky position occupied by the hostiles. I had a strong feeling of relief, for I certainly was very tired. We had marched continuously eighteen hours over a country so difficult that when we reached their camp Geronimo said he felt that he had no longer a place where the white man would not pursue him.

"The command was now quickly disposed for an attack, our first object being to surround the hostile camp. I was sent around to the farther side. Noiselessly, scarcely breathing, we crept along. It was still dark. It seemed strange to be going to attack these Indians with a force of their own kindred who but a short time before had been equally as criminal. I had nearly reached the farther side, intending to cut off the retreat, when the braying of some burros was heard. These watch-dogs of an Indian camp are better than were the geese of Rome. I hurried along.

"The faint light of the morning was just breaking, and I held my breath for fear the alarm would be given, when all at once the flames bursting from the rifles of some of the hostiles who had gone to investigate the cause of the braying of the *burros*, and the echoing and re-echoing of the rifle reports through the mountains, told me that the camp was in arms. Dim forms could be seen rapidly descending the mountain sides and disappearing below. A large number came my way within easy range—less than 200 yards. We fired many shots, but I saw no one fall.

"One Indian attempted to ride by me on a horse; I fired twice at him, when he abandoned the horse and disappeared; the horse was shot, but I never knew what became of the Indian. We pursued for a time, but as few of our Indian scouts could have gone farther, we had to give up the pursuit. The hostiles, like so many quail, had disappeared among the rocks. One by one our scouts returned. We had captured the entire herd, all the camp effects and what little food they had. consisting of some *mescal*, some fresh pony meat, a small part of a deer and a little dried meat, which the scouts seized and began to devour. I had no desire for food. Everyone was worn out and it was cold and damp.

"In a little while an Indian woman came in and said that Geronimo and Natchez desired to talk. She begged food, and left us bearing word that Captain Crawford would see the chiefs the next day. The conference was to be held about a mile away on the river below our position, and he desired me to be present. What would have been the result of this conference will never be known on account of the unfortunate attack of the Mexicans next day. It was fortunate that we occupied the strong position of the hostile camp. Our packs, as well as the doctor and interpreter, had been sent for. hut unfortunately they did not arrive that night.

"We built fires and tried to obtain a little rest, but I could not sleep on account of the intense cold, and, besides, we had been without food for many hours; in fact, we had not partaken of cooked food for days. With the continual marching day and night no wonder our Indians were tired out, and now threw themselves among the rocks to sleep, failing to maintain their usual vigilance. We had no fear of an attack.

"At daylight next morning the camp was aroused by loud cries from some of our scouts. Lieutenant Shipp and I, with a white man named Horn, employed as chief of scouts for my companies, ran forward to ascertain the cause of alarm. We thought at first that the disturbance must have been occasioned by the scouts of Captain Wirt Davis. A heavy fog hung over the mountains, making the morning light very faint. But by ascending the rocks we could see the outlines of dusky forms moving in the distance.

"Then all at once there was a crash of musketry and the flames from many rifles lighted up the scene. In that discharge three of our scouts were wounded, one very badly, and we quickly sought cover. The thought that it was our own friends who were attacking us was agonizing, and we had not the heart to retaliate, but the scouts kept up a desultory fire until Captain Crawford, whom we had left lying by the camp fire, shouted to us to stop. In about fifteen minutes the firing ceased, and it now became known that the attacking party were Mexicans, a detachment of whom, about thirteen, were seen approaching, four of them coming toward the rocks where we were.

"As I spoke Spanish, I advanced about fifty or seventy-five yards to meet them and was followed by Captain Crawford. F told them who we were and of our fight with the hostiles, that we had just captured their camp, etc. Captain Crawford, who did not speak Spanish, now asked if I had explained all to them. I told him I had. At this time we were all standing within a few feet of each other.

"The officer commanding the Mexicans was Major Corredor, a tall, powerful man over six feet high, and he acted as spokesman. Looking to the rocks we could see the heads of many of our Indian scouts with their rifles ready, and could hear the sharp snap of the breech-blocks as the cartridges were inserted. I can well recall the expression on the faces of these Mexicans, for they thought our scouts were going to fire: indeed, I thought so myself. At the same time I noticed a party of Mexicans marching in a low ravine toward a high point which commanded and enfiladed our position, about 400 yards distant.

EARLY MORNING WORK FOR TROOPERS

"I called Captain Crawford's attention to this as well as to the aspect of our own scouts. He said: 'For God's sake, don't let them fire!' Major Corredor also said: '*No tiras*—Don't fire.'

"I said to him, 'No,' and told him not to let his men fire. I then turned to the scouts, saying in Spanish, 'Don't fire,' holding my hand toward them. They nearly all understood Spanish, while they did not speak it. I had taken a few steps forward to carry out the captain's instructions when one shot rang out distinct and alone; the echoes were such that I could not tell where it came from, but it sounded like a death-knell, and was followed by volleys from both sides.

"As we all sought cover I looked back just in time to see the tall Mexican throw down his rifle and fall, shot through the heart. Another Mexican, Lieutenant Juan de La Cruz, fell as he ran, pierced by thirteen bullets. The other two ran behind a small oak, but it was nearly cut down by bullets and they were both killed. Nine or ten others who were in view rapidly got close to the ground or in hollows behind rocks, which alone saved them, as they were near, and formed a portion of the party that advanced.

"Upon reaching the rocks where I had sought shelter I found Captain Crawford lying with his head pierced by a ball. His brain was running down his face and some of it lay on the rocks. He must have been shot just as he reached and mounted the rocks. Over his face lay a red handkerchief at which his hand clutched in a spasmodic way. Dutchy stood near him. I thought him dead, and sick at heart, I gave my attention to the serious conditions existing. The fall of Captain Crawford was a sad and unfortunate event, greatly to be deplored, and cast a gloom over us which we could not shake off.

"Being next in command, I hastened to send scouts to prevent the attack at tempted on our right above referred to, and after an interval of about two hours the Mexicans were entirely routed and the firing gradually ceased. They now occupied a strong line of hills, with excellent shelter, were double our strength, and were armed with 44-calibre Remington rifles, which carried a cartridge similar to our own. Our command was without rations and nearly without ammunition, the one beltful supplied to each scout having in many cases been entirely exhausted in the two fights. It was true that many of them had extra rounds, but I estimated that between 4,000 and 5,000 rounds had been fired and that some of the men had none left.

"The Mexicans now called to us saying they would like to talk, but they were too cautious to advance. When Mr. Horn and I went forward to talk to them, three or four advanced to meet us about 150 yards from our position. The brother of the lieutenant who had been killed was crying bitterly, and the whole party seemed a most forlorn company of men, and sincere in saying that they thought we were the hostiles. All their officers were killed, and I believe others besides, but how many we never knew. The fact that our command was composed almost entirely of Indians was a most unfortunate one. With regular soldiers all would have been clear.

"Our position at this time, confronted as we were by a hostile Mexican force, while behind us was the entire hostile band of Indians evidently enjoying the situation, is unparalleled. We had scarcely any ammunition, no food, and our supplies were with the pack-train almost unprotected—no one knew where—while we were many days march from our own country, which could only be reached through a territory hostile to our Indians. The governor of Sonora had made serious charges against the Indians for depredations committed on the march down, and besides, there was a bitter feeling caused by this fight. If the Mexicans had attacked us in the rear, where we were entirely unprotected, our position would have been untenable. Had such an attack been made the result would probably have been the scattering of our command in the mountains, our Chiricahuas joining the hostiles.

"It looked very serious, and my future course was governed by the condition. I was bound to protect the lives of the white men of the command, the pack-train, and our Indian scouts, if it were possible. Lieutenant Shipp and I were in accord, he appreciating as I did our desperate position. The first attack had been a mistake, and the second had been brought on before the Mexicans could know what had been said to their officers who had been killed.

"The Mexicans deplored the affair and seemed sincere. I felt a pity for them. They asked me to go with them while they carried their dead away. A small detail took the bodies one by one to their lines, and I went with each body. They then asked me to send our doctor to care for their wounded, and to loan them enough of the captured stock to carry their wounded back. I agreed to do this, but could give them no food, which they also asked. Late in the day the doctor arrived, and after he had attended to our wounded I sent him to look after theirs, some of whom were in a dangerous way. He attended five of them.

"The next day I decided to move on, as the surgeon said that the death of Captain Crawford was a matter of but a little time, and our condition made it necessary for us to try and reach our pack-train for supplies and ammunition. I was afraid that the Mexicans might take our pack-train, as it had but a poor escort of the weak and sick. Besides, most of the packers had been armed with 50-calibre carbines (Sharps), while they had been supplied with 45-calibre ammunition. I was in hopes that when away from the Mexicans I might succeed in effecting a conference with the hostile chiefs, and possibly a surrender.

"This could not be done while the Mexicans were near and they would not move before we did, as they said they were afraid they might be attacked by the scouts. In order to move Captain Crawford I had to make a litter and have him carried by hand. As there was no wood in the country, I sent to the river and got canes, which we bound together to make the side rails, using a piece of canvas for the bed.

"While busy attending to the making of this I heard someone calling, and going out a short distance saw Concepcion, the interpreter, standing with some Mexicans about 200 yards away. He beckoned to me and I went forward to talk to the men, as I was the only one who could speak Spanish, Horn being wounded. I had sent Concepcion to drive back some of the captured Indian stock which had wandered off during the fight. As I advanced toward the Mexicans they saluted me very courteously, and in a friendly way said that before they left they wanted to have a talk. It was raining and they asked me to step under a sheltering rock nearby; this was the very point from which they had first fired.

"On stepping under the rock I found myself confronted with about fifty Mexicans, all armed with Remington, rifles, and a hard looking lot, I would here state that I had sent them, according to my promise, six of the captured Indian horses, which, however, they had not received, as they said the horses were no good, being wounded and worn out; but of this I did not know at the time. Old Concepcion was detained by them. He was a Mexican who had been stolen by the Apaches when a boy, and was employed as an interpreter, as he knew the Apache language.

"The manner of the Mexicans when they found me in their power had undergone a marked change. They became insolent, stating that we had killed their officers and that we were marauders and had no authority in their country. They demanded my papers. I explained that there was a treaty between Mexico and the United States, but that I had no papers, as Captain Crawford had left all our baggage with the pack-train. Their language was insolent and threatening.

"I now appreciated my position and realized that the consequence of my being away from the command with the interpreter was that there was no one with the scouts who could make himself understood by them. The Mexicans stated that I had promised them animals to take back their wounded, and had not furnished them, as those I had sent were worthless. I told them I would send them other animals on my return, and started to go, when they surrounded me, saying that I must remain until I had sent the mules.

"By this time our Indians were yelling and preparing to fight. A few shots would have precipitated matters. The Mexicans called my attention to the action of my scouts, and I told them that the Indians evidently feared treachery, and that I could not control them while away. They then said I could go if I would send them six mules, after which they would leave the country. This I promised I would do, but they would not trust my word of honour and held old Concepcion a prisoner till I sent them the mules. I demanded a receipt, which they gave, and afterward Mexico paid our government the full value of the animals.

"It was now too late in the day to move, but the next morning I proceeded on the homeward march, carrying Captain Crawford by hand. The Indians, always superstitious, did not want to help, but were persuaded, Lieutenant Shipp and I also assisting. To add to the difficulty, it was the rainy season, and the steep mountain sides were climbed most laboriously. It would be difficult to describe this march. With great effort, the first day we only made two or three miles. The wounded Indian was placed on a pony, and although badly hurt, seemed to get along very well. The two other wounded scouts and Mr. Horn were so slightly injured that they moved with no trouble.

"An Indian woman came into camp that night and said that Geronimo wanted to talk. I concluded to meet him, and the next morning, after moving about two miles, I left the command and went with the interpreter, Mr. Horn, and rive scouts, to a point about a mile or so distant. We went without arms, as this was expressly stipulated by Geronimo as a condition.

"The chiefs did not appear, but I had a talk with two of the men, who promised that the chiefs would meet me the next day. They said I must come without arms. The next day I went to meet them and found Geronimo, Natchez, Nana and Chihuahua with fourteen men. They came fully armed with their belts full of ammunition, and as I had come unarmed, according to agreement, this was a breach of faith, and I did not think it argued well for their conduct. Apparently suspicious of treachery, every man of them sat with his rifle in an upright position, forming a circle nearly around me, with Geronimo in the centre. He sat there for fully a minute looking me straight in the eyes. Finally he got up and said to me:

I CAME TO CAPTURE OR DESTROY YOU AND YOUR BAND

"'Why did you come down here?'

"'I came to capture or destroy you and your band,' I answered.

"He knew perfectly well that this was the only answer I could truthfully make. He then walked up to me and shook my hand, saying that he could trust me, and then asked me to report to the department commander what he had to say. He enumerated his grievances at the agency, all of which were purely imaginary or assumed. I advised him to surrender and told him that if he did not neither the United States troops nor the Mexicans would let him rest. He agreed to surrender to me Nana, one other man, his (Geronimo's) wife, and one of Natchez's wives, with some of their children—nine in all—and promised to meet General Crook near San Bernardino in two moons to talk about surrendering.

"With this understanding I returned to camp. In a short time he sent the prisoners with the request that I give him a little sugar and flour. This request I complied with, having in the meantime sent some of my scouts for the pack-train, which they had found and brought back. Here, almost at midnight, I was awakened by the scouts who had assembled saying that they had seen the Mexicans approaching to attack us, and that they must have ammunition. I had not intended to issue any more just then, as we only had about 3,000 rounds left, but they begged so hard that I finally issued 1,000 rounds, though I could hardly believe this report. No Mexicans appeared. The hostiles had plenty of money, and it was afterwards reported that our scouts had sold them ammunition at the rate of one dollar per round.

"The next day we continued our march, which was very difficult on account of our being encumbered with our wounded. On the 17th of January, while sitting with Captain Crawford, he opened his eyes and looked me straight in the face and then pressed my hand. No doubt he was conscious, and I tried to get him to speak or write, but he could not. I assured him I would do all in my power to arrange his affairs, and he put his arm around me and drew me to him, but could only shake his head in answer.

"This conscious interval only lasted about five minutes, and then the look of intelligence seemed to pass away forever. The next day he died while we were on the march, passing away so quietly that no one knew the exact time of his death. We wrapped the body in canvas and placed it on one of the pack mules. We now moved more rapidly, but when we reached the Satachi River we could not cross it, as it was swollen by the late rains and was deep and turbulent. We were thus forced to go into camp and lose a day.

"In the meantime the body of Captain Crawford began to decompose, so we hurried on, crossing the river the next day, and on the day following reached Nacori. Here we buried Captain Crawford, putting his body in charge of the *presidente* of the town and marking well the place of his burial. I could only get four boards (slabs) in the town, and used them in making a coffin, the body being wrapped securely in canvas.

"The disposition of the people was decidedly unfriendly, and at Baserac and Bavispe about 200 of the local troops were assembled with hostile intent. To add to the trouble, the scouts obtained mescal and were very unruly. I had to use great care to prevent a conflict at Baserac. I was obliged to pass through the town, as there was a mountain on one side and a river on the other. The officials refused at first to let me pass, but I moved some of the troops through, supported by the remainder, and avoided a conflict. At Bavispe the Indians obtained a large quantity of *mescal*, and the civil authorities tried to take our captured stock. I sent them out of the camp, and had they not left when they did I am sure the intoxicated Indians would have fired upon them.

"Here occurred a quarrel between a company of White Mountain Indian scouts and one of Chiricahuas. They loaded their rifles to fire upon each other, while the first sergeants of the two companies fought between the lines, but I finally succeeded in quelling the disturbance. The next day I hurried away, and without further difficulty reached Lang's Ranch, arriving there on February 1st. Up to that time we had marched over 1,000 miles.

"I was ordered to return, February 5th, to Mexico and look out for the hostiles who had agreed to signal their return. I camped about ten miles south of the line on the San Bernardino River, and remained there until the 15th of March, when a signal was observed on a high point about twenty miles south. I went out with four or five scouts and met some messengers from Geronimo and Natchez, near the point from which the signal had been made. They informed me that the entire band of hostiles were then about forty miles away, camped in the mountains near Fronteras.

"I told them to return and bring Geronimo and his band at once, as the Mexicans were in pursuit and liable to attack them at any time. On the 19th the entire band came and camped about half a mile from my command. One more warrior with his wife and two children gave themselves up, and I now had thirteen prisoners. I endeavoured to persuade Geronimo and his band to go into Fort Bowie, telling them they were liable to be attacked by Mexican troops, but could only induce them to move with me to the Canyon de Los Embudos, about twelve miles below the border, where they camped in a strong position among the rocks half a mile away.

"I had notified the department commander upon the arrival of the messengers on the 15th, and on the 26th he arrived at my camp. In the interval, however, before General Crook arrived, Geronimo had almost daily come into my camp to talk to me and ask when the general would get there. On his arrival a conference was held and the hostiles promised they would surrender. General Crook then returned, directing me to bring them in. This I endeavoured to do, but this surrender was only an agreement, no arms being taken from them, nor were they any more in my possession than when I had met them in the Sierra Madre Mountains.

"It was believed, however, that they would come in. Unfortunately they obtained liquor, and all night on the 27th I could hear firing in their camp a mile or so away. I sent my command on, and, accompanied only by the interpreter, waited for the hostiles to move, but they were in a bad humour.

"They moved their camp at noon that day and I then left. I met Geronimo and a number of warriors gathered together nearby on Elias Creek, many of them being drunk, and Geronimo told me they would follow, but that I had better go on or he would not be responsible for my life. I then proceeded to my camp. I had ordered the battalion to camp at a point ten miles on the way back on the San Bernardino. That afternoon the hostiles came up and camped about half a mile above me in a higher position.

"I went into their camp and found trouble. Natchez had shot his wife, and they were all drinking heavily. I sent Lieutenant Shipp with a detail to destroy all the *mescal* at a ranch nearby, where they had previously obtained all their liquor. During the day all seemed quiet, but at night a few shots were heard. I sent to find out the cause and found the trouble was over some women; this trouble soon ceased, however, and quiet was restored. I felt anxious about the next day's march, as I would then cross the line and be near troops. The next morning I was awakened and told that the hostiles were gone.

"I caused a careful search to be made, and ascertained that Geronimo and Natchez, with twenty men, thirteen women and two children had gone during the night, and not a soul, as far as I could ascertain, knew anything of the time they had gone, or that they had intended to go. Chihuahua, Ulzahney, Nana, Catley, nine other men, and forty-seven women and children remained. The herd was brought in, and only three of their horses were missing. I directed Lieutenant Faison, with a sufficient detail, to take the remaining hostiles to Fort Bowie; then, with all the available men left, Lieutenant Shipp and I at once started in pursuit.

"About six miles from camp we struck the trail going due west over a chain of high mountains. This gave us a full view of the mountains in all directions, but the trail suddenly changed its direction to the south and went down a steep and difficult descent, across a basin so dense with chaparral and cut up with ravines as to make travel very difficult and slow, especially as every bush was full of thorns which tore ourselves and animals.

"Across this basin, about ten miles, the trail ascended a high mountain, very steep and rocky. The trail of the one horse with the hostiles induced us to think it might be possible to ride, but after reaching the top we found this horse stabbed and abandoned among the rocks; they were unable to take it farther. Beyond, the descent was vertical and of solid rock from 50 to 300 feet high for miles each away. Here the trail was lost, the Indians having scattered and walked entirely on the rocks.

"No doubt our pursuit had been discovered from this point when we crossed the mountain on the other side of the basin, ten miles away. These Indians were well supplied with telescopes and glasses, and a watch had doubtless been maintained here according to their usual custom. It is in this way, by selecting their line of march over these high points, that their retreat can always be watched and danger avoided. In the same way they watch the country for miles in advance. These never-failing precautions may serve to show how difficult is the chance of catching these men, who once alarmed are like wild animals, with their sense of sight and of hearing as keenly developed.

"We could not descend here, so we were obliged to retrace our steps down the mountain and make a circuit of ten miles to again strike the trail beyond. This we did, but when the stream beyond was reached it was dark, and further pursuit that night was impossible. Next morning we moved down the creek, cutting the trails which had come together about four miles below, and we followed this for about ten miles to the south. The hostiles had not stopped from the time they had left, and now had made about forty-five miles and had good ten hours the start. The trail here split and one part, the larger, crossed over the broken mountains north of Bavispe, into the Sierra Madres, while the other crossed into the mountains north of Fronteras.

"The scouts now seemed discouraged. Their *moccasins* were worn out by the constant hard work of the past five months, and the prospect of returning to the scenes of their last trials was not inviting. Besides, their discharge would take place in about one month. They appealed to me to go no farther, telling me that it was useless, etc. This I appreciated and decided to return. We then retraced our way and continued the homeward march. While returning, two of the escaped hostiles joined me and gave themselves up. I arrived at Fort Bowie on the 3rd of April. The results of the expedition were by no means unimportant, as we had secured the larger part of the hostiles, seventy-nine in all, of whom fifteen were warriors."

The Indian at Last Subdued

With the close of the year 1886 the Indian wars practically came to end. Not that there were no uprisings of the tribesmen after that, or that all was peace and happiness. Trouble was still brewing constantly and peace was maintained only at the price of constant vigilance on the part of the government. And that future outbreaks were not avoided is seen by the uprising in 1890, which assumed a most threatening aspect, and demanded extraordinary efforts on the part of the military authorities; but after all they were no more than the last convulsive movements of a dying race, the last delirious effort of a people doomed to extinction. The result was never in serious doubt. The epoch of real Indian armed resistance ended in 1886.

It was then that he was subdued, conquered, overpowered. Brought into the reservations, the Indian was caged and kept under control. True, the reservations were vast areas of land, and furnished the savage son of the wilderness with ample space to create the illusion that he could still roam about in nature's freedom. But it was a mere illusion. He simply had a large cage, which, year after year, was made smaller, imperceptibly at first, gradually at the beginning, but with less regard for his feelings later on and always systematically and methodically. And thus one reservation after the other was taken from the Indians and opened to the wild scramble of the white settler—opened up for civilization, and the confines of the savages became narrower and narrower.

Sentimental people might deplore the fate of the Indian as

something intensely tragic. As a matter of fact his fate was but the result of that inexorable rule which has been called the survival of the fittest. The Indian race's fate was sealed when the first white man set his foot upon the virgin soil of this great continent. His doom thereafter was only a question of time. The two races met, barbarism and the civilization of a new era clashed and the outcome could only be the survival of the fittest. There is no sentiment about this law of nature; it is inexorable, unchangeable.

In 1886 the subjugation was complete. The Indian was no longer a menace to the safety of the country. From a foe, who spread terror and fear, he had degenerated into a "ward of the nation," the object of the government's care and solicitude; to be petted upon good conduct, spanked when refractory.

There were a few among the Indians who felt the humiliation which this condition brought upon their nation. Unable to view the situation philosophically and submit to the inevitable with resignation, imbued, too, with a true spirit of Indian patriotism they once more decided to throw off the white man's yoke and invoked the religious prejudices of their kinsmen to inflame their spirit of war. And then the great outbreak of 1890 followed.

The Memorable Outbreak of 1890

CHARLES A. VARNUM

Religious fanaticism was primarily the cause of those Indian troubles which in 1890 and 1891 commanded the attention of the entire country and placed the Indian question in the foreground of public discussion. The uprising assumed such threatening proportions that the largest and most formidable Indian war in the history of this country seemed inevitable. Happily for the people of the United States the fears were not realized, and the anticipated war was averted; happily for the white people of the United States, but happily also for the Indians themselves. The result would never have been in doubt and the extermination of whole tribes would have been the outcome. The timely death of Sitting Bull, than whom there has never been a craftier or shrewder Indian chief, averted the threatened danger and caused a complete collapse of all hostile preparations.

The religious fanaticism spoken of was created by the appearance of a Messiah among the various Indian tribes. Early in 1890 religious fervour suddenly seized the Utes. A white man appeared in their midst who by his assumed or genuine piety soon gained the respect and friendship of the Indians.

He pretended to have inspirations from above and predicted the coming of an Indian Messiah who would deliver his race from the bondage of the white man, resuscitate the spirits of the departed dear ones and restore the oppressed and enslaved tribes to the full possession of their hunting grounds and the dominion of their ancestors.

As the wish is father to the thought, so does the human mind accept for true whatever conforms to its longings and wishes.

The white man had no trouble in finding willing believers of his prophecies among the Indians, since they gratified so much their innermost and eager desires.

In order to prepare themselves for the arrival of this Messiah the Indians instituted a so-called "Messiah" or "ghost" dance, and thus lent their newly-created religious fervour a more forcible expression.

During the summer of 1890 the Sioux and Arapahoes paid the Utes their customary annual visit, and on that occasion became acquainted with the strange white preacher, the prophecy of the red Messiah and the ghost dance. They, too, readily fell victims to the new religion and carried its fascinating ceremony—the dance—to their homes in their own reservations.

Then the Messiah doctrine began to spread and extend from one tribe to another, and before it could be explained how the myth had travelled or how it could have been carried to such far-away tribes, the whole Indian race in the northwest and west became infected with the craze, for such it had now become. Every tribe expected deliverance from its own Messiah, every lodge was eager to outdo the other in preparing for the coming of this Redeemer.

Half consciously the Indian realized that his race was doomed to utter destruction. Once his nation was powerful and strong, the undisputed master of this vast country. The white man came, and with him came another civilization. Unable to either cope with the intruder or accept his civilization, he saw his race decline and decay. His powers vanished and his glory disappeared. As civilization progressed, the Indian retreated; territory after territory was taken from him by force, by fraud, by trade and barter, by promises, by any and all means, no matter how.

Thus was the Indian compelled to recede, to relinquish the ancestral ground, the land where from time immemorial his tribe had lived, hunted, made merry and buried its dead. True, the Indian sometimes revolted, resisted, went to battle the palefaced intruder; but each war only accentuated his helplessness in a more glaring light, and sullenly he submitted to the inevitable fate, to be ruled by the white man and to await the final extinction before the relentless march of a death-bringing civilization. Left to his own resources the Indian was doomed.

Now came the new religion and a ray of hope sprung up in the heart of the despairing Indian. Heaven itself was to bring him salvation. It was to send him the Messiah. Where he was helpless the Messiah would act.

Was it strange that the new creed spread like wildfire, that it found followers? Was it so singular that the Messiah or ghost dance should be performed in every Indian camp and village?

At first the dance and the accompanying ceremonies bore a purely religious character, free from any political tinge. Soon, however, the medicine men and political schemers, ambitious chiefs and intriguing warriors seized upon the opportunity and used the dances to further their own selfish plans and ends, and ere long the movement turned into one huge political conspiracy—death and destruction to the white conqueror became the aim, America for the Indians the slogan.

The Messiah dance has been variously described, but the manner in which it is most generally indulged in is as follows:

A high priest, a leading medicine man, has entire charge of the ceremonies. He is assisted by four helpers, who have to start or stop the dance as they see fit; they are empowered to inflict punishment on any person who disobeys their orders.

Those who are to participate in the dance prepare themselves by a sweat-bath, while the high priest and his assistants engage in prayer.

The sweat-baths are taken in tents erected for this purpose. Poles are stuck m the ground and the tops are bent and securely tied. Blankets and robes are thrown over this frame-work to such thickness as to render the interior as nearly air-tight as possible. A fire is then started inside in a hole in the ground and good-sized stones are heated. The participants now enter the tent and proceed to force the perspiration by sitting almost naked upon these heated stones.

The atmosphere is made still more disagreeable by pouring water on the stones and thus filling the interior of the tightly-closed tent with steam and vapour. Attendants keep hot stones in readiness as long as the youths are able to stand the confinement. The pipe is vigorously smoked during the sweat, and smoke, heat, vapour and steam all con tribute to produce a peculiar effect upon the participants and prepare their minds for the approaching exultation at the dance.

Finally the young men emerge from the enclosure, perspiration fairly streaming from every pore.

Weather permitting, they plunge into a pool in the creek nearby, but if the air be too chilly blankets are thrown about their bodies.

The high priest wears eagle feathers in his hair and a short skirt reaches from the waist nearly to the knees; the assistants are similarly dressed.

An invocation or prayer is then chanted by the high priest, while the multitude gather about the young fellows who are to execute the dance.

A sacred tree is the centre of the scene, around which the terpsichorean evolutions are executed. Dancing, singing, praying, groaning and crying are kept up from beginning to end—a weird and ghost-like scene, especially at night, impressive in its earnestness, awe-inspiring in the ugliness of the participants and their peculiar motions. The dance is continued for hours, until the dancers fall to the ground exhausted and worn out.

The attitude of the authorities and those in charge of the Indians toward this new craze was such as to invite criticism. It seems to have been the general consensus of opinion that the Indian agents failed to grasp the significance of this outbreak of fanaticism, that they lacked in firmness and energy in meeting the situation, that by their own actions they themselves were responsible for the ghost dance being converted from a religious ceremony into a war dance.

Among the many Indian chiefs who from patriotic and ambitious motives were active in promoting and spreading the new movement the irreconcilable Sitting Bull was the leader.

He saw in the outburst of religious fervour a chance to arouse the warlike spirit of the noble sons of the great Wakautanka, to unite the many tribes of his great nation, the Sioux, and to he liberated from the yoke of the white oppressor.

Sitting Bull has been called an intriguer, a treacherous savage, a schemer, an Indian demagogue, a disturber, and yet, granting that he merited all these epithets, the memory of his gigantic, martial figure and commanding personality reflects him before the eyes of the world as one of the ablest and cleverest Indians that race has produced and a man whose very meanness—from the white man's standpoint—was inspired by the loftiest motives of love for the people of his nice.

While condemning him, nobody who has studied his remarkable career will withhold his admiration for him. True, he fomented trouble, incited his followers to rebel, inspired the war and brought misery and disaster to his people, but his aim and ideal were the liberty and independence of his race. "God Almighty made me an Indian, and he did not make me an agency Indian, and I do not intend to be one," he said on one occasion to General Miles, and now, when the Indians all over the northwest were agitated and uneasy, and he was surrounded by thousands of followers, he tried to impress this same sentiment upon the minds of the warriors.

Sitting Bull became the soul of the whole movement, the acknowledged leader of the dissatisfied tribes.

The first impetus to the general upheaval emanated from the Pine Ridge Reservation in South Dakota. The agent there, ac-

The Battle of Wounded Knee Creek

companied by fourteen Indian police, rode into White Bird's camp and attempted to stop the Messiah dance, which he considered to be a hostile demonstration.

But the Indians of the village met him with Winchesters and compelled him to return under penalty of death.

When the story of the boldness of these Indians and the display of weakness on the part of the agent was told it spread like wildfire. The Indians at the Rosebud and Standing Rock Reservations began to flock to the vicinity of Pine Ridge and the excitement among the whites and redskins increased.

The seat of the trouble was a tract of country embraced within the boundaries made by the Cannon Ball, Missouri and Niobrara Rivers and by a line north extending from Forts Robinson and Meade to the Cannon Ball. The number of Indians who were considered to be on the warpath was estimated at 4,000, while 6,000 others were regarded as doubtful and in need of constant observation.

At first the military force which had to cope with the situation consisted of one cavalry and two infantry regiments at Pine Ridge, one cavalry and one infantry regiment at the mouth of the Beele Fouche River, one regiment of infantry at Fort Pierre, one at Fort Yates, and one cavalry and two infantry regiments at Fort Keogh. The position of these forces was in the nature of a huge cordon that could be tightened or extended according to requirements. General Miles had charge of the military operations.

The presence of these troops was used by the Indian leaders to still further incense their warriors. "What are the soldiers here for?" they argued. "Are we to be molested even at our religious devotions?"

Large bands of Sioux had tied to the extreme north of the reservation and into the adjoining Bad Lands, where camps had been established.

The policy of the government was to mass troops, overawe the Indians and to avoid, if possible, a clash, counting upon the salutary effect which a skilful display of strength has upon a weaker foe.

General Miles was especially qualified to carry out the intentions of the government, and proved himself equal to the occasion. The campaign which was now inaugurated had for its final object the hemming in of the hostiles, and by cutting off all avenues of escape it was intended to force them to surrender in preference to death by starvation. As winter was near and the Indians were not provided any too well with supplies, it was but a question of time till they would be forced to lay down their arms and ask for peace.

During the month of November the excitement continued with unabated strength.

Several attempts to induce the warriors by conference and persuasion to return to their reservations and villages failed.

By December 1st the government began to change its Indian agents, replacing incompetents with men of known integrity and ability. General Miles and Buffalo Bill, who had been given a commission as brigadier-general, agreed that the arrest of Sitting Bull would help to break the backbone of the rebellion and restore peace and quietness.

On December 7th General Miles reported that Lieutenant Gaston, Eighth United States Cavalry, had conferred with the Cheyennes at the Tongue River Mission, and General Brooke with a number of hostile chiefs whose warriors had gotten beyond reach in the Bad Lands. Both conferences, like all previous ones, failed of success, but the presence of so many troops and the activity of the commanders had an intimidating effect on many chiefs, and from December 12th to 15th the reports of Generals Ruger, Carr and Brooke showed that quite a number of tribes were delivering up their arms and coming in.

On December 15th it was learned that Sitting Bull was about to start out to join the hostiles in the Bad Lands, and a body of Indian police, followed by a troop of cavalry under Captain Fouchet and infantry under Colonel Drum, was sent to apprehend the Indian chief.

It was a dreary and difficult march, but the fatigues of the long and dangerous journey had been sufficiently provided against, and when the dawn of the first day appeared the expedition was within easy reach of its destination. The Indian police were the first to sight the *tepees* on the bank of the Grand River. The detail put the spurs to the horses and were at Sitting Bull's camp before the redoubtable chief or his warriors could realize what was about to happen. Bull Head, lieutenant, and Shaved Head, first sergeant, were in command of the police.

No time was lost in *parleying*. The chief was hustled out of his tent and hoisted upon a waiting horse. The squad was ready to take up the return march. Sitting Bull at first raged and struggled, then, suddenly changing his mind, straightened up and began to shout commands for his own rescue. The police attempted to force him to silence by pointing their Winchesters at his head, but Sitting Bull refused to be intimidated and continued giving orders. Presently there was a shot. The policeman to the prisoner's right reeled in his saddle and fell dead to the ground. The police now became incensed and replied with a volley that had a deadly effect upon the frenzied warriors. Firing became general on both sides.

In the confusion Sitting Bull's voice could be heard directing the battle, though himself a captive, he was calling upon his sons and warriors, his gaunt form far overreaching everybody else. Suddenly he dropped limp on the hard prairie, shot dead. Sitting Bull had given his last command, fought his last battle. It was some time before the police realized the great Indian's death—they thought he was shamming. His followers in the meantime began closing in from all sides, and matters assumed critical form for the brave little band of policemen. Captain Fouchet arrived just at the opportune time to assist them, and the appearance of the infantry and cavalry forced the Indians to bolt for the river.

With Sitting Bull, his two sons, Blackbird and Crowfoot, the latter a mere boy of twelve, were killed.

The death of the famous chief gave rise to considerable comment and much criticism. There was, too, another version of the occurrence, according to which Sitting Bull was shot down as he emerged from his tent in reply to a summons from a policeman and after his son, not knowing the purport of the presence of the armed force, had cried for assistance. It was also stated that one of the police lifted the old leader's scalp as a proud trophy and left his mangled body on the field, a horrible sight to behold.

It is unnecessary to state that the news of Sitting Bull's death had a depressing effect upon the hostiles in every camp. On December 17th fully 1,000 Indians surrendered. The next day skirmishes were reported at a ranch near Smithville.

On December 20th 500 friendlies left Pine Ridge to urge the hostiles in the Bad Lands to come in. A band of thirty-nine of Sitting Bull's followers also gave up their arms.

During the next week the situation became more favourable, large bands of hostiles continuing to come in.

December 27th the hostiles made two attempts to break up a camp of Cheyenne scouts on Battle Creek. Both attacks were repulsed, with several killed and wounded on both sides.

Colonel Forsyth, Seventh United States Cavalry, on December 29th located the camp of Big Foot, who, after having been captured, had made his escape and settled near Wounded Knee. Among the 150 male Indians of his camp, about one-third were refugees from Sitting Hull's dispersed band. There was likewise a large number of women and children in the *tepees*. In pursuance of orders from General Miles, Colonel Forsyth decided to disarm the Indians and ordered that the whole number appear before him, as he wanted to talk to them.

With the sullenness characteristic of their race, the Indians obeyed and ranged themselves in a semi circle in front of the tent of Big Foot, who lay sick with pneumonia. By twenties they were ordered to give up their arms. The first batch went to their tents and returned with only two guns. This irritated Major Whiteside, who was charged with the execution of the order, and after a brief consultation with the colonel he ordered the cavalrymen, who were dismounted and formed in almost a square of about twenty-five paces, to close in. This was done and the Indians were now completely encircled. A detachment was then sent to search the *tepees*.

What happened next is a matter of conjecture, since it is impossible to get at the facts from the mass of conflicting statements. Two facts are, however, beyond controversy; namely, that the Indians had in their possession many arms, which they had secreted, and that the cavalrymen of the Seventh, Custer's regiment, had a grudge against the Indians. It is further beyond dispute that a shot was fired and fired by one of the Indians. At the same time the warriors made a rush for the troopers.

And then ensued what can be termed only a carnage. Maddened by the sudden and unexpected shot and attack, without waiting for the command they reached for their rifles, and in an instant the whole front was one sheet of fire, above which the smoke rolled and obscured the scene from view. That first volley left few Indians to tell the awful story. When the atmosphere had cleared, the ground, saturated with blood, was found strewn with the bodies of wounded and dead warriors, while a few were seen to hurry away toward the bluffs to a place of safety. The wounded fought on the ground, till a blow from the butt-end of a rifle or a shot ended their miserable existence.

Big Foot lay in his tent killed, his body riddled with bullets. All about the narrow place the horribly-mangled bodies of the savages lay. Thus far the fighting was so close that the field guns could not be trained without danger to the soldiers. Now they were called into action after the fleeing Indians.

For an hour a most destructive fire was kept up, when the guns were silenced and the rifles dropped; the war of extermination had been carried out to the end. There was nothing left to shoot at.

Of the 150 male Indians only a few escaped with their lives, and these few were captured. Of the thirty-nine women captured twenty-one were wounded, while a number of them were killed on the field, together with several children.

The troops, too, lost heavily. Captain Wallace and twenty-five men were killed and two officers and thirty-four men were wounded, the probability being that owing to the close range

CORPORAL WEINERT WORKING HIS HOTCHKISS

at which the shooting was done many of the cavalrymen were struck by the bullets of their own comrades.

That during the fight many a heroic deed was performed by the troopers is certain, that more than one of the soldiers did not allow himself to be carried away by blind hatred and passion is admitted even by the unfortunate savages, and amidst the many acts of unpardonable slaughter and butchery there were, too, those of humanity and true soldierly virtues which serve to throw a ray of brighter light upon this gloomy battlefield.

Especially is this true of the following:

First Lieutenant Ernest A. Garlington, Troop A, Seventh United States Cavalry, and Second Lieutenant H. L. Hawthorne, Second United States Artillery, both of whom were severely wounded. First Sergeants Jacob Trautman, Troop I, and Frederick E. Toy, Troop G, Sergeant George Lloyd, Troop 1, and Private James Ward. Troop B, the latter receiving a serious and painful wound, and Privates Mosheim Feaster, Troop E, Matthew H. Hamilton, Troop G, Marvin C. Hillock, Troop B, George Hobday, Troop A, Herman Ziegner, Troop E, and Adam Neder, Troop A, all of the Seventh United States Cavalry, the last-named hero being severely injured.

Private John Clancey, Battery E, First United States Artillery, distinguished himself by truly heroic work in caring for his wounded comrades, and Private Joshua B. Hartzog, of the same battery, won general admiration and praise, when amidst the tumult and confusion he came to the assistance of his wounded artillery lieutenant and carried him away from the field of battle to a place of safety. All these men received the Medal of Honour.

Corporal Paul H. Weinert, Battery E, First United States Artillery, rendered himself conspicuous by the calm and cool manner in which he served his gun, when all was excitement and confusion.

In referring to the incident, for which he was granted the Medal of Honour, Corporal Weinert says:

"After the heaviest part of the fight at Wounded Knee a lot of Indians got into a ravine, from which they were shooting

PAUL H. WEINERT

with awful effect. The Seventh couldn't get at them. I then took my little Hotchkiss down to the entrance of the ravine and blazed away. When I started I had three men. All of the Indians opened fire on us. One of my men went for ammunition and didn't come back. Everybody ran from the mouth of the ravine where I was to the top of and behind a hill about fifty yards away, excepting Joshua B. Hartzog and George Green. My captain called to me to come back, but I kept moving nearer the Indians, and kept on shooting.

"Seeing that I would not come, Lieutenant Hawthorne came toward me and was calling, when suddenly I heard him say: 'Oh, my God!' Looking around, I saw him lying on his side, and I then knew he had been hit. Hartzog ran to him and carried him back behind the hill. That left me alone with Green. I said: 'By God! I'll make 'em pay for that,' and ran the gun fairly into the opening of the ravine and tried to make every shot count. The Hotchkiss was a single-shot affair and had to be pulled off with a lanyard. They kept yelling at me to come back, and I kept yelling for a cool gun there were three more on the hill not in use.

"Bullets were coming like hail from the Indians Winchesters. The wheels of my gun were bored full of holes and our clothing was marked in several places. Once a cartridge was knocked out of my hand just as I was about to put it in the gun, and it's a wonder the cartridge didn't explode. I kept going in farther, and pretty soon everything was quiet at the other end of the line. Then the other guns came down. I expected a court-martial, but what was my surprise when gruff old Allyn Capron, my captain, came up to me and grasped me by the shoulders and said to the officers and men: 'That's the kind of men I have in my battery.'"

As has been stated before, a party of Indians, after the first few volleys, managed to break through the troops and escape to the ravine nearby. They were pursued, and during the fighting that occurred here many acts of bravery were performed, notably by First Lieutenant John C. Gresham, who voluntarily led the pursuing party, and Sergeants William J. Austin, Albert H. McMillan and Private Thomas Sullivan, all of Troop E, Seventh United States Cavalry, who were also awarded the Medal.

Following this battle, reports of which had aroused the hostiles to the highest pitch of excitement, came an attack on the Catholic Mission at Clay Creek, December 30th. The Seventh Cavalry had just gone into camp after having repulsed an attack upon its supply train, when a courier brought the news of a fire at the Catholic Mission and a massacre of the teachers and pupils. Within twenty minutes the exhausted and worn-out cavalry were once more in motion on the way to the scene of action, a few miles distant. The Indians, 1,800 in number, under Little Wound and Two Strike, were found about a mile beyond the mission.

The fighting commenced at once, but on the part of the Indians peculiar tactics were followed, squads of forty warriors fighting at a time and the main body slowly retreating. Colonel Forsyth expected another ambush and refused to be drawn into dangerous ground. The Indians became cognizant of the fact that their ruse would not work and thereupon began to close in upon the regiment. They greatly outnumbered the troops and were already drawing their characteristic circle preparatory to a charge, when Colonel Henry, with the Ninth United States Cavalry, appeared on the scene and attacked the redskins in the rear. This forced the whole band of savages to flee.

In this engagement Captain Charles A. Varnum, Troop B, Seventh United States Cavalry, performed an act of great bravery, and thereby gained the Medal of Honour.

The order to retire had been given and was being carried out in the face of the steadily advancing savages. Captain Varnum realized that a further retreat would result in the cutting off of one of the troops, so disregarding orders he took the lead of his company and made a dashing charge upon the Indians, driving them back and gaining a commanding position, which he held until the Ninth Cavalry came to the assistance of the regiment.

First Sergeant Theodore Ragnar and Sergeant Bernhard Jetter, Troop K, Seventh United States Cavalry; Corporal William O. Wilson, Troop I, Ninth United States Cavalry, and Farrier Richard J. Nolan, Troop I, Seventh United States Cavalry, also displayed on this occasion, as throughout the campaign, qualities of the most conspicuous bravery and gallantry, for which they, were granted the Medal of Honour.

The Perils of Winter Campaigning

BENJAMIN H. CHEEVER

Two days after the last engagement mentioned in the preceding story, on January 1, 1891, a short but sharp encounter occurred on the banks of the White River, at the mouth of the Little Grass Creek, in South Dakota.

Troop K, Sixth United States Cavalry, fifty-three men strong, was escorting a supply train to the camp of the regiment, on Wounded Knee Creek, several miles away. The day was intensely cold, the thermometer twenty degrees below zero. A sharp wind was blowing, which made the atmosphere still more icy and added to the hardships of the mid winter march. The train had covered considerable distance when presently a large band of Indians, estimated at from three to four hundred, approached.

From close observation it soon became apparent that the redskins were on the warpath and came prepared to open hostilities. Second Lieutenant Robert L. Howze, who was in command of the detachment, decided on a becoming reception for the braves, whose war-cries and howls rent the air as they came nearer and nearer. The country was slightly hilly and the lieutenant selected one of the highest knolls, which offered the best advantages for an effective defence.

This knoll was about 300 yards from the banks of the river, which was lined on both sides by a slight growth of woods.

Howze parked his horses and wagons and fortified himself as well as circumstances and time would permit. Then he calmly awaited the approach of the warriors. They made a sudden dash as if about to charge, but when within 600 yards were met with such a heavy and well-directed fire from within the barricades that they abandoned their intention and instead scattered in all directions.

Soon, however, they again collected, and now began to surround the pent-up troop. At various points they became aggressive and made determined attacks, which were repulsed through the cool bravery of the men. Sergeant Frederick Myers and Corporal Cornelius C. Smith, by choosing advanced positions, with the aid of four or five men each succeeded in frustrating several well-planned attacks of the savages.

The woods along the river offered the Indians protection from the fire of the soldiers and enabled them to maintain an annoying and threatening position.

With almost reckless bravery Lieutenant Howze with a small force made a sortie and charged the Indians concealed behind the trees, clearing the strip of woods completely. Accompanied by two brave troopers he then broke through the cordon of redskins and dispatched the two soldiers to the camp to notify the commander

CORNELIUS C. SMITH

of the attack and apprise him of the siege. He then returned to his post and continued to hold the bloodthirsty Indians at bay until relief came.

The couriers arrived safely at the camp. They delivered their message to First Lieutenant Benjamin H. Cheever, Jr., who, after the hardships of a protracted campaign, was complacently sitting in his tent writing a letter to a friend. He was congratulating himself on a day of rest at last, and he had just penned the words: "Well, everything is quiet today, but there is no telling what moment something will pop," when he was disturbed by the couriers bringing the news of the attack on Troop K. A moment later a picket rushed by on his way to the tent of Colonel E. A. Carr. He reported heavy firing to the right of the camp, and said that it sounded like volley firing.

The young lieutenant immediately reported the fact to Major T. C. Tupper, who was in command of the squadron to which he was attached, Troops F and I, and both officers ordered their horses saddled, for they knew that that squadron would be the first ordered out for detached service.

The captain of Cheever's troop was in a distant part of the camp, leaving the lieutenant in command. He ordered the men of the troop to get saddles and bridles ready, for the order was expected at once. It came a moment later, and in less than five minutes from the time the first alarm had been brought to camp the two troops were ready to go to the relief. Lieutenant Cheever sent an orderly to notify his captain of what had happened, and started out at a ringing gallop through the chilling winter air. Time was precious, and delay might jeopardize valued lives a few miles away. Waiting was not to be thought of.

A mile and a half had been quickly covered when Major Tupper, commanding the squadron, ordered the young officer to throw out an advance skirmish line of twenty men. He obeyed, taking charge of it himself, and leaving the troop in command of the second lieutenant, knowing that the captain would soon overtake his men. So quickly had the order been given, and so rapidly had it been executed, that Lieutenant

WITH ALMOST RECKLESS BRAVERY LIEUTENANT HOWZE WITH A SMALL FORCE MADE A SORTIE

Cheever had not been able to determine how many men he had with him, until the little force were deployed as skirmishers, when he found that there were but thirteen, sometimes considered an unlucky number. But he had no time just then to make inquiries and dashed ahead at a run till he and his small command were nearly two miles in advance of the main body of troops. The sound of firing in front became more and more distinct as they rushed on.

Arriving at the top of a high bluff he discovered the Indians on the opposite side of the White River. They reviled him and dared him to come up with his force. Between him and them, where the beleaguered troop was also located, flowed the river, half frozen and filled with floating ice, flanked on both sides by precipitous cliffs, which towered to a height of several hundred feet directly in front of the troopers.

There was only one descent to the valley below, and that was by a narrow trail, so that the men had to close in on the centre and proceed with great care, expecting any moment to be ambushed. The Indians were in every direction. On reaching the valley the troop was deployed in order that the banks of the river might be reconnoitred and a suitable ford found. No such ford was there, and knowing that the Indians would be upon him at any moment, and that if he remained where he was till the main body of troops came up he would be at a great disadvantage, both in numbers and position for should the Indians get possession of the opposite bank of the river he could not hold his position Lieutenant Cheever gave the order to advance.

Notwithstanding the great danger of crossing the frozen river, which must be done by swimming, the plunge was made. It was something awful, the crossing of that river, men and horses swimming and scrambling in the water and battling with the ice.

For a time it looked as if half the little force would be carried away, but at last, after moments that seemed hours, all stood on the farther bank, their clothes soaked and freezing to their skins. There was no time to build fires, no time to

Men and horses battling with the ice

think of anything but their beleaguered comrades ahead, so they pushed on till they stood on the crest of the hill, and there the action opened at once.

It was short and vigorous. Hardly fifteen minutes elapsed before the main body of Major Tupper's command came in sight, and the Indians, knowing that they were almost equally matched in numbers, were afraid to give a fair fight. They soon commenced a rapid retreat, carrying off their dead and disabled. The troops captured three ponies from the redskins, who numbered about 800. Troop K was relieved without the loss of a man.

It was a very cold day, and as the march back to camp was about fourteen miles, it was a decidedly worn out and hungry lot of troopers that arrived there just before midnight. The clothing of many was frozen stiff.

In addition to Lieutenant Cheever, Captain John B. Kerr and Sergeant Joseph F. Knight fought with such distinction and gallantry as to receive the highest praise from the general commanding, General Miles, besides being awarded the Medal of Honour. Others who won the Medal in this engagement were Lieutenant Howze, Sergeant Frederick Myers and Corporal Cornelius C. Smith.

Following this affair there were numerous other engagements and encounters, but lack of provisions, internal dissensions, the death of Sitting Bull and, above all, General Miles's masterly handling of the situation displaying his strength rather than using it—soon had their effect upon the Indians and it was not long before it became clear that the backbone of the movement was broken and the reaction had set in. Tribe by tribe came in and surrendered; one chief after another submitted to the inevitable, until at the end of January the war, which had threatened to assume gigantic proportions, was completely ended and General Miles closed the campaign with a magnificent midwinter parade of the troops under his command—a military spectacle such as the assembled and completely cowed Indians had never seen before, and in all probability will never see again.

So much adverse criticism of the methods employed in treating with the Indians was directed against the authorities that steps were taken by the latter to give the Indians fair and better treatment, and consequently there were fewer uprisings, this campaign of 1890-91 being the last war against the Sioux and in fact the last against the Indians in general, for the government has them under such control as to quell any outbreak at the very start. No serious uprisings of Indians have therefore occurred between 1891 and 1898 when, during the War with Spain, the last one was promptly subdued.

In the interim occasional raids were made by hostile bands through the sparsely populated sections of the west, which were always checked by small detachments of the military and the offenders punished. These raids cannot be regarded as wars or uprisings, for they were no more warlike in character than the raids by white desperadoes which likewise had to be checked by the troops, although whenever they occurred there was hard work for the troops engaged in the pursuit, testing their endurance to the utmost.

Particularly troublesome were Mexican bandits and rebels who came across the border into the States and terrorized the inhabitants by their plundering, an incident of which is related on the following page.

Fought Three Mexicans Single-Handed

Allen Walker

The Garza rebellion in Mexico in 1891, which was a revolt against the government of President Diaz, caused considerable trouble to the United States troops stationed along the Texas border line.

The rebels and other Mexican outlaws had established their rendezvous in the country on both sides of the frontier, and whenever pressed by the troops of the Mexican government crossed on to United States territory, where they were safe from further pursuit. Here they would assemble and gather their heterogeneous forces and map out their plans for the overthrow of the established government.

To put an end to the machinations of these conspirators the United States authorities were appealed to for the rigid enforcement of the neutrality laws. This led to the display of a considerable military force in southern Texas and gave the troops ordered thither much arduous duty, coupled with hardships and adventures which furnished many good stories for the campfires.

Private Walker searched his prisoners

It fell to the good fortune of Private Allen Walker, of Troop C. Third United States Cavalry, to distinguish himself during this time. On December 30, 1891, he was sent with dispatches from one post to another, and was riding along at a good speed when he encountered three well-armed Mexicans whom he knew to be in league with the rebel cause and to have violated the laws of this country.

The young soldier appreciated that their very presence on United States territory was in open defiance of the authority of his own government, and he said to himself: "These fellows may trifle with the laws of their own country, but by God they won't do it with mine!" And with almost reckless boldness he dashed right up to the three rebels and demanded their surrender. When his demand was ignored he opened up on them, and in a sharp but short conflict had one of them wounded, the horse of another killed and the third one put to flight.

He searched his prisoners and took from them some papers which proved to be documents of extreme importance concerning the Garza rebellion, and which contained the details of a plan for an organized invasion of United States territory. So important was the seizure of these papers that Walker received the Medal of Honour as a fitting reward.

The Bear Island Uprising

Early in October, 1898, an Indian uprising occurred at the Bear Island, Reservation of the Chippewas, in Minnesota, which caused much more excitement than it deserved, and was squelched within a week. In its scope it was really nothing more serious than an armed resistance of several hundred Indians against the execution of an order from the government, but it led to a fierce fight and for a time threw the whole country into a state of anxiety, because a repetition of the Custer massacre was feared. When reliable information from the seat of the trouble reached the War Department, and not only failed to confirm the first wild rumours, but brought news of the safety of the military detachment, the minds of the people were relieved and public excitement died away. The cause of this disturbance was a peculiar one, and dated back at least one year. An unscrupulous white man was arrested and taken to Duluth, Minn., for selling whisky to Indians on the reservation. Among the Indians who were produced as witnesses against the defendant was one who was a real "bad Injun." Such at least was his reputation.

He is described as a man of imposing physique, tall as a pine, bony and strong. He was the typical Indian in all his ways and actions. He wore the blanket, lived in a tent or the hollow of a tree, loved to roam about, despised work and hated the palefaces. He was the ideal Indian. The United States authorities had some difficulty in inducing him to appear as a witness at Duluth, and succeeded only after promising him plenty of money, good treatment and the means to reach his home after the trial.

The promises, which were unquestionably unauthorized and certainly illegal, were not kept, and the Indian from the Bear Island Reservation was sorely disappointed. He had to walk and beg his way home, and reached his destination in a deplorable condition. This treatment of course was not conducive to a state of good feeling on the part of the Indian. When the second trial of the same defendant came off in the fall of 1897 the United States Marshal made much less ado about securing his testimony—he simply went to the reservation and took him to Duluth, where, after the testimony had been given, the Chippewa brave was once more turned loose to shift for himself.

He again returned to his home, his heart filled with hatred for the white man, and determined to get even for the insults to which he had been subjected. He vowed vengeance and kept his word. Henceforth he followed the life of an outlaw. He stole, plundered, robbed, and, the authorities say, murdered. It is said he slew an old and prominent Indian chief. This conduct had a two-fold result: first, to inspire fear and terror; second, to surround him with a number of sympathizing followers.

And so he gradually became a power among the Indians of the reservation. He created discontent and fanned it by calling attention to the conduct of certain officials who were taking advantage of the inexperienced Indians in their commercial dealings. It was not long until his agitation and reckless conduct became a real menace to the white settlers in the vicinity and the military authorities, and a warrant for his arrest was finally issued and placed in the hands of the United States Marshal for execution.

Anticipating trouble, General John M. Bacon with a detachment of 100 regulars accompanied the marshal on his errand.

On the approach of the military force the Indians became uneasy. Many of them did not know the significance of the expedition; others, especially those of troubled conscience, feared for their safety. The result was that some 400 Indians deserted their places of abode and flocked together, all armed to the teeth and incited by the previously-mentioned hostile brave to offer resistance.

General Bacon reached Bear Island in the forenoon of October 5, 1898. The day was sombre and dreary and intensely cold as the force landed at Leech Lake, having crossed the small lake in rowboats.

There wasn't an Indian in sight when General Bacon and his men arrived; ominous silence prevailed as far as could be seen or heard. Scouts were sent out, but came back with the report that no traces of Indians could be found. At noon the general assembled his small force and gave the order for dinner. The men dispersed, and some of them were about to prepare their frugal meal when suddenly and without warning a shot fired from an Indian hut near the shore struck a soldier in the breast, killing him instantly. As if this fatal shot had been the signal agreed upon, a band of Indians emerged from the woods and came yelling and dashing upon the surprised troopers. However, the soldiers, although taken completely unawares, were men of the true military stamp. Most of them had faced the savage many times before and were well acquainted with the tactics of the redskin.

They at once sought shelter behind stumps of trees and opened a well-directed fire at the oncoming Indians. A few volleys and the advance was checked. The men then retreated to the shore and there took up a strong and unassailable position. Once more the Chippewas made a dash, but were forced to retreat before the fire of the plucky little squad. Then the battle was ended and no further hostilities were offered.

The loss to the troopers during this short engagement was rather severe. Major Melville Wilkinson, Sergeant William Buller and Privates Ed. Lowe, John Olmstead, John Swallenstock and Alfred Zebell were killed and sixteen men sustained injuries more or less severe, while the loss to the Indians was very much smaller. However, the news of the battle brought re-enforcements to the scene almost immediately, and within less than a week quiet was restored and the ringleaders in the hands of the authorities.

General Bacon received the commendation of the whole

country for the cool and energetic manner in which he faced an unexpected emergency. Hospital Steward Oscar Burkhard was awarded the Medal of Honour in recognition of his services during the engagement and in rendering aid to the wounded.

This battle concludes the history of the Indian wars. Their end was contemporaneous with the war with Spain. No outbreak by the hostiles worthy of recording in this history has occurred since this affair, and, as civilization is spreading among even the most savage tribes of the West, it probably will be recorded as the last armed resistance in force against the United States authorities. The red man has at last approached the stage of common reason, and this tells him that he has to abandon all hope of again following the nomadic life his fathers lived, and that he and his kin must adopt the mode and morals of living of the white man if their kind is not to be exterminated.

Whether or not civilization means death and extermination to the entire Indian race cannot be prophesied as yet. The truth is that the uncivilized Indian is dying off rapidly as he is brought into proximity with the white man and no effort is made on his part to adopt civilization. However, when once successful in changing his nomadic mode of living he and his children will prosper and increase in number. The Indian race of this type is not dying out.

Our later Indian wars had constantly grown more fierce. The courageous and wily hostile, a born hunter and warrior, became accustomed to the most modern weapons and no one understood and estimated his strength better than the soldier who confronted him in battle. Fighting single-handed, oftentimes without direction of an officer and relying on his individual tactics and resources, was the lot of our soldiers in these affairs, and it can be truthfully stated that the military methods employed in our later Indian wars have been used as a basis of military tactics in modern warfare. The individual soldier is expected to depend more on his own resources in battle than formerly, and, therefore, deeds of heroism and self-sacrifice will increase rather than decrease in coming wars.

An Officer's Devotion to His Men

On the 23rd of April, 1882, a detachment consisting of six men and six Indian scouts, commanded by Lieutenant McDonald, Fourth Cavalry, was attacked by a large band of Chiricahua Apaches, about twenty miles south of Stein's Pass, near the boundary line between Arizona and New Mexico. The men put up a brave tight, holding off the Indians with rare skill and courage. By dint of rapid firing and skilful manoeuvring the men held the howling fiends in check and their trusty carbines made several of them measure their lengths upon the ground.

One by one the brave men of this little squad fell wounded. Escape was impossible. Annihilation was in sight unless re-enforcements were brought up. As a last resort one of the scouts slipped away from the detachment and succeeded in making his escape from the desperate situation, and notified Lieutenant-Colonel G. A. Forsyth of the plight his comrades were in. Colonel Forsyth immediately set out at a gallop with Troops C, F, G, H and M, of the Fourth Cavalry, to the relief of the rest of Lieutenant McDonald's little party.

The sixteen miles which the troops had to travel to reach McDonald's command were covered in an incredibly short time, and when they arrived at the scene of action they found McDonald's men still defending themselves against the onslaughts of the Indians, but on the approach of the column the redskins fled. Pursuit was at once taken up and the hostiles were overtaken in a strongly entrenched position in Horseshoe Canyon, New Mexico The command dismounted and promptly attacked them among the rocky ridges, varying from 400 to 1,600 feet high.

While climbing one of these narrow gorges in the mountains two soldiers, one of whom was Private Edward Leonard, asked permission to secure an Indian pony just discovered some distance up the mountain at the side of a high boulder. The men were told that it was probably an ambuscade, but not heeding the advice they started. They had not gone very far, however, when to their surprise a volley was fired from the top of the boulder, and then only did they realize that the officers surmise of an ambuscade was correct, and they hurried back over the jagged rocks. Leonard slipped and fell partly behind a rock, and was immediately shot through both his exposed legs. The other man rejoined the command.

First Lieutenant Wilber E. Wilder, of the Fourth Cavalry, seeing Leonard's plight, at once advanced along the gorge to his assistance. The entire distance he was subjected to a severe fire from the Indian sharpshooters, but luckily he arrived at Leonard's side in safety, and then, with the ultimate assistance of Leonard's comrade, who had followed Wilder, he carried the wounded man down over the rocks amid generous volleys from the hidden Apaches. For his intrepidity in rescuing Leonard, Lieutenant Wilder was awarded the Medal of Honour.

The Indians were driven from rock to rock among the mountains, until they dispersed in every direction and further immediate pursuit was impracticable, They left behind them in this engagement thirteen Indians killed and several wounded. A number of their animals were also captured.

ALSO FROM LEONAUR
AVAILABLE IN SOFTCOVER OR HARDCOVER WITH DUST JACKET

A HISTORY OF THE FRENCH & INDIAN WAR by *Arthur G. Bradley*—The Seven Years War as it was fought in the New World has always fascinated students of military history—here is the story of that confrontation.

WASHINGTON'S EARLY CAMPAIGNS by *James Hadden*—The French Post Expedition, Great Meadows and Braddock's Defeat—including Braddock's Orderly Books.

BOUQUET & THE OHIO INDIAN WAR by *Cyrus Cort & William Smith*—Two Accounts of the Campaigns of 1763-1764: Bouquet's Campaigns by Cyrus Cort & The History of Bouquet's Expeditions by William Smith.

NARRATIVES OF THE FRENCH & INDIAN WAR: 2 by *David Holden, Samuel Jenks, Lemuel Lyon, Mary Cochrane Rogers & Henry T. Blake*—Contains The Diary of Sergeant David Holden, Captain Samuel Jenks' Journal, The Journal of Lemuel Lyon, Journal of a French Officer at the Siege of Quebec, A Battle Fought on Snowshoes & The Battle of Lake George.

NARRATIVES OF THE FRENCH & INDIAN WAR by *Brown, Eastburn, Hawks & Putnam*—Ranger Brown's Narrative, The Adventures of Robert Eastburn, The Journal of Rufus Putnam—Provincial Infantry & Orderly Book and Journal of Major John Hawks on the Ticonderoga-Crown Point Campaign.

THE 7TH (QUEEN'S OWN) HUSSARS: Volume 1—1688-1792 by *C. R. B. Barrett*—As Dragoons During the Flanders Campaign, War of the Austrian Succession and the Seven Years War.

INDIA'S FREE LANCES by *H. G. Keene*—European Mercenary Commanders in Hindustan 1770-1820.

THE BENGAL EUROPEAN REGIMENT by *P. R. Innes*—An Elite Regiment of the Honourable East India Company 1756-1858.

MUSKET & TOMAHAWK by *Francis Parkman*—A Military History of the French & Indian War, 1753-1760.

THE BLACK WATCH AT TICONDEROGA by *Frederick B. Richards*—Campaigns in the French & Indian War.

QUEEN'S RANGERS by *Frederick B. Richards*—John Simcoe and his Rangers During the Revolutionary War for America.

AVAILABLE ONLINE AT **www.leonaur.com**
AND FROM ALL GOOD BOOK STORES

ALSO FROM LEONAUR
AVAILABLE IN SOFTCOVER OR HARDCOVER WITH DUST JACKET

JOURNALS OF ROBERT ROGERS OF THE RANGERS *by Robert Rogers*—The exploits of Rogers & the Rangers in his own words during 1755-1761 in the French & Indian War.

GALLOPING GUNS *by James Young*—The Experiences of an Officer of the Bengal Horse Artillery During the Second Maratha War 1804-1805.

GORDON *by Demetrius Charles Boulger*—The Career of Gordon of Khartoum.

THE BATTLE OF NEW ORLEANS *by Zachary F. Smith*—The final major engagement of the War of 1812.

THE TWO WARS OF MRS DUBERLY *by Frances Isabella Duberly*—An Intrepid Victorian Lady's Experience of the Crimea and Indian Mutiny.

WITH THE GUARDS' BRIGADE DURING THE BOER WAR *by Edward P. Lowry*—On Campaign from Bloemfontein to Koomati Poort and Back.

THE REBELLIOUS DUCHESS *by Paul F. S. Dermoncourt*—The Adventures of the Duchess of Berri and Her Attempt to Overthrow French Monarchy.

MEN OF THE MUTINY *by John Tulloch Nash & Henry Metcalfe*—Two Accounts of the Great Indian Mutiny of 1857: Fighting with the Bengal Yeomanry Cavalry & Private Metcalfe at Lucknow.

CAMPAIGN IN THE CRIMEA *by George Shuldham Peard*—The Recollections of an Officer of the 20th Regiment of Foot.

WITHIN SEBASTOPOL *by K. Hodasevich*—A Narrative of the Campaign in the Crimea, and of the Events of the Siege.

WITH THE CAVALRY TO AFGHANISTAN *by William Taylor*—The Experiences of a Trooper of H. M. 4th Light Dragoons During the First Afghan War.

THE CAWNPORE MAN *by Mowbray Thompson*—A First Hand Account of the Siege and Massacre During the Indian Mutiny By One of Four Survivors.

BRIGADE COMMANDER: AFGHANISTAN *by Henry Brooke*—The Journal of the Commander of the 2nd Infantry Brigade, Kandahar Field Force During the Second Afghan War.

BANCROFT OF THE BENGAL HORSE ARTILLERY *by N. W. Bancroft*—An Account of the First Sikh War 1845-1846.

AVAILABLE ONLINE AT www.leonaur.com
AND FROM ALL GOOD BOOK STORES

ALSO FROM LEONAUR
AVAILABLE IN SOFTCOVER OR HARDCOVER WITH DUST JACKET

AFGHANISTAN: THE BELEAGUERED BRIGADE by G. R. Gleig—An Account of Sale's Brigade During the First Afghan War.

IN THE RANKS OF THE C. I. V by Erskine Childers—With the City Imperial Volunteer Battery (Honourable Artillery Company) in the Second Boer War.

THE BENGAL NATIVE ARMY by F. G. Cardew—An Invaluable Reference Resource.

THE 7TH (QUEEN'S OWN) HUSSARS: Volume 4—1688-1914 by C. R. B. Barrett—Uniforms, Equipment, Weapons, Traditions, the Services of Notable Officers and Men & the Appendices to All Volumes—Volume 4: 1688-1914.

THE SWORD OF THE CROWN by Eric W. Sheppard—A History of the British Army to 1914.

THE 7TH (QUEEN'S OWN) HUSSARS: Volume 3—1818-1914 by C. R. B. Barrett—On Campaign During the Canadian Rebellion, the Indian Mutiny, the Sudan, Matabeleland, Mashonaland and the Boer War Volume 3: 1818-1914.

THE KHARTOUM CAMPAIGN by Bennet Burleigh—A Special Correspondent's View of the Reconquest of the Sudan by British and Egyptian Forces under Kitchener—1898.

EL PUCHERO by Richard McSherry—The Letters of a Surgeon of Volunteers During Scott's Campaign of the American-Mexican War 1847-1848.

RIFLEMAN SAHIB by E. Maude—The Recollections of an Officer of the Bombay Rifles During the Southern Mahratta Campaign, Second Sikh War, Persian Campaign and Indian Mutiny.

THE KING'S HUSSAR by Edwin Mole—The Recollections of a 14th (King's) Hussar During the Victorian Era.

JOHN COMPANY'S CAVALRYMAN by William Johnson—The Experiences of a British Soldier in the Crimea, the Persian Campaign and the Indian Mutiny.

COLENSO & DURNFORD'S ZULU WAR by Frances E. Colenso & Edward Durnford—The first and possibly the most important history of the Zulu War.

U. S. DRAGOON by Samuel E. Chamberlain—Experiences in the Mexican War 1846-48 and on the South Western Frontier.

AVAILABLE ONLINE AT www.leonaur.com
AND FROM ALL GOOD BOOK STORES
07/09

ALSO FROM LEONAUR
AVAILABLE IN SOFTCOVER OR HARDCOVER WITH DUST JACKET

THE 2ND MAORI WAR: 1860-1861 *by Robert Carey*—The Second Maori War, or First Taranaki War, one more bloody instalment of the conflicts between European settlers and the indigenous Maori people.

A JOURNAL OF THE SECOND SIKH WAR *by Daniel A. Sandford*—The Experiences of an Ensign of the 2nd Bengal European Regiment During the Campaign in the Punjab, India, 1848-49.

THE LIGHT INFANTRY OFFICER *by John H. Cooke*—The Experiences of an Officer of the 43rd Light Infantry in America During the War of 1812.

BUSHVELDT CARBINEERS *by George Witton*—The War Against the Boers in South Africa and the 'Breaker' Morant Incident.

LAKE'S CAMPAIGNS IN INDIA *by Hugh Pearse*—The Second Anglo Maratha War, 1803-1807.

BRITAIN IN AFGHANISTAN 1: THE FIRST AFGHAN WAR 1839-42 *by Archibald Forbes*—From invasion to destruction-a British military disaster.

BRITAIN IN AFGHANISTAN 2: THE SECOND AFGHAN WAR 1878-80 *by Archibald Forbes*—This is the history of the Second Afghan War-another episode of British military history typified by savagery, massacre, siege and battles.

UP AMONG THE PANDIES *by Vivian Dering Majendie*—Experiences of a British Officer on Campaign During the Indian Mutiny, 1857-1858.

MUTINY: 1857 *by James Humphries*—Authentic Voices from the Indian Mutiny-First Hand Accounts of Battles, Sieges and Personal Hardships.

BLOW THE BUGLE, DRAW THE SWORD *by W. H. G. Kingston*—The Wars, Campaigns, Regiments and Soldiers of the British & Indian Armies During the Victorian Era, 1839-1898.

WAR BEYOND THE DRAGON PAGODA *by Major J. J. Snodgrass*—A Personal Narrative of the First Anglo-Burmese War 1824 - 1826.

THE HERO OF ALIWAL *by James Humphries*—The Campaigns of Sir Harry Smith in India, 1843-1846, During the Gwalior War & the First Sikh War.

ALL FOR A SHILLING A DAY *by Donald F. Featherstone*—The story of H.M. 16th, the Queen's Lancers During the first Sikh War 1845-1846.

AVAILABLE ONLINE AT **www.leonaur.com**
AND FROM ALL GOOD BOOK STORES

ALSO FROM LEONAUR
AVAILABLE IN SOFTCOVER OR HARDCOVER WITH DUST JACKET

THE FALL OF THE MOGHUL EMPIRE OF HINDUSTAN by H. G. Keene—By the beginning of the nineteenth century, as British and Indian armies under Lake and Wellesley dominated the scene, a little over half a century of conflict brought the Moghul Empire to its knees.

LADY SALE'S AFGHANISTAN by Florentia Sale—An Indomitable Victorian Lady's Account of the Retreat from Kabul During the First Afghan War.

THE CAMPAIGN OF MAGENTA AND SOLFERINO 1859 by Harold Carmichael Wylly—The Decisive Conflict for the Unification of Italy.

FRENCH'S CAVALRY CAMPAIGN by J. G. Maydon—A Special Correspondent's View of British Army Mounted Troops During the Boer War.

CAVALRY AT WATERLOO by Sir Evelyn Wood—British Mounted Troops During the Campaign of 1815.

THE SUBALTERN by George Robert Gleig—The Experiences of an Officer of the 85th Light Infantry During the Peninsular War.

NAPOLEON AT BAY, 1814 by F. Loraine Petre—The Campaigns to the Fall of the First Empire.

NAPOLEON AND THE CAMPAIGN OF 1806 by Colonel Vachée—The Napoleonic Method of Organisation and Command to the Battles of Jena & Auerstädt.

THE COMPLETE ADVENTURES IN THE CONNAUGHT RANGERS by William Grattan—The 88th Regiment during the Napoleonic Wars by a Serving Officer.

BUGLER AND OFFICER OF THE RIFLES by William Green & Harry Smith—With the 95th (Rifles) during the Peninsular & Waterloo Campaigns of the Napoleonic Wars.

NAPOLEONIC WAR STORIES by Sir Arthur Quiller-Couch—Tales of soldiers, spies, battles & sieges from the Peninsular & Waterloo campaingns.

CAPTAIN OF THE 95TH (RIFLES) by Jonathan Leach—An officer of Wellington's sharpshooters during the Peninsular, South of France and Waterloo campaigns of the Napoleonic wars.

RIFLEMAN COSTELLO by Edward Costello—The adventures of a soldier of the 95th (Rifles) in the Peninsular & Waterloo Campaigns of the Napoleonic wars.

AVAILABLE ONLINE AT **www.leonaur.com**
AND FROM ALL GOOD BOOK STORES

ALSO FROM LEONAUR
AVAILABLE IN SOFTCOVER OR HARDCOVER WITH DUST JACKET

AT THEM WITH THE BAYONET by *Donald F. Featherstone*—The first Anglo-Sikh War 1845-1846.

STEPHEN CRANE'S BATTLES by *Stephen Crane*—Nine Decisive Battles Recounted by the Author of 'The Red Badge of Courage'.

THE GURKHA WAR by *H. T. Prinsep*—The Anglo-Nepalese Conflict in North East India 1814-1816.

FIRE & BLOOD by *G. R. Gleig*—The burning of Washington & the battle of New Orleans, 1814, through the eyes of a young British soldier.

SOUND ADVANCE! by *Joseph Anderson*—Experiences of an officer of HM 50th regiment in Australia, Burma & the Gwalior war.

THE CAMPAIGN OF THE INDUS by *Thomas Holdsworth*—Experiences of a British Officer of the 2nd (Queen's Royal) Regiment in the Campaign to Place Shah Shuja on the Throne of Afghanistan 1838 - 1840.

WITH THE MADRAS EUROPEAN REGIMENT IN BURMA by *John Butler*—The Experiences of an Officer of the Honourable East India Company's Army During the First Anglo-Burmese War 1824 - 1826.

IN ZULULAND WITH THE BRITISH ARMY by *Charles L. Norris-Newman*—The Anglo-Zulu war of 1879 through the first-hand experiences of a special correspondent.

BESIEGED IN LUCKNOW by *Martin Richard Gubbins*—The first Anglo-Sikh War 1845-1846.

A TIGER ON HORSEBACK by *L. March Phillips*—The Experiences of a Trooper & Officer of Rimington's Guides - The Tigers - during the Anglo-Boer war 1899 - 1902.

SEPOYS, SIEGE & STORM by *Charles John Griffiths*—The Experiences of a young officer of H.M.'s 61st Regiment at Ferozepore, Delhi ridge and at the fall of Delhi during the Indian mutiny 1857.

CAMPAIGNING IN ZULULAND by *W. E. Montague*—Experiences on campaign during the Zulu war of 1879 with the 94th Regiment.

THE STORY OF THE GUIDES by *G.J. Younghusband*—The Exploits of the Soldiers of the famous Indian Army Regiment from the northwest frontier 1847 - 1900.

AVAILABLE ONLINE AT **www.leonaur.com**
AND FROM ALL GOOD BOOK STORES

ALSO FROM LEONAUR
AVAILABLE IN SOFTCOVER OR HARDCOVER WITH DUST JACKET

ZULU:1879 *by D.C.F. Moodie & the Leonaur Editors*—The Anglo-Zulu War of 1879 from contemporary sources: First Hand Accounts, Interviews, Dispatches, Official Documents & Newspaper Reports.

THE RED DRAGOON *by W.J. Adams*—With the 7th Dragoon Guards in the Cape of Good Hope against the Boers & the Kaffir tribes during the 'war of the axe' 1843-48'.

THE RECOLLECTIONS OF SKINNER OF SKINNER'S HORSE *by James Skinner*—James Skinner and his 'Yellow Boys' Irregular cavalry in the wars of India between the British, Mahratta, Rajput, Mogul, Sikh & Pindarree Forces.

A CAVALRY OFFICER DURING THE SEPOY REVOLT *by A. R. D. Mackenzie*—Experiences with the 3rd Bengal Light Cavalry, the Guides and Sikh Irregular Cavalry from the outbreak to Delhi and Lucknow.

A NORFOLK SOLDIER IN THE FIRST SIKH WAR *by J W Baldwin*—Experiences of a private of H.M. 9th Regiment of Foot in the battles for the Punjab, India 1845-6.

TOMMY ATKINS' WAR STORIES: 14 FIRST HAND ACCOUNTS—Fourteen first hand accounts from the ranks of the British Army during Queen Victoria's Empire.

THE WATERLOO LETTERS *by H. T. Siborne*—Accounts of the Battle by British Officers for its Foremost Historian.

NEY: GENERAL OF CAVALRY VOLUME 1—1769-1799 *by Antoine Bulos*—The Early Career of a Marshal of the First Empire.

NEY: MARSHAL OF FRANCE VOLUME 2—1799-1805 *by Antoine Bulos*—The Early Career of a Marshal of the First Empire.

AIDE-DE-CAMP TO NAPOLEON *by Philippe-Paul de Ségur*—For anyone interested in the Napoleonic Wars this book, written by one who was intimate with the strategies and machinations of the Emperor, will be essential reading.

TWILIGHT OF EMPIRE *by Sir Thomas Ussher & Sir George Cockburn*—Two accounts of Napoleon's Journeys in Exile to Elba and St. Helena: Narrative of Events by Sir Thomas Ussher & Napoleon's Last Voyage: Extract of a diary by Sir George Cockburn.

PRIVATE WHEELER *by William Wheeler*—The letters of a soldier of the 51st Light Infantry during the Peninsular War & at Waterloo.

AVAILABLE ONLINE AT **www.leonaur.com**
AND FROM ALL GOOD BOOK STORES

ALSO FROM LEONAUR
AVAILABLE IN SOFTCOVER OR HARDCOVER WITH DUST JACKET

OFFICERS & GENTLEMEN by Peter Hawker & William Graham—Two Accounts of British Officers During the Peninsula War: Officer of Light Dragoons by Peter Hawker & Campaign in Portugal and Spain by William Graham.

THE WALCHEREN EXPEDITION by Anonymous—The Experiences of a British Officer of the 81st Regt. During the Campaign in the Low Countries of 1809.

LADIES OF WATERLOO by Charlotte A. Eaton, Magdalene de Lancey & Juana Smith—The Experiences of Three Women During the Campaign of 1815: Waterloo Days by Charlotte A. Eaton, A Week at Waterloo by Magdalene de Lancey & Juana's Story by Juana Smith.

JOURNAL OF AN OFFICER IN THE KING'S GERMAN LEGION by John Frederick Hering—Recollections of Campaigning During the Napoleonic Wars.

JOURNAL OF AN ARMY SURGEON IN THE PENINSULAR WAR by Charles Boutflower—The Recollections of a British Army Medical Man on Campaign During the Napoleonic Wars.

ON CAMPAIGN WITH MOORE AND WELLINGTON by Anthony Hamilton—The Experiences of a Soldier of the 43rd Regiment During the Peninsular War.

THE ROAD TO AUSTERLITZ by R. G. Burton—Napoleon's Campaign of 1805.

SOLDIERS OF NAPOLEON by A. J. Doisy De Villargennes & Arthur Chuquet—The Experiences of the Men of the French First Empire: Under the Eagles by A. J. Doisy De Villargennes & Voices of 1812 by Arthur Chuquet.

INVASION OF FRANCE, 1814 by F. W. O. Maycock—The Final Battles of the Napoleonic First Empire.

LEIPZIG—A CONFLICT OF TITANS by Frederic Shoberl—A Personal Experience of the 'Battle of the Nations' During the Napoleonic Wars, October 14th-19th, 1813.

SLASHERS by Charles Cadell—The Campaigns of the 28th Regiment of Foot During the Napoleonic Wars by a Serving Officer.

BATTLE IMPERIAL by Charles William Vane—The Campaigns in Germany & France for the Defeat of Napoleon 1813-1814.

SWIFT & BOLD by Gibbes Rigaud—The 60th Rifles During the Peninsula War.

AVAILABLE ONLINE AT **www.leonaur.com**
AND FROM ALL GOOD BOOK STORES

ALSO FROM LEONAUR
AVAILABLE IN SOFTCOVER OR HARDCOVER WITH DUST JACKET

ADVENTURES OF A YOUNG RIFLEMAN by *Johann Christian Maempel*—The Experiences of a Saxon in the French & British Armies During the Napoleonic Wars.

THE HUSSAR by *Norbert Landsheit & G. R. Gleig*—A German Cavalryman in British Service Throughout the Napoleonic Wars.

RECOLLECTIONS OF THE PENINSULA by *Moyle Sherer*—An Officer of the 34th Regiment of Foot—'The Cumberland Gentlemen'—on Campaign Against Napoleon's French Army in Spain.

MARINE OF REVOLUTION & CONSULATE by *Moreau de Jonnès*—The Recollections of a French Soldier of the Revolutionary Wars 1791-1804.

GENTLEMEN IN RED by *John Dobbs & Robert Knowles*—Two Accounts of British Infantry Officers During the Peninsular War Recollections of an Old 52nd Man by John Dobbs An Officer of Fusiliers by Robert Knowles.

CORPORAL BROWN'S CAMPAIGNS IN THE LOW COUNTRIES by *Robert Brown*—Recollections of a Coldstream Guard in the Early Campaigns Against Revolutionary France 1793-1795.

THE 7TH (QUEENS OWN) HUSSARS: Volume 2—1793-1815 by *C. R. B. Barrett*—During the Campaigns in the Low Countries & the Peninsula and Waterloo Campaigns of the Napoleonic Wars. Volume 2: 1793-1815.

THE MARENGO CAMPAIGN 1800 by *Herbert H. Sargent*—The Victory that Completed the Austrian Defeat in Italy.

DONALDSON OF THE 94TH—SCOTS BRIGADE by *Joseph Donaldson*—The Recollections of a Soldier During the Peninsula & South of France Campaigns of the Napoleonic Wars.

A CONSCRIPT FOR EMPIRE by *Philippe as told to Johann Christian Maempel*—The Experiences of a Young German Conscript During the Napoleonic Wars.

JOURNAL OF THE CAMPAIGN OF 1815 by *Alexander Cavalié Mercer*—The Experiences of an Officer of the Royal Horse Artillery During the Waterloo Campaign.

NAPOLEON'S CAMPAIGNS IN POLAND 1806-7 by *Robert Wilson*—The campaign in Poland from the Russian side of the conflict.

AVAILABLE ONLINE AT **www.leonaur.com**
AND FROM ALL GOOD BOOK STORES

ALSO FROM LEONAUR
AVAILABLE IN SOFTCOVER OR HARDCOVER WITH DUST JACKET

OMPTEDA OF THE KING'S GERMAN LEGION *by Christian von Ompteda*—A Hanoverian Officer on Campaign Against Napoleon.

LIEUTENANT SIMMONS OF THE 95TH (RIFLES) *by George Simmons*—Recollections of the Peninsula, South of France & Waterloo Campaigns of the Napoleonic Wars.

A HORSEMAN FOR THE EMPEROR *by Jean Baptiste Gazzola*—A Cavalryman of Napoleon's Army on Campaign Throughout the Napoleonic Wars.

SERGEANT LAWRENCE *by William Lawrence*—With the 40th Regt. of Foot in South America, the Peninsular War & at Waterloo.

CAMPAIGNS WITH THE FIELD TRAIN *by Richard D. Henegan*—Experiences of a British Officer During the Peninsula and Waterloo Campaigns of the Napoleonic Wars.

CAVALRY SURGEON *by S. D. Broughton*—On Campaign Against Napoleon in the Peninsula & South of France During the Napoleonic Wars 1812-1814.

MEN OF THE RIFLES *by Thomas Knight, Henry Curling & Jonathan Leach*—The Reminiscences of Thomas Knight of the 95th (Rifles) by Thomas Knight, Henry Curling's Anecdotes by Henry Curling & The Field Services of the Rifle Brigade from its Formation to Waterloo by Jonathan Leach.

THE ULM CAMPAIGN 1805 *by F. N. Maude*—Napoleon and the Defeat of the Austrian Army During the 'War of the Third Coalition'.

SOLDIERING WITH THE 'DIVISION' *by Thomas Garrety*—The Military Experiences of an Infantryman of the 43rd Regiment During the Napoleonic Wars.

SERGEANT MORRIS OF THE 73RD FOOT *by Thomas Morris*—The Experiences of a British Infantryman During the Napoleonic Wars-Including Campaigns in Germany and at Waterloo.

A VOICE FROM WATERLOO *by Edward Cotton*—The Personal Experiences of a British Cavalryman Who Became a Battlefield Guide and Authority on the Campaign of 1815.

NAPOLEON AND HIS MARSHALS *by J. T. Headley*—The Men of the First Empire.

AVAILABLE ONLINE AT **www.leonaur.com**
AND FROM ALL GOOD BOOK STORES

ALSO FROM LEONAUR
AVAILABLE IN SOFTCOVER OR HARDCOVER WITH DUST JACKET

COLBORNE: A SINGULAR TALENT FOR WAR *by John Colborne*—The Napoleonic Wars Career of One of Wellington's Most Highly Valued Officers in Egypt, Holland, Italy, the Peninsula and at Waterloo.

NAPOLEON'S RUSSIAN CAMPAIGN *by Philippe Henri de Segur*—The Invasion, Battles and Retreat by an Aide-de-Camp on the Emperor's Staff.

WITH THE LIGHT DIVISION *by John H. Cooke*—The Experiences of an Officer of the 43rd Light Infantry in the Peninsula and South of France During the Napoleonic Wars.

WELLINGTON AND THE PYRENEES CAMPAIGN VOLUME I: FROM VITORIA TO THE BIDASSOA *by F. C. Beatson*—The final phase of the campaign in the Iberian Peninsula.

WELLINGTON AND THE INVASION OF FRANCE VOLUME II: THE BIDASSOA TO THE BATTLE OF THE NIVELLE *by F. C. Beatson*—The final phase of the campaign in the Iberian Peninsula.

WELLINGTON AND THE FALL OF FRANCE VOLUME III: THE GAVES AND THE BATTLE OF ORTHEZ *by F. C. Beatson*—The final phase of the campaign in the Iberian Peninsula.

NAPOLEON'S IMPERIAL GUARD: FROM MARENGO TO WATERLOO *by J. T. Headley*—The story of Napoleon's Imperial Guard and the men who commanded them.

BATTLES & SIEGES OF THE PENINSULAR WAR *by W. H. Fitchett*—Corunna, Busaco, Albuera, Ciudad Rodrigo, Badajos, Salamanca, San Sebastian & Others.

SERGEANT GUILLEMARD: THE MAN WHO SHOT NELSON? *by Robert Guillemard*—A Soldier of the Infantry of the French Army of Napoleon on Campaign Throughout Europe.

WITH THE GUARDS ACROSS THE PYRENEES *by Robert Batty*—The Experiences of a British Officer of Wellington's Army During the Battles for the Fall of Napoleonic France, 1813.

A STAFF OFFICER IN THE PENINSULA *by E. W. Buckham*—An Officer of the British Staff Corps Cavalry During the Peninsula Campaign of the Napoleonic Wars.

THE LEIPZIG CAMPAIGN: 1813—NAPOLEON AND THE "BATTLE OF THE NATIONS" *by F. N. Maude*—Colonel Maude's analysis of Napoleon's campaign of 1813 around Leipzig.

AVAILABLE ONLINE AT **www.leonaur.com**
AND FROM ALL GOOD BOOK STORES

ALSO FROM LEONAUR
AVAILABLE IN SOFTCOVER OR HARDCOVER WITH DUST JACKET

BUGEAUD: A PACK WITH A BATON by *Thomas Robert Bugeaud*—The Early Campaigns of a Soldier of Napoleon's Army Who Would Become a Marshal of France.

WATERLOO RECOLLECTIONS by *Frederick Llewellyn*—Rare First Hand Accounts, Letters, Reports and Retellings from the Campaign of 1815.

SERGEANT NICOL by *Daniel Nicol*—The Experiences of a Gordon Highlander During the Napoleonic Wars in Egypt, the Peninsula and France.

THE JENA CAMPAIGN: 1806 by *F. N. Maude*—The Twin Battles of Jena & Auerstadt Between Napoleon's French and the Prussian Army.

PRIVATE O'NEIL by *Charles O'Neil*—The recollections of an Irish Rogue of H. M. 28th Regt.—The Slashers—during the Peninsula & Waterloo campaigns of the Napoleonic war.

ROYAL HIGHLANDER by *James Anton*—A soldier of H.M 42nd (Royal) Highlanders during the Peninsular, South of France & Waterloo Campaigns of the Napoleonic Wars.

CAPTAIN BLAZE by *Elzéar Blaze*—Life in Napoleons Army.

LEJEUNE VOLUME 1 by *Louis-François Lejeune*—The Napoleonic Wars through the Experiences of an Officer on Berthier's Staff.

LEJEUNE VOLUME 2 by *Louis-François Lejeune*—The Napoleonic Wars through the Experiences of an Officer on Berthier's Staff.

CAPTAIN COIGNET by *Jean-Roch Coignet*—A Soldier of Napoleon's Imperial Guard from the Italian Campaign to Russia and Waterloo.

FUSILIER COOPER by *John S. Cooper*—Experiences in the 7th (Royal) Fusiliers During the Peninsular Campaign of the Napoleonic Wars and the American Campaign to New Orleans.

FIGHTING NAPOLEON'S EMPIRE by *Joseph Anderson*—The Campaigns of a British Infantryman in Italy, Egypt, the Peninsular & the West Indies During the Napoleonic Wars.

CHASSEUR BARRES by *Jean-Baptiste Barres*—The experiences of a French Infantryman of the Imperial Guard at Austerlitz, Jena, Eylau, Friedland, in the Peninsular, Lutzen, Bautzen, Zinnwald and Hanau during the Napoleonic Wars.

AVAILABLE ONLINE AT **www.leonaur.com**
AND FROM ALL GOOD BOOK STORES

ALSO FROM LEONAUR
AVAILABLE IN SOFTCOVER OR HARDCOVER WITH DUST JACKET

CAPTAIN COIGNET *by Jean-Roch Coignet*—A Soldier of Napoleon's Imperial Guard from the Italian Campaign to Russia and Waterloo.

HUSSAR ROCCA *by Albert Jean Michel de Rocca*—A French cavalry officer's experiences of the Napoleonic Wars and his views on the Peninsular Campaigns against the Spanish, British And Guerilla Armies.

MARINES TO 95TH (RIFLES) *by Thomas Fernyhough*—The military experiences of Robert Fernyhough during the Napoleonic Wars.

LIGHT BOB *by Robert Blakeney*—The experiences of a young officer in H.M 28th & 36th regiments of the British Infantry during the Peninsular Campaign of the Napoleonic Wars 1804 - 1814.

WITH WELLINGTON'S LIGHT CAVALRY *by William Tomkinson*—The Experiences of an officer of the 16th Light Dragoons in the Peninsular and Waterloo campaigns of the Napoleonic Wars.

SERGEANT BOURGOGNE *by Adrien Bourgogne*—With Napoleon's Imperial Guard in the Russian Campaign and on the Retreat from Moscow 1812 - 13.

SURTEES OF THE 95TH (RIFLES) *by William Surtees*—A Soldier of the 95th (Rifles) in the Peninsular campaign of the Napoleonic Wars.

SWORDS OF HONOUR *by Henry Newbolt & Stanley L. Wood*—The Careers of Six Outstanding Officers from the Napoleonic Wars, the Wars for India and the American Civil War.

ENSIGN BELL IN THE PENINSULAR WAR *by George Bell*—The Experiences of a young British Soldier of the 34th Regiment 'The Cumberland Gentlemen' in the Napoleonic wars.

HUSSAR IN WINTER *by Alexander Gordon*—A British Cavalry Officer during the retreat to Corunna in the Peninsular campaign of the Napoleonic Wars.

THE COMPLEAT RIFLEMAN HARRIS *by Benjamin Harris as told to and transcribed by Captain Henry Curling, 52nd Regt. of Foot*—The adventures of a soldier of the 95th (Rifles) during the Peninsular Campaign of the Napoleonic Wars.

THE ADVENTURES OF A LIGHT DRAGOON *by George Farmer & G.R. Gleig*—A cavalryman during the Peninsular & Waterloo Campaigns, in captivity & at the siege of Bhurtpore, India.

AVAILABLE ONLINE AT **www.leonaur.com**
AND FROM ALL GOOD BOOK STORES

ALSO FROM LEONAUR
AVAILABLE IN SOFTCOVER OR HARDCOVER WITH DUST JACKET

THE LIFE OF THE REAL BRIGADIER GERARD VOLUME 1—THE YOUNG HUSSAR 1782-1807 *by Jean-Baptiste De Marbot*—A French Cavalryman Of the Napoleonic Wars at Marengo, Austerlitz, Jena, Eylau & Friedland.

THE LIFE OF THE REAL BRIGADIER GERARD VOLUME 2—IMPERIAL AIDE-DE-CAMP 1807-1811 *by Jean-Baptiste De Marbot*—A French Cavalryman of the Napoleonic Wars at Saragossa, Landshut, Eckmuhl, Ratisbon, Aspern-Essling, Wagram, Busaco & Torres Vedras.

THE LIFE OF THE REAL BRIGADIER GERARD VOLUME 3—COLONEL OF CHASSEURS 1811-1815 *by Jean-Baptiste De Marbot*—A French Cavalryman in the retreat from Moscow, Lutzen, Bautzen, Katzbach, Leipzig, Hanau & Waterloo.

THE INDIAN WAR OF 1864 *by Eugene Ware*—The Experiences of a Young Officer of the 7th Iowa Cavalry on the Western Frontier During the Civil War.

THE MARCH OF DESTINY *by Charles E. Young & V. Devinny*—Dangers of the Trail in 1865 by Charles E. Young & The Story of a Pioneer by V. Devinny, two Accounts of Early Emigrants to Colorado.

CROSSING THE PLAINS *by William Audley Maxwell*—A First Hand Narrative of the Early Pioneer Trail to California in 1857.

CHIEF OF SCOUTS *by William F. Drannan*—A Pilot to Emigrant and Government Trains, Across the Plains of the Western Frontier.

THIRTY-ONE YEARS ON THE PLAINS AND IN THE MOUNTAINS *by William F. Drannan*—William Drannan was born to be a pioneer, hunter, trapper and wagon train guide during the momentous days of the Great American West.

THE INDIAN WARS VOLUNTEER *by William Thompson*—Recollections of the Conflict Against the Snakes, Shoshone, Bannocks, Modocs and Other Native Tribes of the American North West.

THE 4TH TENNESSEE CAVALRY *by George B. Guild*—The Services of Smith's Regiment of Confederate Cavalry by One of its Officers.

COLONEL WORTHINGTON'S SHILOH *by T. Worthington*—The Tennessee Campaign, 1862, by an Officer of the Ohio Volunteers.

FOUR YEARS IN THE SADDLE *by W. L. Curry*—The History of the First Regiment Ohio Volunteer Cavalry in the American Civil War.

AVAILABLE ONLINE AT **www.leonaur.com**
AND FROM ALL GOOD BOOK STORES

ALSO FROM LEONAUR
AVAILABLE IN SOFTCOVER OR HARDCOVER WITH DUST JACKET

LIFE IN THE ARMY OF NORTHERN VIRGINIA by Carlton McCarthy—The Observations of a Confederate Artilleryman of Cutshaw's Battalion During the American Civil War 1861-1865.

HISTORY OF THE CAVALRY OF THE ARMY OF THE POTOMAC by Charles D. Rhodes—Including Pope's Army of Virginia and the Cavalry Operations in West Virginia During the American Civil War.

CAMP-FIRE AND COTTON-FIELD by Thomas W. Knox—A New York Herald Correspondent's View of the American Civil War.

SERGEANT STILLWELL by Leander Stillwell —The Experiences of a Union Army Soldier of the 61st Illinois Infantry During the American Civil War.

STONEWALL'S CANNONEER by Edward A. Moore—Experiences with the Rockbridge Artillery, Confederate Army of Northern Virginia, During the American Civil War.

THE SIXTH CORPS by George Stevens—The Army of the Potomac, Union Army, During the American Civil War.

THE RAILROAD RAIDERS by William Pittenger—An Ohio Volunteers Recollections of the Andrews Raid to Disrupt the Confederate Railroad in Georgia During the American Civil War.

CITIZEN SOLDIER by John Beatty—An Account of the American Civil War by a Union Infantry Officer of Ohio Volunteers Who Became a Brigadier General.

COX: PERSONAL RECOLLECTIONS OF THE CIVIL WAR--VOLUME 1 by Jacob Dolson Cox—West Virginia, Kanawha Valley, Gauley Bridge, Cotton Mountain, South Mountain, Antietam, the Morgan Raid & the East Tennessee Campaign.

COX: PERSONAL RECOLLECTIONS OF THE CIVIL WAR--VOLUME 2 by Jacob Dolson Cox—Siege of Knoxville, East Tennessee, Atlanta Campaign, the Nashville Campaign & the North Carolina Campaign.

KERSHAW'S BRIGADE VOLUME 1 by D. Augustus Dickert—Manassas, Seven Pines, Sharpsburg (Antietam), Fredricksburg, Chancellorsville, Gettysburg, Chickamauga, Chattanooga, Fort Sanders & Bean Station.

KERSHAW'S BRIGADE VOLUME 2 by D. Augustus Dickert—At the wilderness, Cold Harbour, Petersburg, The Shenandoah Valley and Cedar Creek..

AVAILABLE ONLINE AT **www.leonaur.com**
AND FROM ALL GOOD BOOK STORES

ALSO FROM LEONAUR
AVAILABLE IN SOFTCOVER OR HARDCOVER WITH DUST JACKET

THE RELUCTANT REBEL *by William G. Stevenson*—A young Kentuckian's experiences in the Confederate Infantry & Cavalry during the American Civil War..

BOOTS AND SADDLES *by Elizabeth B. Custer*—The experiences of General Custer's Wife on the Western Plains.

FANNIE BEERS' CIVIL WAR *by Fannie A. Beers*—A Confederate Lady's Experiences of Nursing During the Campaigns & Battles of the American Civil War.

LADY SALE'S AFGHANISTAN *by Florentia Sale*—An Indomitable Victorian Lady's Account of the Retreat from Kabul During the First Afghan War.

THE TWO WARS OF MRS DUBERLY *by Frances Isabella Duberly*—An Intrepid Victorian Lady's Experience of the Crimea and Indian Mutiny.

THE REBELLIOUS DUCHESS *by Paul F. S. Dermoncourt*—The Adventures of the Duchess of Berri and Her Attempt to Overthrow French Monarchy.

LADIES OF WATERLOO *by Charlotte A. Eaton, Magdalene de Lancey & Juana Smith*—The Experiences of Three Women During the Campaign of 1815: Waterloo Days by Charlotte A. Eaton, A Week at Waterloo by Magdalene de Lancey & Juana's Story by Juana Smith.

TWO YEARS BEFORE THE MAST *by Richard Henry Dana. Jr.*—The account of one young man's experiences serving on board a sailing brig—the Penelope—bound for California, between the years 1834-36.

A SAILOR OF KING GEORGE *by Frederick Hoffman*—From Midshipman to Captain—Recollections of War at Sea in the Napoleonic Age 1793-1815.

LORDS OF THE SEA *by A. T. Mahan*—Great Captains of the Royal Navy During the Age of Sail.

COGGESHALL'S VOYAGES: VOLUME 1 *by George Coggeshall*—The Recollections of an American Schooner Captain.

COGGESHALL'S VOYAGES: VOLUME 2 *by George Coggeshall*—The Recollections of an American Schooner Captain.

TWILIGHT OF EMPIRE *by Sir Thomas Ussher & Sir George Cockburn*—Two accounts of Napoleon's Journeys in Exile to Elba and St. Helena: Narrative of Events by Sir Thomas Ussher & Napoleon's Last Voyage: Extract of a diary by Sir George Cockburn.

AVAILABLE ONLINE AT **www.leonaur.com**
AND FROM ALL GOOD BOOK STORES

ALSO FROM LEONAUR
AVAILABLE IN SOFTCOVER OR HARDCOVER WITH DUST JACKET

ESCAPE FROM THE FRENCH *by Edward Boys*—A Young Royal Navy Midshipman's Adventures During the Napoleonic War.

THE VOYAGE OF H.M.S. PANDORA *by Edward Edwards R. N. & George Hamilton, edited by Basil Thomson*—In Pursuit of the Mutineers of the Bounty in the South Seas—1790-1791.

MEDUSA *by J. B. Henry Savigny and Alexander Correard and Charlotte-Adélaïde Dard*—Narrative of a Voyage to Senegal in 1816 & The Sufferings of the Picard Family After the Shipwreck of the Medusa.

THE SEA WAR OF 1812 VOLUME 1 *by A. T. Mahan*—A History of the Maritime Conflict.

THE SEA WAR OF 1812 VOLUME 2 *by A. T. Mahan*—A History of the Maritime Conflict.

WETHERELL OF H. M. S. HUSSAR *by John Wetherell*—The Recollections of an Ordinary Seaman of the Royal Navy During the Napoleonic Wars.

THE NAVAL BRIGADE IN NATAL *by C. R. N. Burne*—With the Guns of H. M. S. Terrible & H. M. S. Tartar during the Boer War 1899-1900.

THE VOYAGE OF H. M. S. BOUNTY *by William Bligh*—The True Story of an 18th Century Voyage of Exploration and Mutiny.

SHIPWRECK! *by William Gilly*—The Royal Navy's Disasters at Sea 1793-1849.

KING'S CUTTERS AND SMUGGLERS: 1700-1855 *by E. Keble Chatterton*—A unique period of maritime history-from the beginning of the eighteenth to the middle of the nineteenth century when British seamen risked all to smuggle valuable goods from wool to tea and spirits from and to the Continent.

CONFEDERATE BLOCKADE RUNNER *by John Wilkinson*—The Personal Recollections of an Officer of the Confederate Navy.

NAVAL BATTLES OF THE NAPOLEONIC WARS *by W. H. Fitchett*—Cape St. Vincent, the Nile, Cadiz, Copenhagen, Trafalgar & Others.

PRISONERS OF THE RED DESERT *by R. S. Gwatkin-Williams*—The Adventures of the Crew of the Tara During the First World War.

U-BOAT WAR 1914-1918 *by James B. Connolly/Karl von Schenk*—Two Contrasting Accounts from Both Sides of the Conflict at Sea During the Great War.

AVAILABLE ONLINE AT **www.leonaur.com**
AND FROM ALL GOOD BOOK STORES

ALSO FROM LEONAUR
AVAILABLE IN SOFTCOVER OR HARDCOVER WITH DUST JACKET

IRON TIMES WITH THE GUARDS *by An O. E. (G. P. A. Fildes)*—The Experiences of an Officer of the Coldstream Guards on the Western Front During the First World War.

THE GREAT WAR IN THE MIDDLE EAST: 1 *by W. T. Massey*—The Desert Campaigns & How Jerusalem Was Won---two classic accounts in one volume.

THE GREAT WAR IN THE MIDDLE EAST: 2 *by W. T. Massey*—Allenby's Final Triumph.

SMITH-DORRIEN *by Horace Smith-Dorrien*—Isandlwhana to the Great War.

1914 *by Sir John French*—The Early Campaigns of the Great War by the British Commander.

GRENADIER *by E. R. M. Fryer*—The Recollections of an Officer of the Grenadier Guards throughout the Great War on the Western Front.

BATTLE, CAPTURE & ESCAPE *by George Pearson*—The Experiences of a Canadian Light Infantryman During the Great War.

DIGGERS AT WAR *by R. Hugh Knyvett & G. P. Cuttriss*—"Over There" With the Australians by R. Hugh Knyvett and Over the Top With the Third Australian Division by G. P. Cuttriss. Accounts of Australians During the Great War in the Middle East, at Gallipoli and on the Western Front.

HEAVY FIGHTING BEFORE US *by George Brenton Laurie*—The Letters of an Officer of the Royal Irish Rifles on the Western Front During the Great War.

THE CAMELIERS *by Oliver Hogue*—A Classic Account of the Australians of the Imperial Camel Corps During the First World War in the Middle East.

RED DUST *by Donald Black*—A Classic Account of Australian Light Horsemen in Palestine During the First World War.

THE LEAN, BROWN MEN *by Angus Buchanan*—Experiences in East Africa During the Great War with the 25th Royal Fusiliers—the Legion of Frontiersmen.

THE NIGERIAN REGIMENT IN EAST AFRICA *by W. D. Downes*—On Campaign During the Great War 1916-1918.

THE 'DIE-HARDS' IN SIBERIA *by John Ward*—With the Middlesex Regiment Against the Bolsheviks 1918-19.

AVAILABLE ONLINE AT **www.leonaur.com**
AND FROM ALL GOOD BOOK STORES

www.ingramcontent.com/pod-product-compliance
Lightning Source LLC
Chambersburg PA
CBHW030217170426
43201CB00006B/115